*Daring to Dissent*

A *new series of books from Cassell's Sexual Politics list,* Women on Women *provides a forum for lesbian, bisexual and heterosexual women to explore and debate contemporary issues and to develop strategies for the advancement of feminist culture and politics into the next century.*

COMMISSIONING:

**Roz Hopkins**
**Liz Gibbs**
**Christina Ruse**

# *Daring to Dissent*

*Lesbian Culture
from Margin
to Mainstream*

**Edited by Liz Gibbs**

CASSELL

Cassell
Villiers House, 41/47 Strand
London WC2N 5JE

387 Park Avenue South
New York, NY 10016–8810

First published 1994

**British Library Cataloguing-in-Publication Data**
A catalogue record for this book is available from the British Library.

Library of Congress CIP Data available.

ISBN 0-304-32794-8 (hardback)
    0-304-32796-4 (paperback)

Typeset by York House Typographic Ltd, London
Printed and bound in Great Britain by Mackays of Chatham Plc

# Contents

# About the Contributors

### Rose Collis

Following work as an untrained performer, musician and writer in theatre from 1979 to 1986, Rose Collis then became an equally untrained, but more successful, journalist. Her interviews, features and reviews on a wide variety of subjects have been published in *City Limits*, *Time Out*, *The Independent*, *Gay Times* and *Spare Rib*, among others. She was a member of the team who produced the award-winning TV documentary, *Framed Youth* (1983), and was the first lesbian co-editor of *City Limits'* influential 'Out in the City' section, working with the late Brian Kennedy. Her first book, *Portraits to the Wall*, is published by Cassell in 1994 and her second, a biography of Nancy Spain, will be published in 1995.

### Liz Gibbs

Liz Gibbs works in a number of publishing guises, usually in the field of press and marketing. En route she has been a fundraiser in the voluntary sector and a psychology teacher to 18-year-olds. She now works for Cassell as a list consultant on the lesbian and gay studies list, and for Scarlet Press and *Diva*, a new women's magazine published by Millivres, on promotion.

### Nicola Godwin

Nicola Godwin studied media and psychology in South Africa and London and worked for the BBC for three years before moving into print journalism and freelance radio production. She is currently researching an anthology with the working title *Lesbian Others*, due for publication by Cassell in 1995.

## Veronica Groocock

Veronica Groocock is a freelance journalist and author who has contributed to a wide range of national publications, including *The Times, Independent, Guardian* and *Observer*, and women's magazines such as *Marie Claire* and *Options*. She has written three books, one as sole author – *Women Mean Business* (Ebury Press, 1988) – and two as co-author, and has contributed to *Out of Focus*, an anthology exploring images of women in the media (The Women's Press, 1987). She also reviews non-fiction for *New Statesman & Society* and *Everywoman*.

## Belinda Hollowes

Belinda Hollowes graduated from Manchester University in 1987 with a degree in audio-visual communications and sociology. She works as a radio studio manager at BBC Westminster and is currently researching an anthology of contemporary lesbian cultural issues, due for publication by Cassell in 1995. She was part of the team responsible for the first lesbian and gay magazine programme on BBC Radio 4.

## Shameem Kabir

Shameem Kabir used to work in television and now works in women's publishing. Hers was the title story of *In and Out of Time* (ed. Patricia Duncker, Onlywomen Press, London, 1990). Her other published work includes album sleeve notes and television, music and book reviews. Forthcoming publications include: 'Lesbian representation in film: mermaids in the desert . . . must be seeing things', in *Volcanoes and Pearl Divers* (ed. Suzanne Raitt, Onlywomen Press) and a lesbian vampire story inspired by seeing *The Hunger*, appropriately called 'Hunger', in *Unknown Territory*, a forthcoming Onlywomen Press anthology. She has also written romantic pop-rock songs and hopes one day to get a break as a songwriter.

## Sheridan Nye

After working for the BBC for six years as an engineer in News and Current Affairs, Sheridan Nye studied journalism at the University of Westminster. Her work has been published in *Shebang*, the *Pink Paper* and *Feminist Review*. She is currently working with Belinda Hollowes and Nicola Godwin on an anthology of alternative lesbian lifestyles due to be published by Cassell in spring 1995.

## Nina Rapi

Nina Rapi is a playwright and translator. She studied at the London School of Economics and Essex University, where she received an MA in Drama. Her plays – *Ithaka*, *Dream House*, *Dance of Guns*, and the monologues *Johnny Is Dead* and *Dangerous Oasis* have been staged in a number of London venues. *Ithaka*, her critical work and poems have been published in *Seven Plays by Women*, *Women Writers' Handbook* (Aurora Metro), *New Theatre Quarterly* (Cambridge University Press), *Serious Pleasure* (Sheba), *Rouge*, *Square Peg* and other publications. She researched and scripted the documentary *Greek Love and Sapphic Sophistication*, screened on Channel 4 in April 1990. She is also a tutor at Birkbeck College and a visiting lecturer at Goldsmiths' College, London University.

## Cherry Smyth

Cherry Smyth is a journalist and poet living in London. Her non-fiction book, *Queer Notions*, was published by Scarlet Press in 1992, and her fiction appears in several anthologies. Her poetry is published in *Frankenstein's Daughter* (ed. Sara Boyes, Stride Publications, 1993), and *Virago New Poets* (Virago Press, 1993). An essay on lesbian pornography, 'The pleasure threshold' was published in *Feminist Review*, no. 34, spring 1990, and an essay on 'The transgressive sexual subject' is forthcoming in *Queer Romance*, from Routledge.

## Barbara Wilson

Barbara Wilson is the author of the Pam Nilsen mystery series: *Murder in the Collective, Sisters of the Road* and *The Dog Collar Murders*. She has written two novels, *Ambitious Women* and *Cows and Horses*, and a collection of short stories, *Miss Venezuela*. Her fourth mystery, *Gaudi Afternoon*, won both the 1990 Lambda Literary Award for Best Lesbian Novel and the 1991 British Crime Writing Association Award for Best Mystery Set in Europe. She has translated several works from Norwegian and received the Columbia Translation Prize for her work on Norwegian author Cora Sandel. Her work has been translated into Italian, Finnish and German. She is a co-founder of Seal Press and, more recently, the non-profit publishing house, Women in Translation.

## Mary Wings

Mary Wings has written three novels to date, *She Came Too Late* (named *City Limits*' Best Novel of the Year), *She Came in a Flash* and *Divine Victim*, all published in the UK by The Women's Press. She currently lives in San Francisco and her work has been translated into Dutch, German, Japanese and Spanish. She has been nominated for the Raymond Chandler Fulbright Award in Detective and Spy Fiction in the UK.

## Liz Yorke

Liz Yorke worked for six years as a general nurse before having three children and then returning as a mature student to Manchester Metropolitan University, where she worked as a part-timer teaching women's writing (among other things). She is also interested in using creative writing and poetry as therapy and now works full time as a counsellor at Nottingham Trent University. Her book, *Impertinent Voices: Subverting Strategies in Contemporary Women's Poetry* was published by Routledge in 1992. Her recently completed PhD thesis is entitled 'Re-visionary mythmaking in the work of Adrienne Rich and other women poets'.

*For Celia,*
*with love*

# Introduction

*Mama exhorted her children at every opportunity to 'jump at de sun'. We might not land on the sun, but at least we would get off the ground.*
Zora Neale Hurston, *Dust Tracks on a Road*

THESE essays were commissioned to examine and investigate the notion of lesbian genre. But what, one may ask, is 'lesbian genre' and what relevance does it have to contemporary media?

I have used a definition of lesbian genre to represent the broadest possible spectrum of work. This collection includes critical essays on the gamut of media including television, radio, journalism, theatre, literature, poetry and film. Clearly, this cannot be a comprehensive critique of every aspect of the arts, merely a starting-point.

Genre, strictly speaking, is defined as 'kind' or 'style' by the *Oxford English Dictionary*. In working on this book it fast became obvious that there is no single lesbian style, rather a startling and dazzling diversity which is growing rapidly and in many directions. There are, however, some discernible traits and it is with this in mind that I began commissioning the contributions, to map some territory of our burgeoning lesbian culture, a culture which, due to its oppositional stance, has created some of the most challenging and innovative media forms. This refusal to accept the bland face of a common doctrine has fuelled a spirit of creativity: lesbians are amongst the few who are *Daring to Dissent*.

Defining the word 'lesbian' is not as simple as referring to a dictionary. In charting the lives and passions of lesbians in the seventeenth and eighteenth centuries, Emma Donoghue's *Passions between Women*[1] reveals that texts of this time were full of words that dictionary compilers did not include. These were often the very words which later became associated with descriptions of lesbians today: 'The compilers of the Oxford English Dictionary assume that early uses of the word Lesbian/lesbian, especially when the poet Sappho is mentioned, simply mean "of or pertaining to the island of Lesbos".'[2] Clearly, though, definitions which were used at this time covered a multitude of meanings, incorporating both platonic and sexual ones. This contradicts Lillian Faderman's definition in *Surpassing the Love of Men*,[3] which describes pre-modern women's love as 'romantic friendship' in which 'two women are devoted to each other above anyone else'.[4] Faderman convincingly portrays romantic friendships as the epitome of social propriety. This avoids the political danger zones of contemporary definitions and the associated pejorative claims that lesbians are mad, bad, dangerous and definitely not nice girls to know!

However, Faderman's definition could be seen as an exclus- ive one, ignoring, as it does, women who experience lesbian culture as something other than coupledom. Interestingly, Faderman de- velops her definition further in her later book, *Odd Girls and Twilight Lovers*[5] and adopts a pluralist stance: 'in keeping with my definition of post-1920s lesbianism, you are a lesbian if you say (at least to yourself) that you are'.[6]

Prevailing concepts of sexuality vary according to the time, culture and most prominent moralities. So, for the purposes of this book, the definition of 'lesbian' is one of identity and community rather than simply sexual acts. To some extent these changes in definition are products of the political climate, and I would argue that definitions of 'lesbian' must be diverse in order to be accurate. Janice Raymond's definition acknowledges the wider sense of community: 'to extend a "sexual preference" beyond the realm and reality of a sexual category to a state of social and political existence'.[7]

At a time when the concept of 'community' has been steadily and deliberately eroded by 15 years of Conservative governments in the UK, the lesbian community is one which has strengthened and matured. In the face of adversity, diversity has hardened the political and creative lesbian muscles. Toni Morrison similarly describes women's inventiveness and the creative originality of black women:

'She has nothing to fall back on; not maleness, not whiteness, not ladyhood, not anything. And out of the profound desolation of her reality she may well have invented herself.'[8] Oppression can unify and act as a creative catalyst. At a time of little political cohesion, lesbian culture has become ever more vibrant perhaps because we have so little to lose – we can only go forwards.

The catalysts of this development are numerous, but I would suggest that part of this change flows from the political influence of the latest impact of feminism. The lesbian (and gay) liberation movements were informed and strengthened by the women's movement and many women experimented widely with different art forms. In recent years the women's movement has become less unified, and the lesbian community has diversified and strengthened. In this twenty-fifth anniversary year of New York's Stonewall riots, this diversification has created a myriad of lesbian styles, attitudes, philosophies and politics, reaching a cultural maturity. It could be argued that the lesbian and gay community, as a whole, now represents one of the few cohesive 'political' movements at large within the UK. It has proved mercurial in its flexibility and ability to organize fast and fight back. One can see the legislative threats to lesbian and gay liberty as political thermometers, and in recent years, as the temperature has risen, so has the level of political organization within our communities.

The political heat rose in the UK in 1988, with the (unsuccessful) reactive campaign against Section 28 of the Local Government Act (which prohibits 'promotion' of homosexuality within local authorities and adds the word 'lesbian' to the statute book for the first time). Yet, the proactive campaign to equalize the age of consensual sex between gay men with that of heterosexuals was narrowly defeated in the House of Commons in February 1994. This campaign was characterized by a high level of political lobbying and political allegiances being made with, of all people, right-wing MPs!

Despite the consistent deprivation of financial life-blood to arts organizations in the UK throughout the Tory years, lesbian culture has still managed to extend, diversify and strengthen. Perhaps it is this very oppression which has helped the process of growth.

This collection attempts to reflect some of the richness of

lesbian culture and to analyse our approaches to creating and the boundaries within which we operate. The fact that this book is one of the first lesbian titles published by Cassell, a mainstream publisher, epitomizes one of the themes debated in this anthology. Cassell's lesbian and gay studies list is, indeed, a newcomer to lesbian and gay publishing and one that ten years ago would have seemed unlikely. However, if one delves further back in Cassell's history, we find that Oscar Wilde was an employee of the very same publishing house. Cassell remains today the only large-scale independent publishing house in the UK. What on first inspection seems mainstream may at times be exactly the injection of resources and unexpected sources of independence which we need.

The contributors to this book are indicative of this growth and represent new voices and established names alike. They are journalists, playwrights, publishers, critics, crime writers, radio producers and technicians. The variety of their professions is echoed in the diversity of perspective and, often, of political outlook. The contributors are, however, unified in their innovative contributions to lesbian culture.

Mary Wings sets the scene with a fresh reappraisal of Daphne du Maurier's life and work in her chapter entitled 'Rebecca Redux'. There is a potential danger in re-reading past texts without an awareness of the pitfalls of our modern minds imposing modern meanings. However, if one approaches texts with an open mind and a knowledge of the writer's language, encodings, and cultural and political frameworks, it is possible to decipher lesbian meanings and subtexts. These may not always be explicit. An accurate reading of du Maurier's *Rebecca* requires an understanding of how and when it was written. This can be fully understood only by examining her own journals, diaries and private notes, as Mary Wings has done. Gillian Hanscombe describes this phenomenon as donning her 'lesbian specs': 'it is important to look at the structures of a writer's imagination in order to understand more accurately the specific way in which a particular image is used'.[9]

Mary Wings pursues the meaning of *Rebecca* by piecing together du Maurier's human condition, concerns and preoccupations and by charting their impact on her life. This notion of subtext is reiterated as Mary Wings reveals that Alfred Hitchcock, the producer of the film version of du Maurier's *Rebecca*, always used a subtext which was regarded as taboo in order to heighten the dramatic intensity of his films. In the case of *Rebecca*, this taboo was lesbianism.

The debate rages as to whether lesbians can maintain control and autonomy if they work within the constraints of male-owned and dominated commercial business. Veronica Groocock's chapter on lesbian journalism offers an interesting approach to this dilemma. Veronica Groocock is an experienced and established journalist who has worked both inside and outside mainstream print media. In her chapter she examines the full spectrum of community publications, comparing them with the mainstream and their (apparent) new-found obsession with lesbian chic. Interestingly, Lillian Faderman traces this term to the 1920s when the media turned its gaze to the lesbian and gay communities in the USA. This euphoria was an attempt to push the last vestiges of the Victorian era out of the door.[10] Interviewing some of the most influential editors of glossy women's magazines with a combined monthly readership in the UK of over three million, Veronica Groocock presents fascinating material which sheds a unique light on the 'Pink Pound' and lesbian chic debates.

Rose Collis's 'Screened Out' continues these themes with a timely appraisal of the portrayal of lesbians in British and US television. Mad, bad, sad and predatory are the major characteristics of the majority of television lesbians, thankfully strongly contrasting with the increasing number of positive visions created by the independent sector. This bodes well for the future representation of lesbians on television in the UK, due to the BBC's new-found commitment to offering broadcasting choice. This may result in an increase in the number of independent production companies which are franchised. However, the power of the visual is massive as we become increasingly a visually oriented society. As Shameem Kabir proposes in her chapter, 'Lesbian Desire on the Screen: *The Hunger*', it is vital to seek affirmation in the few mainstream sources that are available. Even though Shameem Kabir has political reservations about the film *The Hunger*, she gives an intriguing and complex analysis of the avant-garde techniques of the film and how this approach positively enhances the film. Clearly, it is time that more films were produced for lesbian audiences, which means that funding must be made available to film makers, and film distribution must extend internationally.

It is not good enough to make do with what we already have. Proponents of a new autonomy are also found in 'Twisting the Dials', written by Sheridan Nye, Nicola Godwin and Belinda Hollowes, who have wide experience as technicians, producers and researchers working both within the BBC and independent radio. Their chapter gives an astute and contemporary vision of lesbians both on the radio and as producers. After an informal overview of the recent history of lesbians on the radio in every capacity, the authors examine the political climate and legislative changes which are making radio a very different beast. Since the BBC's Director General John Birt's ground-breaking document 'Extending Choice' (1993), the Corporation has been forging ahead into fresh fields – driven by the necessity to offer innovation and distinctive broadcasting.

Refreshingly, 'Birtism' is opening doors which have long been closed to lesbian broadcasters, and the framework itself seems to be changing to allow a greater level of diversification. The authors welcome the increasing number of lesbian (and some gay) radio ventures, and are enthusiastic in their encouragement of lesbians to become involved in these new stations and programmes. Independence seems to be the key to the future in radio.

It is clear that lesbians are creating new contexts within the structures which exist, but the dynamic is not as simple as revisionism. The heralding of an ultratext, in the sense of going beyond previous constraints of existing media, is a rare and heady brew which lesbians are busy creating, resulting in some of the most fascinating media forms. Liz Yorke charts some of this new territory in 'Primary Intensities: Lesbian Poetry and the Reading of Difference'. From Audre Lorde's 'word countries' to Adrienne Rich's development of language, this is poetry which goes beyond the commonly accepted structures. Nina Rapi also perceives that mapping new lands in our culture is a most powerful tool. From her perspective as an established playwright, Nina Rapi welcomes the multifaceted nature of contemporary lesbian theatre. From lesbian pastiche to Dykenoir, she believes that the time is ripe to move from the margins to the mainstream as we begin to reinvent our lesbian selves.

In 'Beyond Queer Cinema', Cherry Smyth defies polarities of margin and mainstream and proposes that queer cinema has set its own agendas, creating a different sphere in which social change can be unleashed. As one of the programmers of the London Lesbian and Gay Film Festival, Cherry Smyth gives an erudite overview of queer cinema and its new departures.

Finally, Barbara Wilson's 'The Outside Edge' gives the private world of the writer a public airing. Discussing her own metamorphosis as a lesbian writer, Barbara Wilson questions the need for a genre-based analysis of lesbian writing. She highlights the snobbery that is rife in literary circles, particularly concerning popular lesbian genres such as crime and science fiction: 'if one pushes hard enough at the outside edge, the boundaries change, and what was once outside is now inside'.

Writing revolutions seems possible and the pure exhilaration of setting off into this uncharted land is a catalyst which will lead who knows where. Lesbians are undoubtedly at the cutting edge of the creative process, developing and designing an ever more colourful culture, one which has the potential to inform and alter wider society.

## Notes

1. Emma Donoghue, *Passions between Women: British Lesbian Culture 1668–1801*. Scarlet Press, London, 1993.
2. *Ibid.*, p. 3.
3. Lillian Faderman, *Surpassing the Love of Men*. The Women's Press, London, 1981.
4. *Ibid.*, p. 19.
5. Lillian Faderman, *Odd Girls and Twilight Lovers: A History of Lesbian Life in Twentieth-Century America*. Penguin, Harmondsworth, 1992.
6. *Ibid.*, p. 8.
7. Janice Raymond, *A Passion for Friends: Towards a Philosophy of Female Affection*. The Women's Press, London, 1986, p. 14.
8. Toni Morrison, 'What the Black woman thinks about women's lib'. *New York Times Magazine*, 22 August 1971, p. 63.

9.   Gillian Hanscombe, 'Katherine Mansfield's pear tree', in E. Hobby and C. White (eds), *What Lesbians Do in Books*. The Women's Press, London, 1991, p. 113.
10.  Faderman, *Odd Girls and Twilight Lovers*, p. 63.

# Part One
# Rereadings

Chapter one

# Rebecca Redux: Tears on a Lesbian Pillow[1]

**Mary Wings**

## 'Why don't you just do it?'

THERE is one scene in the gothic film genre which has always stuck in my mind, a moment where a young bride stares at the initial on an embroidered pillow and thinks about the woman it represents – a woman of almost superhuman strength and power, majestic beauty and deviant sexual passion. She is gone from us and the young bride is sobbing uncontrollably.

She's pretty, this newly-wed. Her blonde sausage curls jiggle as quick breathy sobs escape from her lips. She's still staring at that initial, as if it would tell her something. Her tears catch the light like diamonds; her sobs are sweet, excited. She is crying beautifully. Twinkling down her perfect rosy cheeks her tears are probably making little circular stains on the pillow, dotting the symbol she is fixated upon. That symbol is an embroidered 'R' for Rebecca, an 'R' embroidered with lesbian love in every stitch by Rebecca's maid, Danny.

The bride gazes with agony, with longing. But what kind of agony? What kind of longing? Underneath the Sapphic tapestry is

Rebecca's nightgown, a nightly veil for Rebecca's body. A black lace see-through affair. It represents sex, forbidden but to be fulfilled. And enjoyed. While Rebecca is absent from the filmy black lace, she is huge in the young woman's mind.

Where is Rebecca? She's dead.

The lesbian lover of Rebecca goads the young woman to jump out of the window.

'No man got the better of her, no woman – only the sea!' she says, confirming the impression that Rebecca was a supernatural bisexual. If only the young bride would leap out of the window, she could find Rebecca, join her in a land where you don't even wear négligés.

*Rebecca*, both the novel by Daphne du Maurier published in 1938 and the later film made by Alfred Hitchcock, reeks of lesbian intent and punishment.

I've always been fascinated by gothics, and by *Rebecca* in particular, because of the enormous sexual tension between the female characters, in both the film and the novel. This is the story of my research into the lesbian atmosphere of Rebecca and how I came to write *my* lesbian gothic novel, *Divine Victim*, updated, I hope, to the 1990s.

I wanted to place a narrator in the gothic claustrophobic interior that threatens. I wanted a gothic plot where the past informs the present, where nothing moves forward without moving backward. I wanted to write a novel where the narrator's actions are reactive. Where the narrator's concern is more to survive the suffocation of atmosphere and attacks from the unknown than to solve a mystery.

The more I thought about what I did and didn't want to write, the more I turned to the charged atmosphere of *Rebecca*, film and novel, in recreating the queer gothic. The nice thing about gothics is that the setting is never any further away than home. Kate Ellison writes:

> The typical conception of 'domestic happiness' emerged toward the end of the eighteenth century, as the middle-class home, distanced in ideology, and increasingly in fact, from the

place where money was made, became a 'separate sphere' from the 'fallen world of work'.

Focusing on the crumbling castles as sites of terror, and on homeless Narrators who wander the face of the earth, the Gothic, too is preoccupied with the home. But it is the failed home that appears on its pages, the place from which some (usually 'fallen men') are locked out, and others (usually 'innocent' women) are locked in.[2]

Ellison was speaking primarily of nineteenth-century novels. But the gothic formula offers many possibilities. In *Rebecca* both the locked in and locked out are women. And the fall, replacing nineteenth-century sins of blasphemy, greed and cruelty, is, I believe in the case of *Rebecca*, homosexuality. The punishment was Rebecca's execution.

Is the narrative of *Rebecca* an elaborate defence against homosexuality? Was *Rebecca* an inner drama related to du Maurier herself? Was killing Rebecca symbolically killing the lesbian impulse? Were the people responsible for adapting the novel for film aware of this?

For years I've watched the film in fascination as the love-struck Mrs Danvers sadistically toys with the wimpy narrator, played with true bottom cringiness by Joan Fontaine. I wondered what a twentieth-century gothic for queers would present as fear and terror.

I asked the queer question of *Rebecca* (was she or wasn't she?) and of all the people related to the book *and* the film. I came up with information about du Maurier, Alfred Hitchcock and du Maurier's sister, Angela.

I will first look at the original text of the book to give examples of the coded passages which identify Rebecca as a lesbian character.

Recent biographies of du Maurier have confirmed my suspicions of lesbian content in the film. I'm going to reveal the facts about the bisexual literary and theatrical figures of the time who were connected with *Rebecca*. I'm going to do the dangerous thing of interpreting an author's text through her life. In the end you can decide for yourself if Rebecca was truly queer.

## 14: *Daring to Dissent*

In case you haven't read the book or seen the film, here's how it goes. A young woman, whom I will call the narrator, as she's never named throughout the story, comes to Monte Carlo as a companion to a vulgar American woman, Mrs Van Hopper. There she meets Maxim de Winter, a handsome, wealthy, older man. His late wife, the beautiful and talented Rebecca, is dead, drowned at sea in a tragic accident.

Maxim proposes marriage and after a hasty wedding the two go to his imposing country estate, Manderley. The narrator is intimidated by the wealth of the place and overshadowed by the memory of Rebecca. Mrs Danvers, Rebecca's former servant, succeeds in making the heroine feel inadequate.

The narrator attempts to gain control of the domestic situation by organizing a costume ball.

Mrs Danvers suggests to her that she dress up in a costume designed after a portrait of one of Maxim's relatives. The night of the ball the heroine descends the great staircase only to be greeted by her horror-stricken husband. It turns out Rebecca had worn the same costume at a previous ball. When she runs up to Rebecca's room she confronts Mrs Danvers who nearly persuades her to commit suicide. Just then fireworks signal a shipwreck. Rebecca's boat is discovered.

We learn that Maxim does not love Rebecca, he hated her and, in the novel, he killed her. In the film this is made into an unfortunate accident, but more about that later.

Maxim confesses to the narrator and reveals Rebecca's true nature. A trial ensues where he is publicly exonerated and the couple, now released from Rebecca's spectre, are united.

## 'You've been touching it, haven't you?'

The first and most obvious lesbian in the film is Mrs Danvers (a 'Mr Danvers' is never identified); Mrs Danvers is frequently referred to as 'Danny'. The film critic Robin Wood describes the eerie servant and questions her role in the film:

Danny is both neurotic and a villainess: one cannot gloss over the fact that she tries to drive Joan Fontaine to suicide. Yet how we read her depends to a degree on how we read the film as a whole. Is it about the construction of the 'good wife' and the ideologically correct heterosexual couple? Or is it about the male's fear of an *adult and autonomous female sexuality?* [emphasis added][3]

. . . which I would describe as lesbian sexuality.

In the book du Maurier describes the thoughts of the narrator, a voice missing from the film. The narrator has a conversation with a friendly relation who tries to excuse Mrs Danvers's behaviour. The relative explains: 'Did you not know? She [Mrs Danvers] simply adored Rebecca.' And the narrator responds by thinking:

> The words had shocked me at the time. Somehow I had not expected them. But when I thought it over I began to be sorry for Mrs. Danvers. I could imagine what she must feel. It just hurt her every time she heard me called 'Mrs. de Winter'. Every morning when she took up the house telephone and spoke to me, and I answered, 'Yes, Mrs. Danvers,' she must be thinking of another voice [Rebecca's voice]. Mrs. Danvers knew the colour of her eyes, her smile, the texture of her hair.[4]

# 'You've always wanted to see this room, haven't you?'

The bond between Danny and Rebecca is constantly underscored in both the text and the action of the film. An overtly sexual scene takes place in Rebecca's bedroom. This unconsumated clothing-only orgy scene is an emotional high point in the story. To the throbbing of violins the narrator steals into Rebecca's bedroom, a forbidden place for her, guarded by Rebecca's dog.

Billows of organdy curtains confront her. She can just see the shadows of flowers and a glint of gold through the floor-length veils. She pulls aside the filmy gauze to enter an immense room of draped walls, rococo furnishings, curving legs with golden stockings supporting huge vases of spring flowers at every turn. Getting a sudden chill, she walks towards the bed when she is interrupted.

'Do you wish anything, madam?'

Mrs Danvers parts the curtains and opens the window; light spills into the room. We see that the chamber is lined with brocade, velvet, with a huge rococo bedstead, swathed in curtains; it looks like a stage.

'You've always wanted to see this room haven't you? Why didn't you just ask. I was always ready to show it to you.'

Indeed, show it to her she does. But more than that, Mrs Danvers is ready to commune with Rebecca, by fondling her furs, underwear and other intimate apparel. With her hypnotizing voice Danny treats the narrator to the sensual delights of Rebecca's clothing. She pulls out a fur coat, and brings a big cuff up to stroke the narrator's cheek. The narrator feels the chinchilla and struggles between pleasure and horror as Danny notes her excitement with a smile.

Next on the agenda: lingerie. At the brush of a fingertip on a hidden latch Mrs Danvers reveals what else but Rebecca's underwear. It glows in the dark, like silk, like satin, like it's still alive. Ah, the power of Rebecca's knickers!

Mrs Danvers touches the tiny folded items; the narrator is denied this pleasure and just stares fixated by the intimate apparel. Danny informs her that the underwear was made by 'the Nuns of the convent of St. Clare'. Only holy vestal virgins are qualified to touch the cloth that would cover Rebecca's sex.

Mrs Danvers closes the drawer quickly against the longing gaze of the narrator. The underwear drawer is closed and she may not come closer. The chinchilla coat, yes, but not the underwear – not yet!

Danny leads the narrator to the dressing table and holds Rebecca's brush over her hair, the bristles of Rebecca's brush almost making their way to her scalp, allowing the narrator to feel exactly what Rebecca would feel: Danny's brushstroke. Is Rebecca's hair still caught in the bristles, perhaps mingling with the narrator's own?

Mrs Danvers next goes to the bed and picks up Rebecca's monogrammed pillow, informing us that she has embroidered the initial herself. Replacing it gently on the bed, her fingers reach inside. Out of this cocoon emerges, light as a butterfly wing, a black see-through négligé! In the 1940s there was no more potent symbol of overt female sexuality. Mrs Danvers draws the gown out by the shoulders, holding it aloft with reverence. It floats like a body before us, half reclining on the bed. It was once the outer skin of Rebecca, collapsed now, but waiting to be filled.

Danny slips her hand inside the nightgown and beckons – insists – that the narrator approach. Her hand fills the black lace, just where Rebecca's breast would be. 'Look,' she cries excitedly, 'You can see my hand through it!'

But the implication is more than Danny's hand. In staring at flesh through the gown the emotional impact tells us (aided by a small symphony), 'Look, you can almost see *Rebecca's* body! *Rebecca's* naked flesh!'

But everyone is denied that pleasure. The narrator will not have Rebecca, nor will Danny, or Maxim, or the audience. Wanting her and not having her is part of what makes Rebecca work as an absent character. She is every woman's symbol of forbidden sexuality. Uncontrollable, renegade sexuality. Sexuality which feels distinctly lesbian.

'Do you think the dead come back and watch the living?' Mrs Danvers's eyes glide up and down the narrator's body. Mrs Danvers is always doing this. It is a threatening look, but the way her eyes examine the narrator's entire body is also sexual.

I went back to the original text of the book to read the bedroom scene. It is, in fact, racier than the film, although it does not include the delicious line about Rebecca's underwear, made by the nuns of the convent of St Clare.

From the novel, here's how Mrs Danvers describes Rebecca's bed, including her accusing the narrator of fondling Rebecca's underwear:

'That was her bed. It's a beautiful bed, isn't it? I keep the golden coverlet on it always, it was her favourite. Here is her nightdress inside the case. You've been touching it, haven't you? This was the nightdress she was wearing for the last time, before she died. Would you like to touch it again?'

'Feel it, hold it' she said, 'how soft and light it is, isn't it? I haven't washed it since she wore it for the last time . . . These are her slippers. "Throw me my slips, Danny," she used to say . . . put your hand inside the slippers . . . You never would have thought she was so tall, would you?'

'You've seen her brushes haven't you . . . Everyone was angry with her when she cut her hair, but she did not care. "It's nothing to do with anyone but myself," she would say. And of course short hair was much easier for riding and sailing . . . She was wearing slacks, of course, and a shirt when she died. They were torn from the body in the water though . . . ' (p. 156)

This exciting text evokes desire: forbidden desire, over-whelming and lesbian. The film version was no less exciting to me. It was these moments I recall as a teenager, semi-consciously aware of the erotic charge.

## 'Would you like to touch it again?'

What I couldn't put into words, what I didn't understand emotionally, was why the narrator didn't spend the night there with Rebecca's ghost. It still seems like the opportunity of a lifetime. I would even invite Danny in to watch. The novel allows Danny to fill us in on more of Rebecca's character: 'She was never one to stand mute and be wronged. She had all the courage and the spirit of a boy. She ought to have been a boy, I often told her that . . . She did what she liked. She lived as she liked' (p. 158).

Maxim, in both film and novel, describes these qualities quite differently: 'She was clever, damnably clever' (p. 227), and 'She looked like a boy in her sailing kit, a boy with the face of a Botticelli angel' (p. 254).

Leonard J. Leff in his book *Hitchcock and Selznick* says:

> Though no one mentioned the underlying lesbianism of the Rebecca–Danvers relationship Hitchcock sensed it . . . according to numerous observers, sexual aberrance intrigued the director. In *Rebecca*, the unnatural attachment of servant to mistress awaited only [Alfred Hitchcock's] touch.[5]

When the film was considered for production Selznick had to pass a synopsis by Joseph I. Breen. Breen administered the Motion Picture Association's production code, a censorship code heavily enforced in the late 1930s and early 1940s. Breen was concerned about homosexuality and didn't mince words. He warned Selznick:

> Mrs. Danver's description of Rebecca's physical attributes, her handling of the various garments, particularly the nightgown . . . must not [suggest a] perverted relationship . . . if any possible hint of this creeps into this scene we will . . . not be able to approve the picture.[6]

Although much of the text remains the same from novel to big screen there is one major difference. A difference which I think underscores the cultural horror of homosexuality at that time.

Since the Motion Picture Code and the restrictions of the Hays Office declared that no murderer should go unpunished, the murder of Rebecca had to be rewritten so that it became an accident. Rebecca goads Maxim into pushing her; she falls on the floor, her head conveniently hits a piece of fishing tackle and she dies. But we feel she deserves it. The original intention of the author, however, was that the death of Rebecca was the result of out-and-out murder.

Maxim proudly confesses in the novel:

> 'Rebecca was not drowned at all. I killed her. I shot Rebecca in the cottage in the cove. If it had come all over again I should not do anything different. I'm glad I killed Rebecca, I shall never have any remorse for that, never, never.' (p. 250)

This may be one of the *only* romance novels where the male romantic lead gets away with the murder and maintains – perhaps even establishes – his heroic stature with this act. Rebecca's character is described as so heinous we are expected not only to forgive the slaughter but to applaud it. How does this happen?

The film critic Robin Wood asks the question we all ask:

> What of Rebecca's crime? Apart from minor mental cruelty to a harmless lunatic, simply that she resisted male definition, asserting her right to define herself and her sexual desires (including an at least implicit lesbian attachment to Mrs Danvers). The logic of the film would have Rebecca as its heroine.[7]

The only other testimony to Rebecca's evil is her supposed mistreatment of animals, but du Maurier is inconsistent here. Rebecca's dog Jasper still longs for his mistress and sits waiting patiently for her on the rug in the morning room.

Hidden in the subtext of the film is the real crime. In the following examples look for those familiar code words like 'farce', 'shame', 'unspeakable', 'degradation', 'shadow life', 'abnormal', often used to signify homosexuality. Maxim describes Rebecca again: 'Our marriage was a farce from the very first. We never loved each other, never had one moment of happiness together. Rebecca was incapable of love, of tenderness, or decency. She was not even normal' (p. 254). There are frequent allusions to a double life, to persons and groups that were not what they seemed, Rebecca included, and their charms, like drugs, are described as irresistible and addictive. Maxim explains his reasons for killing Rebecca:

> 'No one would guess meeting her that she was not the kindest, most generous, most gifted person in the world. Had she met you . . . you would have been taken in, like the rest. You would have sat at her feet and worshipped her . . .
> 'She was so lovely, so accomplished, so amusing . . . but all the time I had a seed of doubt at the back of my mind. There was something about her eyes. Then the jig-saw pieces

came together piece by piece, and the real Rebecca took shape and form before me, stepping from her shadow world like a living figure from a picture frame, Rebecca seizing life with her two hands . . .

'I found her out once . . . five days after we were married. She sat there, laughing, her black hair blowing in the wind; she told me about herself, she told me things I shall never repeat to a living soul. I knew then what I had done, what I had married. Beauty, brains, and breeding. Oh my God.' (p. 255)

He continues:

'She knew I would sacrifice pride, honour, personal feeling, every damned quality on earth rather than stand before our little world after a week of marriage and have them know the things about her she had told me then. She knew I would never stand in a divorce court and give her away . . .

'I don't want to look back on those years. The shame and degradation. The lie we lived, she and I. The shabby, sordid, farce we played together . . . She would be up at dawn driving to London, streaking to that flat of hers by the river like an animal to its hole in the ditch, coming back here at the end of the week, after five unspeakable days. Oh, I kept to my side of the bargain all right. I never gave her away. Her blasted taste made Manderley the thing it is today . . . The drawing room as it is today – the morning room . . . that's all Rebecca! Those chairs . . . that tapestry . . . Rebecca again.' (p. 257) [An interesting note here: Rebecca may be the first female homosexual in literature to be praised for her interior-decorating abilities]

In the earlier and following references to London I also find a coded homo reference. Large cities have historically been the *only* place where gays and lesbians have been able to find each other and establish a social life. Where would a queer Rebecca go on the weekend? Maxim continues:

'What she did in London did not touch me. And she was careful those first years, there was never a murmur about her, never a whisper. Then little by little she began to grow careless. You know how a man starts drinking? He goes easy at first, just a little at a time. Soon it's every month, every fortnight, every few days. There's no margin of safety and all his cunning goes. It was like that with Rebecca.' (p. 257)

'She began to ask her friends down here. She would have one or two of them and mix them up at a week-end party so that at first I was not quite sure, not quite certain. I came back once, having been away shooting in Scotland, and found her there, with a half-a-dozen of them, people I have never seen before. I warned her and she shrugged her shoulders.

'What's that got to do with you?' she said.

'I nearly killed her then,' he said. 'It would have been so easy . . . ' (p. 258)

And kill her he does.

Whether one reads the novel or watches the film, whether it's murder or accident, it's clear that this was more than a bad marriage. Maxim hates, even loathes, Rebecca. And we're supposed to go along.

The subliminal underscoring of homosexual desire not only justifies the murder but also functions to excite the audience. At a time when the 'love that dare not speak its name' *could not be mentioned*, its cover of namelessness also allowed for more highly charged sexual scenes, such as Danny fondling Rebecca's underwear.

D.A. Miller, in his essay 'Rope', which is based on the film of the same name, directed by Hitchcock, talks about the function of dual plots: 'Until recently, homosexuality offered not the most prominent – it offered the only subject mass culture appertained exclusively to the shadow world of connotation. Connotation exciting the desire for proof . . . '[8]

# 'Why have you never asked me to show it to you before?'

Let's go back to the topic of lesbian excitement. Does Rebecca's room symbolize lesbian desire itself? 'You've always wanted to come here, haven't you?' Mrs Danvers goads the narrator with flawless sadistic certainty, seeming to echo that school of thought which believes homosexuality to be a genetically determined trait.

And what of the suicide scene? The narrator falls weeping on the 'R' embroidered for Rebecca by Mrs Danvers, the symbol of Danny's lesbian attachment. Crying in desperation, the narrator pulls herself up and stares at the curving female initial. At this moment could she be caught in the struggle with lesbian desire, made keener by the asexual heterosexual love offered by the distracted Maxim? Indeed, Maxim shows little affection, much less any sexual desire for the narrator. Is the struggle in the narrative between Rebecca and Maxim for the narrator's soul? Rhona J. Berenstein comments:

> Fontaine's character also assumes a masculine position in the book . . . one associated with . . . the vulnerabilities of male childhood. The masculine traits attributed to Rebecca by Danvers are as powerful as those possessed by Fontaine's authoritative men . . . Fontaine's position as the passive partner invokes another connotation associated with lesbianism . . . she plays the 'Femme' to . . . Rebecca's 'Butch'.[9]

The narrator is a nameless person, an empty vessel waiting to be filled. Could she be caught in a moment of *longing* looking at Rebecca's pillow? She will not be named Rebecca. She will become merely Mrs de Winter.

Du Maurier and Hitchcock couch this ending with all the correct hetero tones. At the end of the film Maxim and narrator are united and return to Manderley to find it in flames.

'It's Mrs Danvers – she's gone mad – she couldn't bear to see us together at Manderley,' she cries to Maxim. (This line is not in the novel.) In the film they embrace while Danny burns, the appropriate punishment for witches. Is the story of Rebecca a lesbian witch hunt, presented in a contradictory fashion? The lesbian element so tantalizing, so sexually endowed that we are meant to be confused? Both titillated and punished? How confused was the author?

## 'Queer creatures . . . freaks of nature'

Before I cite recent biographies of du Maurier there is another novel, another lesbian source, that is out of the closet in the du Maurier past. Few know that Daphne du Maurier's sister, Angela, wrote a novel with lesbianism as its *central theme*, entitled *The Little Less*.

*The Little Less* features an intense lesbian affair and a bisexual narrator, Vivien. Published in 1941, three years after her sister's novel *Rebecca*, the descriptive copy before the title page reads:

> No one had ever touched her heart until she met . . . Clare.
> Virginia, unhappily married, welcomed Vivien's friendship
> but she did not realize that what Vivien was offering was not
> friendship alone but an all-consuming love . . .

*The Little Less*, the jacket assures us, 'handles frankly but sensitively an unusual theme.'[10]

Never attracted to men, Vivien lives in the country by herself, a sort of neutered creature, after she leaves school. An old schoolchum, Phil, comes for a visit some years later and confesses to Vivien that she is having a lesbian relationship with a baroness.

Vivien's ex-schoolteacher, Flora MacDonald, is also on hand for the weekend, and discovers some love letters addressed to the baroness by rooting around in Phil's wastebasket. Flora comes downstairs to give Vivien a piece of her mind.

'I could not bring myself to come downstairs while you had that – that creature with you,' she began.

Vivien flushed. 'Are you talking of Phil?'

'Who else? But I can only imagine that you have no idea of the sort of person she was. Is, in fact. I had always disliked the sound of her. I imagined she was a low woman, a fast woman, but better far she had been, yes, a low street-walker than the foul thing she is . . . But you don't know, you can't know, you poor child. I can't judge you because you've been so horribly taken in, tricked into harbouring creatures that I shudder even to think about . . . When I saw the photographs in her room a feeling of sickness, almost of nausea, came over me. I realized, of course, how blind I had been from the beginning . . . I can generally sense that sort of creature, smell them a mile off . . .'[11]

The homophobic schoolmistress sounds like Maxim describing Rebecca, but in this narrative homophobia itself is cast as ignorant and disagreeable. Once again, illness reverberates through the text, nausea and sickness. And once again the image of the blinded heterosexual, infused with an almost religious purity.

In the novel by Angela du Maurier, the narrator, Vivien, triumphs over such homophobia. She not only falls in love with the novelist, Clare, but she moves in with her (without ever revealing her true feelings, of course). One day Vivien bravely introduces the topic of 'Phil and the baroness', to test the lesbian waters with Clare. Clare is not up for swimming and reveals a more modern, liberal form of homophobia. Homosexuals, reflecting a more liberal attitude on the part of society, reap pity at the tragedy of this misunderstood love. Clare says:

'To me love can't be wrong, but then people commit lots of wrongs and call it love when it's anything but that. I've never come up against loving one's own kind, like the unfortunate Phil. I can't help feeling it's all rather meaningless and pointless. Look at us, for instance. I certainly can't imagine ever feeling like that about another woman. Could you?'

With a tremendous effort Vivien pulled herself

together and laughed. She knew she could never, never tell Clare the truth. No matter how great the temptation, no matter how overwhelming the longing. She looked up and saw Guy stepping over the rocks to them.[13]

Guy is Clare's brutish ex-husband. Because he's a scumbag he can easily recognize Vivien's sick ardour for his wife. He takes Vivien aside and warns her.

'I quite realize you love my wife. [I must warn you] . . . all that sort of thing not only bores her, but nauseates her.'
[Vivien protests] 'I tell you Clare doesn't know . . . '
'She will if you don't mind out. It's pretty obvious! But she's a kind creature, can't bear hurting a friend, especially someone she's grateful to. So . . . I don't want to hurt you, Vivien, but if you really want to know, you're erring on the tactless [and besides] Clare's a perfectly healthy normal woman.'
A look at Vivien's face made him stop. Queer creatures they were, these freaks of nature.[13]

Angela du Maurier and the third du Maurier sister, Jeanne, never married.

## 'Life is queer'

Daphne du Maurier was born in 1907 into a glamorous theatrical family. Her father, Gerald, was a prodigal matinée idol who adored her. Daphne moved to Cornwall and spent years restoring Menabilly, the home that was in part the model for Manderley, Rebecca's house. In 1932 she married 'Boy Browning', a handsome major. Her fourth and fifth novels, *Jamaica Inn* (1936) and *Rebecca* (1938), captured a vast public. Both were made into feature films, as were the novels *My Cousin Rachel*, *Hungry Hill*, *Frenchman's Creek* and *The King's General*, and her short stories, 'The Birds' and 'Don't Look Back'.

There are some interesting clues in Daphne du Maurier's life which support the theory that *Rebecca* is a conscious or unconscious living out, and destroying of, lesbian desire. The main reference I've used here is Margaret Forster's recent biography, *Daphne du Maurier*, and Martyn Shallcross's *The Private World of Daphne du Maurier* (questioned by du Maurier's scholars, Shallcross has been labelled opportunistic).

Both Shallcross and Forster's biographies of du Maurier clearly state the author's gender confusion and sexual torment. According to Shallcross the author was known to dress in men's clothing, the better to assume the identity of her alter ego, 'Eric Avon'. Eric was the author of five of her books with masculine narrators. Du Maurier said that the clothing helped her to write from a masculine point of view. Once again we see an example of cross-dressing among white aristocratic novel-producing British women in the early twentieth century: '[Daphne's] almost mannish attitude to life, with the scant regard she paid to clothes and makeup, caused some people to wonder about her sexual orientation also.'[14]

In 1925 at the age of eighteen du Maurier first had an affair with her schoolmistress, Mlle Fernande Yvon, while attending a finishing school at Camposina.

> Life is queer [she wrote home to her governess]. By the way I've quite fallen for that woman I told you about, Mlle Yvon. She has a fatal attraction . . . she's absolutely kind of lured me on and now I am coiled in the net . . . Venetian I should think. She pops up to the bedroom at odd moments and is generally divine. She's most seductive when coming back from the opera. I get on the back seat with her and she puts her arm round me and makes me put my head on her shoulder then sort of presses me! Ugh! it all sounds too sordid and low, but I don't know, it gives one a sort of extraordinary thrill! I only hope I haven't got any Venetian tendencies.[15]

'Venetian', explains biographer Forster, was the codeword for 'lesbian' (the origin of the term never explained) and 'Cairo' was the codeword du Maurier used for heterosexuals and heterosexual sex.

The film critic Rhona Berenstein writes:

> Historical accounts of the 1930s indicate that it was a period in which the late nineteenth century and early twentieth century gains of the educated and prominent New Woman were negatively transformed . . . earlier commended, they were now criticized; earlier perceived as mildly threatening, they were now deemed a social and sexual menace.[16]

How this climate for homosexuals created self-hatred is evident in the life of du Maurier. Forster goes on to explain:

> In fact Venetian tendencies were precisely what she realized she did have, though the reality was more complex than this . . . attracted by Mlle Yvon and feeling herself respond to her advances, she worried not only that she was a 'Venetian' but that, after all, she really was a boy. Having Venetian tendencies . . . scared her and she fought her 'tendencies' hard. She might want to be male, but she did *not* want to be 'Venetian'. Her attitudes then were distinctly homophobic and she was repelled at the idea of being associated with homosexuals.[17]

# Venice

Forster writes of an overwhelming but unreciprocated infatuation du Maurier had for Ellen Doubleday, wife of her US publisher. *Rebecca* had already been published with great success in the United States and Doubleday was to be her host in New York. Later, du Maurier, in a letter to Ellen, describes her own sexual history:

> . . . growing up with a boy's mind and a boy's heart, so that at eighteen this half-breed fell in love, as a boy would, with

someone quite twelve years older than himself who was French [Mlle Yvon] and had all the understanding in the world and he loved her in every conceivable way . . . by God and by Christ if anyone should call that sort of love by that unattractive word that begins with 'L' I'd tear their guts out.[18]

To add to this confusion, du Maurier thought of Ellen Doubleday as the 'Rebecca of Barberrys [the Doubledays' home]'. She wrote to Ellen:

Watching you at Barberrys was very hard to bear . . . You looked lovelier every day. It just defeated me . . . truly, truly I should have been born a boy . . . I glory in Venice when I am in a Venice mood, and forget about it when I am not. The only chip is the dreary knowledge that there can never be Venice with you.[19]

Rumours have persisted about the novelist having an affair with Gertrude Lawrence, the famous actress. Du Maurier wrote a play, *September Tides*, which reflected an intimate affair. Their close relationship did not go unnoticed.

According to Shallcross, Gertrude Lawrence and du Maurier probably first met around 1932. He writes: 'Eleven years or so older than Daphne, in many ways Gertie was an unlikely friend for her – nevertheless their friendship was a close and intimate one.'[20]

Descriptions of Lawrence's temper recall the character of Rebecca. Michael Gough, an actor who worked with Lawrence, stated:

As much as I admired Gertie, her bouts of temper were sometimes difficult to deal with, especially for a young actor like me. I remember that one day a door had jammed on stage; Gertie's next change was down to her bra and knickers and she did it at the back of the stage.

As soon as she spotted the assistant stage manager, she

yelled at him, 'Fuck off, you shit!' Just because the door had jammed! She could be angelic one minute and quite awful the next. I had never heard an actress use such language. I was fully aware of the importance that Gertie's friendship had on Daphne. She was devoted to and besotted by her.

Every day during the run of the play there would be a small bouquet of flowers for her [with the enclosed card] 'from Daphne in Cornwall'. During the play Gertie got away with blue murder, and Daphne was so smitten she just smiled.[21]

Shallcross mentions that 'Many of their friends thought that Gertie's interest in Daphne was unhealthy. They were inseparable. Daphne appeared to adore Gertie, following her about, sitting and listening to her, loving every moment in her company.'[22] While that doesn't appear unhealthy to me, it apparently does to Shallcross, writing his book, and using *this* codeword, 'unhealthy' in 1992.

Forster, a biographer with fewer qualms about Venice, writes: 'In Florida in the sun, she and Gertie were "like two silly schoolgirls" playing games in the sea, cavorting on the beach, laughing and shrieking and losing all inhibitions. Gertie, unlike Ellen, was not inhibited about any kind of sex . . .'[23]

On a sad note Forster reveals:

'What was distressing for [du Maurier's] children was to discover . . . that their mother had not told them the truth about Gertrude Lawrence . . . the success with which Daphne maintained this subterfuge was striking . . . the revelation that she was so tortured for much of her life has been a shock . . . They are tempted to wonder if perhaps this is another instance of fantasy . . . and none of this inner life need be taken seriously.

I think it should be taken very seriously indeed. The controlling of her 'No. 2' persona . . . was no fantasy. Daphne battled with it all her life and the result is seen in her work.[24]

# *Towards a lesbian gothic*

I sent my RSVP to Mrs Danvers and Rebecca and their invitation to a supernatural *ménage à trois*, and set about releasing the trapped female desire that beckons so in *Rebecca*. I want to follow the long, tenacious fingers that lead up to Manderley; I want to read the menu Mrs Danvers proffers in the morning room; I want to know just how particular Rebecca is with her sauces; I want to lift the black veil of homophobia and find the flesh underneath.

I started making notes for *Divine Victim*. What, for example, if Mrs Danvers had been strikingly beautiful, and the narrator encased in a black dress and her hair sucked into a bun? So the narrator can more easily be seduced by a gorgeous Mrs Danvers?

I thought about literally rewriting *Rebecca* with everyone, Maxim, narrator, Danny, the ghost Rebecca, cast as lesbian.

I thought about a lot of things and eventually I ended up changing the situation and the characters, of course. But I did keep the gothic formula where the past informs the present. The claustrophobic, threatening environment. The constant relationship to the past that cannot be dispelled.

Updating the gothic isn't hard. Conveniently available for the task is the late twentieth-century female academic without tenure. Like the governesses who roam from town to town in gothics she must go where she can be placed in a suitable situation.

As some contemporary feminist academics achieve a kind of super-heroine status, with the commensurate negative gossip to go along with it, they offered themselves as prime candidates for a 1990s Rebecca-like lover. I invented Ilona Jorgenson, a Swedish art historian. She's got the ego of a Camille Paglia, but she is a feminist and a lot more beautiful.

In *Divine Victim* I have also created a nameless narrator who is additionally a world wanderer. Having completed her degree while attending university overseas, she returns to the United States. She is in the hands of fate, university funding and a problematic, Rebecca-like ex-girlfriend, Ilona. Her new girlfriend, like Maxim, is boring. The sex isn't exciting the way it was with Ilona.

I also created roles for the underwear-producing nuns. In fact, I developed an entire subplot for them and gave them a few steamy relationships of their own. Also included is a Marion sighting, similar to the Virgin's comeback appearance in August 1993 in New Jersey. The past still informs the present and it *is* supernatural.

The tears are dry on my pillow now. I have updated the lesbian gothic to current standards of fear and terror. The fear of being the victim. The terror of lost selfhood in being complicit in a victim/abuser relationship and trapped in a terrible dynamic!

In this process I discovered how cathartic the gothic could be. I found, like Daphne du Maurier, that the task of expressing forbidden emotions created an intense lesbian charge, and that the power of unleashing and resolving unspoken lesbian anxieties was a worthy goal.

## Notes

1.  Originally given as a lecture at York University, November 1992.
2.  Kate Ellison, *The Contested Castle*, Introduction, p. ix.
3.  Robin Wood, *Hitchcock's Films Revisited*. Columbia University Press, New York, 1989, p. 347.
4.  Daphne du Maurier, *Rebecca*. Doubleday, New York, 1948, p. 147. All references to subsequent quotations from *Rebecca* will give page number only, in the text.
5.  Leonard J. Leff, *Hitchcock and Selznick*. Weidenfeld & Nicolson, New York, 1987, p. 20.
6.  *Ibid.*, p. 70.
7.  Wood, *Hitchcock's Films Revisted*, p. 232.
8.  D.A. Miller, 'Rope'.
9.  Rhona Berenstein, 'I'm not the sort of person men marry', *Cineaction*, p. 88.
10. Angela du Maurier, *The Little Less*. Doubleday, New York, 1941.
11. *Ibid.*
12. *Ibid.*
13. *Ibid.*
14. Martyn Shallcross, *The Private World of Daphne du Maurier*. St Martin's Press, New York, 1992, p. 103.
15. Margaret Forster, *Daphne du Maurier*. Chatto and Windus, London, 1993, p. 28.
16. Berenstein, 'I'm not the sort of person', p. 96.
17. Forster, *Daphne du Maurier*.

18. *Ibid.*, p. 231.
19. *Ibid.*, p. 223.
20. Shallcross, *The Private World*, p. 110.
21. *Ibid.*, p. 121.
22. *Ibid.*, p. 111.
23. Forster, *Daphne du Maurier*, p. 252.
24. *Ibid.*, p. 419.

# Part Two
# The New Muse

Chapter two

# 'That's Why You Are So Queer': The Representation of Lesbian Sexuality in the Theatre

**Nina Rapi**

'YOU are not a human being like the rest of us. There wasn't enough material to make a man of you and for a woman you've got too much brain. That's why you are so queer!' I could have invented this quote as the most common abuse hurled at lesbians, directly or indirectly: subhuman, a bad imitation of men, in excess of something or other – too aggressive, too sexual, too strong, too intelligent, too rebellious – to qualify as a woman.

While lesbians, when able to set up our own subcultures, can turn the 'excess' around, play with it, create a specifically lesbian *mise-en-scène*, both on and off stage, with our own distinctly dykey costumes, gestures and role-playing, heterosexual representations of lesbian sexuality continue to dominate public cultural space. As a result we continue to be perceived, and may at times perceive ourselves, as 'not there', 'not real' or simply 'beyond bounds'.

One could argue, and it would be a straight man or woman and/or a privileged lesbian who would do so, that with the recent plethora of 'lesbian chic' articles in the national papers and magazines, lesbians have achieved mainstream acceptance. But as Suzanne Moore recently wrote, 'woe betide you if your life extends beyond that of a glossy magazine'.[1]

In that case the introductory quote would be more than likely to apply and it was written over a hundred years ago! It is of course from Wedekind's *Pandora's Box* and is what Lulu, one of the most enduring icons of dangerous female sexuality, throws at Countess Geschwitz, one of the most enduring, dominant lesbian stereotypes. Has nothing changed then? From my experience of working in the theatre, I would argue that very little has. The average heterosexual thespian still holds on to absurd and ludicrous views of lesbians, for example that they are 'too ugly' to get a man, are 'sad and lonely' or 'doomed' in one way or another, hate their father, never have sex or are sex-obsessed and would have *any* straight woman!

What has changed, however, is the emergence of a lesbian body of theatre work which explores a number of forms, structures and genres, and varies widely in content. On the whole, in its representations of lesbian sexuality, it challenges not only pre-conceived notions of lesbianism but also the presumed naturalness of heterosexuality. Nevertheless it remains largely on the margins of the dominant theatre and is thus denied the possibility of entering public consciousness.

Any representation of sexuality on stage inevitably brings up the question of the controlling gaze. Who has the power to represent what and how; who decides 'what can be seen', as Teresa de Lauretis put it. Who defines whose reality? I shall explore here how lesbian sexuality has been represented in the theatre by the 'straight mind', to use Monique Wittig's term, and in contrast, by the lesbian imagination.

# The straight mind

The plays I will look at in this section are: the *Lulu* plays by Wedekind, *Huis Clos* by Sartre, *The Children's Hour* by Lillian

Hellman and *Foreign Lands* by Karen Hope. These are plays which have become 'classics', in the case of the first three, and heralded as 'the best'[2] in the case of the fourth and most contemporary. As such they are meant to speak universal and lasting truths. I will examine how much of that 'universality' and truth extends to the representation of lesbians.

## 'The devil'

Countess Geschwitz is one of the first lesbian characters to appear on a western stage (1898), and as such is worth going into in some detail.

In *Earth Spirit*, the first of the *Lulu* plays, she appears briefly and only in the final act. Her stage presence consists of her discreetly courting Lulu in front of her husband, and later hiding incongruously behind some curtains, where he discovers her and exclaims: 'The devil!' Why he would associate the Countess, whom he knows and has just been civil to, with the devil is a mystery. If, however, we replace 'the Countess' with 'the lesbian' it becomes apparent that 'lesbian as the devil' is something the playwright wants to communicate to his audience, consciously or not.

## Begging to be kicked

Wedekind, in his introduction to *Pandora's Box*,[3] claims that the Countess is in fact the 'tragic central figure' of the play and not Lulu, who is 'entirely passive in all three acts'. The Countess Geschwitz 'in the first act furnishes an example of . . . superhuman self-sacrifice', while in the second act she is forced by the progress of the plot, 'to summon all her spiritual resources in the attempt to conquer the terrible destiny of abnormality with which she is burdened.' In the third act, 'having borne the most fearful torments of soul with stoical composure, she sacrifices her life in defence of her friend'.

Further, Wedekind states that, in writing the play, he was motivated by his desire to rescue 'the powerful human tragedy of exceptional but wholly fruitless spiritual struggles from its fate of ridicule and bring it home to the sympathy and compassion of those not affected by it'. The most effective way of doing that, he asserts, was to include the character Rodrigo, personifying in him the 'most telling possible form of the vulgar mockery and shrill derision which is the uneducated man's reaction to *this tragedy*' (emphasis added). He had, however, to neutralize his mockery by his serious treatment of the Countess's fate, who in the end would emerge 'as the unconditional victor', if his play was to have fulfilled his purpose. Has it?

To begin with, claiming that the Countess is the central figure of the play is amusing in its naive exaggeration. The plot, the dynamics and all the relationships of the play revolve around Lulu, and not the Countess. The play simply could not exist without Lulu. It would, however, survive a re-write quite satisfactorily without the Countess, if not as effectively in terms of assuaging male fears and reassuring male egos that lesbians could never, ever get 'their goods', the female body.

Wedekind might have genuinely intended to present a noble example of 'the curse of abnormality' but what he has achieved instead is a mockery of lesbianism, precisely what he set out to neutralize. Rodrigo is a fool whose crude comments can easily be dismissed.

It is the treatment the Countess receives from Lulu, the object of her desire, which reinforces exactly what Wedekind claims he counteracts. In the first act, Lulu, immediately after the Countess has carried out 'the superhuman self-sacrifice' of taking her place in prison (in a complex plan which includes deliberate contraction of cholera), amuses herself and her lover with a little anecdote about the Countess: 'Do you remember the fancy-dress ball when I was dressed like a page? And how the tipsy women all ran after me? Geschwitz crawled round at my feet and begged me to kick her in the face with my cloth shoes.'

In the second act the Countess somehow manages to get out of prison. She is one of many hangers-on in Lulu's new court. There is a party. Geschwitz confronts Lulu with the promises she has made to her in exchange for her 'sacrifice'. There was a selfish motive there after all, a bargain. Lulu, typically, hisses at her: 'I shudder with disgust at the thought of it ever becoming reality.'

Despite Wedekind's claims, the Countess appears practically to have struck a prostitution deal with Lulu. And while she has kept her side of it, Lulu has, of course, cheated. Not exactly noble, tragic stuff on either side.

## 'Pathetic and loathsome'

Lulu is a complex character, both innocent and evil, freely *and* manipulatively sexual. Her instinct is one of self-preservation, hardly ever consideration for others. She exploits most of her lovers in one way or another. However, not a single one of those males, no matter how repulsive they are or what wrong they do to her, is subjected to the venomous contempt she reserves for the Countess. She is a 'daft creature who crawls around' her feet at best, and 'pathetic and loathsome' at less than worst. The worst is yet to come. At this stage of the play, two-thirds into the second act, Lulu kindly explains to the Countess why she is the way she is: 'You were uncompleted in your mother's womb, either as a man or a woman. You're not a human being like the rest of us . . . that's why you are so queer.' And to add insult to injury she advises: 'Apply to Miss Bianetta. She's to be had for anything so long as she's paid for it.'

Any self-respecting human being would at this point withdraw, at least to lick her wounds. But the Countess is not a human being, even according to her own estimation. She is 'an insignificant worm'. As such she deserves even worse than she has already been subjected to. Lulu manages to persuade her to have sex with the revolting Rodrigo, at some unknown address at the end of town. Lulu has already arranged to have him killed when they arrive there. This information she does not, of course, pass on to the Countess. What she asks her to do is 'to save her life'. In exchange Lulu promises herself. Another prostitution deal. And the Countess falls for it, yet again! At this point she loses any credibility as a character. She becomes a stooge that helps Wedekind move the plot forward.

## Unconditional victim

In the third act Lulu is living as a destitute escapee in another country, with her husband and the man who brought her up. She is forced into prostitution – true and proper this time. Geschwitz appears, apparently having tried to raise money, without success. How she finds them is not explained and it doesn't really matter. What is absurd is that she does look for them, after Lulu's treatment of her, and is grateful to be received! Moreover, she will not let Lulu go on the street alone, but insists on accompanying her. A client spots her and exclaims: 'The devil'! The woman obviously bears a striking resemblance to him.

Just before Lulu arrives with what is to be her last client, the Countess gives a rather touching soliloquy while she is contemplating suicide. She reiterates that she is not human, but here at least she asserts that she has a human soul. Still, she knows that 'it is no merit' if she sacrifices everything. Presumably a worthless worm like her is *expected* to give everything away. It is ironic that through this soliloquy Wedekind strips the Countess of any tragic potential, when he would probably claim to be doing exactly the opposite. An act that is expected of someone is not a tragic act, rather it is a duty. Further, a sacrifice of 'no merit' is no sacrifice at all.

In her second soliloquy, shortly before the end, the Countess voices for the first time a consciousness of Lulu's coldness. But she still hopes to have her 'taste of happiness' after all. Lulu arrives with Jack, her last client. Jack, the perceptive psycho that he is, realizes that Geschwitz is in love with Lulu and says so. Full of sympathy, he strokes her 'as if she were a dog', according to the stage directions.

The only tragic element in relation to the Countess appears in the last two pages of the play. After Jack and Lulu have gone into the next room the Countess decides for the first time to leave 'these people', to go back to Germany, study and 'fight for women's rights'. The moment she makes this decision, however, Lulu screams from the other room. The Countess runs to her rescue, whereupon Jack staggers out and stabs her. He then kills Lulu too, washes his hands and exits.

The first time the Countess makes a positive decision in her life she is called to altruistic, dangerous but necessary action. The first time she decides to live, she has to die. For the first time she rings true as a character. Any dyke would have run to her friend's call for help. However, when at the very end she says: 'My angel! Let me see you once more! – I am near you – will stay near you – in eternity.

Oh, God!' and then dies, she loses credibility again, sounding comic and melodramatic.

The Countess has thus emerged not as the 'unconditional victor' Wedekind would have us believe, but as the unconditional victim and an unconvincing one at that.

## 'Damned bitch'

*Huis Clos* (1944) is a lot subtler in its anti-lesbianism. Perhaps this is because of the fifty years that separate it from *Pandora's Box*. Perhaps it's because Sartre was intellectually more complex than Wedekind. Or perhaps being Simone de Beauvoir's lifelong lover made all the difference!

The premise of *Huis Clos* is simple. Three people are locked up in a room, in hell. They wonder who their torturers are going to be and discover they are each others' torturers. In the process they each reveal their 'crime', their reason for being sent to hell. Garcin, a journalist, turns out to be a coward who has betrayed his cause and his co-fighters. Estelle, a social butterfly, has killed her baby and driven a man to suicide. Both are heterosexual. Inez, who is a lesbian and a post office clerk hasn't committed a crime per se, she is *evil personified*, a 'damned bitch', 'rotten to the core'. She can't get on 'without making people suffer. Like a live coal. A live coal in others' hearts'. When she is alone she flickers out, she can only exist by crawling under people's skins. She is, in other words, a parasite; furthermore, she is a self-admitted torturer.

*Huis Clos* is a beautifully constructed play and very clever. Inez may be the personification of evil but she is also the most intelligent of all three, the one with the fewest self-delusions. It is she who first realizes the game they've been condemned to play for eternity, she who is the most perceptive of the others' psychologies. But it is only she who is 'not human', as this is beyond her range.

The tension in *Huis Clos* is built around the classic triangle situation where A wants B, B wants C, C wants A. One could argue that this is an equal situation where all three want what they can't have. However, a hierarchy emerges which makes transparent Sartre's presumed universality and reveals it to be, rather, his male heterosexual 'axis of categorization', to use another of Wittig's expressions.

Estelle can only exist through being desired by a man, any man. Being a heterosexual female she can only perceive herself and be defined as a sex object. So she wants Garcin. Inez, who is not only female but a lesbian too, can exist only through her desire for another woman. She does not exist in and of herself. She has no self, and so she is constantly 'wanting'. She is a state of being, not a being. So she wants Estelle. Garcin, being a man, can of course define himself only in relation to his actions. He is primarily concerned with what his actions reveal about him: chiefly, whether he is a coward or a hero. But the only person he can thrash this out with is Inez. So he wants Inez.

The reason he wants Inez is because she knows 'wickedness' and shame and fear; she knows 'what evil costs'. While Garcin, Sartre's existential hero, is tortured by the possibility that he may be a coward, that he may have made the wrong existential choice, Inez, his feared/desired Other, is already a coward as part of her non-human condition. She has no choice. Being a coward comes with being a lesbian. Being a lesbian comes with being shameful and fearful – and above all *evil*, pre-destined.

## The lesbotype

*Huis Clos* and *Pandora's Box* are very different plays but when it comes to the representation of 'the lesbian' a number of similarities emerge. Both the Countess and Inez are 'not human' on their own admission. Either they are mistaken for the devil (Geschwitz) or they are evil personified (Inez). Neither is wanted by the object of her desire. Each is constantly found 'wanting' and seen to be repulsive to the woman she desires. While Geschwitz is told so by Lulu, Inez is actually *spat at* by Estelle.

Even though each is repeatedly humiliated by the woman she desires, she always goes back for more. Being dogs, they like a good kicking.

Finally and unsurprisingly, both women are full of self-loathing; only Inez is at least refreshingly caustic and witty with it.

# 45: 'That's Why You Are So Queer'

## 'Sad and dirty'

In Lillian Hellman's *The Children's Hour* (1937) it is clear that Martha Dobie, 'the lesbian', and Karen Wright, the object of her desire, *love* each other, in sharp contrast to the two previous plays.

Martha Dobie is neither evil and repulsive nor humiliated by Karen Wright. The two women run a school for girls and are living together harmoniously, until they are accused by a highly manipulative girl of being lesbians. A scandal erupts. They are taken to court. The case is disproved but their school and reputations are ruined. They are both shattered.

However, Martha Dobie now realizes that she does love Karen '*that way*' and that 'there's always been something wrong' as long as she can remember. Karen tries to persuade her otherwise but to no avail. In the end, Karen comforts her by saying: 'You are tired and *sick*'.[4] Martha, unconsoled, withdraws into herself more and more. She is becoming aware of a big difference between herself and her friend: 'You feel sad and clean; I feel sad and dirty . . . I can't stay with you anymore, darling.'

Despite further protests Martha has now made a final decision. After a few more exchanges she goes into the other room. We hear a shot. Martha has done the decent thing and killed herself. That's exactly what 'sad and dirty' people should do.

The love between the two women aside, there are a number of similarities between this play and the two discussed earlier:

- the lesbian is yet again represented as *desiring* but *not desired*;
- on realizing that she is a lesbian, she is filled with self-loathing;
- while the way for her to come into being as a lesbian is not by experiencing rejection and humiliation, as in the other two plays, she must annihilate herself.

It seems that, as Ellenberger has asserted: 'Most people . . . who are not lesbian people, deeply want lesbians, if not dead, then changed – silent, disguised, muffled, incognito, pushed to the edges of human consciousness and human culture.'[5]

Lesbians, however, always seem to linger in the back of human consciousness, in the back of heterosexual consciousness, as the feared Other, as their collective shadow. Straight writers can't quite erase her from their minds but they can experience the vicarious pleasure of deleting the lesbian by destroying her in their plays.

### 'Are you sure you know who you are kindred spirits with?'

*Foreign Lands* by Karen Hope was one of the theatrical successes of 1993. The play consists of three scenes, taking place over three weeks in the spring of 1986, and is set in the north-east of England. The writer's stated intention in writing the play was to show 'that some people are born evil just as others are born good'.[6]

In the first scene of the play, Rosie, aka Peggie Bow, the protagonist, rents a room in Barbara's house. Barbara has an autistic daughter Ellen, who has a remarkable memory. Ellen and Rosie/Peggie appear to know each other but neither reveals this to Barbara. The three establish a sinister/cosy familiarity.

In the second scene Madeleine, a hoorah Henrietta type, visits Rosie/Peggie. It emerges that the two women met in prison and became lovers. While Rosie was a lifer, Madeleine was in briefly for refusing to pay a fine. The two had a plan. Rosie, released through Madeleine's contacts, was to write a book in a foreign country, courtesy of Madeleine's rich daddy. Rosie has, however, come up north instead, standing up the 'poor, rich girl', who is now understandably angry. But this doesn't seem to bother Rosie. She has the power in the relationship, knows it and exploits it.

She is another 'damned bitch'. But she has redeeming qualities, unlike Inez. Her heart is forever given to her adolescent sweetheart, her partner-in-crime, now dead, whose grave she is here to visit. She asks Madeleine to find it for her.

Rosie is a 'born' lesbian as much as she is born evil. No explanations needed, no questions asked. With Madeleine we get the impression that lesbianism is a 'phase she's going through', part of her rebellion against her over-privileged family. She is the least developed character in the play and hence least convincing in everything, including her absurd naivety about Rosie.

In the third and last scene the two wake up in Rosie's bed. Rosie continues to tease/torture Madeleine, who claims, despite all evidence to the contrary, that they are 'kindred spirits'. Rosie responds with the threatening question 'Are you sure you know who you're kindred spirits with?', while at the same time subjecting Madeleine to sexual sadism, to accompany the mental and emotional sadism. Following this, we learn that Rosie is a murderess and has returned to the town of her crimes.

## A psychopathic serial killer 'touched by God'

While in prison Rosie/Peggie gained a social sciences degree and a rather odd 'warmth and compassion' (according to Madeleine), which drove the other prisoners wild with lust (a straight woman's lesbian fantasy?), a conviction that she was 'touched by God' and a sense of mission to state her side of the story to the world. It is now revealed that Rosie/Peggie and her girlfriend killed five little boys in this town twenty years ago, and have become folklore heroines/villains, hence the reason that Peggie Bow is posing as Rosie here. In a brilliant ironic twist it is also revealed that Ellen was the little girl they always took with them in the car, as a 'mnemonic device', sworn to secrecy.

However, Madeleine now discovers that it wasn't just little boys that the lesbian lovers killed – in which case 'there was a reason' – but little girls too – in which case it was just for fun and hence unacceptable!

Furious, Madeleine shouts that she has found the grave but that it was desecrated and daubed with foul graffiti. With this information, Rosie's 'dream' appears to collapse.

Barbara enters with Rosie's framed degree – written in the name of Peggie Bow, the local murderess. Madeleine realizes that now not only Barbara but the framer – and probably the whole town – know Rosie's real identity.

The play climaxes with heavy religious symbolism – it is Good Friday and Rosie/Peggie has been making a 'stained-glass' window out of tissue paper with Ellen. There is talk of the holy day, forgiveness and Christ dying to save us. Tension builds. Rosie/Peggie stands by the window, 'her hair up from the nape of her neck, her head flung back – an attitude of sexual, rather than spiritual ecstasy', according to the stage directions. A brick comes through the window. Her hands and arms are cut from glass; they are bleeding. She won't pull away from the window. She asks the others one by one to open the door. They are all frozen to the spot. The banging continues. Rosie/Peggie smiles and goes to answer the door herself. We all know what will happen to her. Blackout.

## Contradictions

Structurally, *Foreign Lands* is admirably skilful, if conventional, but its fundamental premise is dubious. While I do not doubt Hope's integrity, I wonder how 'innocent' is the choice of 'the lesbian as a born psychopath' by a straight writer.

The representation of lesbian sexuality in *Foreign Lands* does indicate a shift in straight perceptions of lesbian sexuality in the theatre, in that it presents 'the lesbian' *as not only loved but desired too*, if in a rather naive and unconvincing way.

However, Hope's honourable conscious intentions of wanting to show lesbian love as 'pure' (even though it is hard to imagine that a love so 'pure' would kill children for kicks), and 'the lesbian' as possessing 'a calm centre', charisma and a sharp mind, are seriously undermined by her unquestioned use of the 'born evil' and 'damned bitch' lesbian clichés.

Even though we hear of a beautiful love (the reservations above notwithstanding), what we witness *on stage* is a 'sick love'; a sadistic lesbian who uses, abuses and tortures her 'victim'. And yet, again, one who in the end must simply stop existing – in this case by being lynched.

In conclusion, it's as if the straight mind can conceive of and represent the lesbian only in certain ways: as unloved, undesired, rotten to the core, parasitic, a victim – and preferably *dead*.

# The lesbian imagination

At the same time as Sartre was writing *Huis Clos* (1944) and in the same city, Paris, Gertrude Stein was writing her idiosyncratic plays. Ironically, while the straight man felt free to represent an openly lesbian character in his play, the lesbian writer felt under censorious pressure to veil and code her lesbian references.

In 1993, while Karen Hope, a heterosexual woman, created a serial child-murderer lesbian protagonist without inhibition *or* criticism,[7] I, a lesbian playwright, when under commission by straight companies, am under pressure to eliminate or code my lesbian references. Totally different writers and contexts, similar power inequalities.

While straights fall back into familiar stereotypes when representing lesbian sexuality, lesbians struggle to represent it in all its complexity, including its dark underbelly, without encouraging homophobia. As Holly Hughes said in *Sins of Omission* (1993), 'Do I censor myself? Every day! . . . I don't want them [homophobes] to see my pain and use it against me . . . against us.'[8]

While there is no denying that lesbians *are* boldly occupying *and* being given public cultural space in a number of spheres – especially photography, fiction and stand-up comedy – censorship and self-censorship continue to inhibit full artistic expression by lesbians.

Furthermore, in the theatre, despite the myth that it is ruled by homosexuals, lesbians remain largely invisible. During *Saturday Night Out*, screened on BBC2 in November 1991, the programme *To Be or Not To Be* (out) interviewed a number of distinguished out male actors (Ian McKellen, Simon Callow, Anthony Sher) but could not find a single 'distinguished' lesbian actress to come out.

The most successful British lesbian playwright is Sarah Daniels, who has, however, written only one lesbian play, *Neaptide* (1986). On the whole, lesbian work remains very much the fringe of the fringe, with the inevitable exceptions that prove the rule, such as *Weldon Rising* (1992) by Phyllis Nagy, which received wide coverage in the national press.

While new and established gay writers are having productions in the most prestigious theatres (from the Hampstead to the Bush, Croydon Warehouse and beyond) and transfers to the National and the West End, and out gay directors are becoming artistic directors of top venues such as the Royal Court and the Lyric Hammersmith, lesbians remain either on the periphery or firmly in the closet. To address the reasons why this is so is beyond the scope of this chapter.

As a playwright, I am constantly aware of externally imposed restrictions on the development of theatre work by lesbians which reduce it to a scale that is not remotely comparable with the work of gay men, let alone straight men and women. However, despite all of these limitations lesbians have created and continue to create theatre.

Defining 'lesbian theatre' is a slippery business. For practical purposes, I shall take it to mean theatre that foregrounds the lesbian experience and is written by out lesbians. The plays I shall focus on are contemporary and have been produced and/or published in the UK. Further, they express the diversity that exists among lesbians in terms of form and content, and of the background of the writers/ theatre makers, even though 'lesbian theatre' is predominantly white and Anglo Saxon at present.

## Lover as friend

The question of how you represent the lesbian on stage – butch/femme/androgynous, angelic, demonic, sexless – is often linked to lesbians' definition of 'the lesbian'. For many, the definition is clear and unambiguous – it is based on mutual sexual desire. For others the picture is more diffuse. Adrienne Rich, the American poet and theorist, articulated the term 'lesbian continuum' which includes 'the sharing of a rich inner life, the bonding against male tyranny, the giving and receiving of practical and political support',[9] not necessarily involving genital sexual experience with another woman.

These two perceptions of the lesbian are reflected in many lesbian plays. I see echoes of Adrienne Rich's views in Maro Green's and C. Griffin's *More*, an exploration of hidden disabilities, anorexia and agoraphobia. The relationship here seems to be based more on a pact of mutual survival rather than sexual desire. Mavro says to Coquino at one point, 'You can call this love or work'. While there is physicality between them, there are no overt sexual gestures. Coquino says to Mavro, 'I want you to touch me', to which Mavro replies 'Yes, and I want more'. This encounter does not lead to a sexual embrace, as might be expected, but to the birth of *More*, the two puppets who become Mavro's and Coquino's uninvited defenders. Mavro calls the body 'Bull', a separate entity, split from her self. When Mavro bares her anorexic body to the waist this is definitely not the female body as the object of desire but the female body as the site of conflicts, unresolved in the outside world.

## Zamis

*The Basin* by Jacqueline Rudet is structured around two lovers and the reactions of their friend to them having sex. It is firmly rooted in the 'lesbian continuum' idea but in the context of black women of West Indian origin. Rudet explores 'zamis', which as she states in her introduction to the play is not 'lesbian in patois' but 'refers more to the universality of friendship between women . . . '

By the end of the first scene Susan, 'the lesbian', has expressed her desire for her childhood friend Mona. At the beginning of scene two, the two women enter one after the other, both wearing dressing-gowns. At the production I saw, by Theatre Noir at the Base Theatre in Camberwell, the predominantly black, female and straight-looking audience burst into knowing sounds and appreciative laughter at this point. It was clear before anything had been said that the two characters had had sex off-stage. Susan's satisfied desire was written all over her body in a rather cheeky and triumphant way. It was this that had brought about the delighted 'you made it' sounds.

Mona, the straight-turned-dyke character, does not want to acknowledge what has happened. She puts the sex down to her being 'too maternal . . . too soft' and making sacrifices for everybody. By the third scene, however, she is wondering, 'Maybe we've always been lovers? I'd never made love to her before, but maybe we've always been lovers? I always turn to her when I need comfort, I always turn to her when I need help. Maybe we've always been lovers.'

In *Memorial Gardens* by Maro Green and Caroline Griffins, the definition of 'lover' is again diffuse and not necessarily linked to sexual desire. 'We've been lovers for two months,' says one of the lovers, to which the other replies, 'Or most of our lives, depending on how you look at it.'

In *The Basin*, being lovers equals forging a pact of survival, as with the lovers of *More*. This is certainly the playwright's intention, but what came across during the Base Theatre production was something different. The sexual element of Susan and Mona's relationship was at the core of the performance, was its 'edge'. The fact that they were lovers as in having sex was what warmed and excited the audience.

## Naming desire

In Jackie Kay's *Chiaroscuro*, which examines 'naming' of both lesbianism and race, 'dream names' and 'desire names', the sexual relationship of two of the characters is at the centre of the play. There is talk of love and sex between them but again there are no explicit sexual gestures on stage (with one exception, where that gesture is a frame up which results in one of the characters being sacked from her job as a nurse).

In Jackie Kay's *Twice Over*, the sexual relationship of two of the central characters again underlines the whole play. These two are older women and one of them, Cora, has just died. Here, however, we witness the women's desire for each other, in flashback, expressed in kisses, dances and language: 'We never made it to bed. Our first passion, on Cora's living room sofa.' The play's emphasis, however, is not so much on the two women's exploration of their sexual lives as on their reasons for being closeted and the reactions of those around them on discovering their lesbianism. *Twice Over* is particularly funny/poignant when Evaki, Cora's adolescent grand-daughter – a baby dyke in the making? – finds through Cora's diaries what her granny was up to. She is overwhelmed by a mixture of fear, anger and sexual curiosity, wondering whether it's hereditary and 'how they did it'.

## Lover as object of desire

Sexuality and the body are almost totally absent from Sarah Daniel's *Neaptide*. The focus is clearly on the battle lesbians have to wage on institutions. Sexual relationships between women obviously exist in the plot but there is never any display of sexual desire on stage.

Holly Hughes's *Dress Suits to Hire*, which has been described as 'dykenoir', a genre of its own, is part of another emerging tradition in lesbian performance, that of centring on sexual desire as a powerful weapon of change. Or, as Audre Lorde writes, 'Recognising the power of the erotic within our lives can give us the energy to pursue genuine change within our world, rather than merely settle for shift of characters in the same weary drama.'[10]

Hughes's language is explicitly but wittily sexual: 'You look hungry. Come on get it, squeeze it outta me, suck it outta me. I wanna be totally Spain when you're done with me.' *Dress Suits to Hire* is centred on Michigan and Deeluxe, two 'sisters'/lovers who never get out of their suits-for-hire shop.

Theirs is a dark, obsessive, totally sexual relationship. The body is, for Michigan at least, a constant source of pleasure, a refuge for when things get bad. The body is separate from the lover: 'And even when I hate her, I love the body', and of uncertain ownership: 'Who does the body belong to? Partly to me. It belongs to her.'

For Deeluxe, however, the body/her body is invaded by Little Peter, a man, who lives inside her. He 'is' one of her hands, and at times controls her life. In the end she 'strangles him'. The two sisters/lovers continue their power battles and game/role playing.

In my own *Ithaka* the passionate but claustrophobic relationship at its centre is unmistakably an arena of sexual desire and, perhaps inevitably, of power. The desire is intense and mutual, the power interchangeable, and in the context of the playfulness and freedom found in lesbian relationships, within the realm of imagination and sexual experience at least. Likewise, and as Kate Davy argues, within *Dress Suits to Hire* power relations are repeatedly redistributed.


## Lesbian metaphors

Lesbian relationships in plays by lesbians are often portrayed through metaphors. While *Dress Suits to Hire* uses the classic sisters/ lovers, *Ithaka* explores the madam/maid, mother/daughter, jailer/ prisoner dualities.

Similarly, Jane Bowles's only play, *In the Summer House* (1953), ostensibly explores three mother/daughter relationships, though the production at the Lyric, Hammersmith (1993), alluded to these as metaphors for lesbian relationships, and certainly for me, as a dyke spectator, the emotional and psychological intensity of the relationships was continuously underlined by psychosexual dynamics which were clearly those of lesbian lovers and not of blood relations.


## The butch/femme dynamic

Two of the longest-running lesbian theatre companies, Split Britches in America and Siren in Britain (the latter now defunct), have separately developed a theatre which dramatizes lesbian desire through the butch/femme dynamic.

As Lois Weaver of Split Britches said in a *Rouge* interview:

> Butch/Femme is a play thing for us . . . we often try to pull from popular culture and popular culture is defined in terms of man and woman. So rather than deal with it as man and woman, which we find limiting, we take it one step away, which is butch and femme. It's . . . something about the imagery we take from those roles and play with them, for erotic and dramatic purposes, for the humour and irony of it.[11]

To this, Peggy Shaw, the other half of Split Britches, added, 'We can only go truthfully. And truthfully, in our hearts of hearts I am butch and she is femme. And we find pleasure in theatricalising it.' Lois Weaver concluded:

> We are theatricalising that part of ourselves to overblow it, to make it huge and go past the stereotypes and go on to the other side of it and claim it and own it and sort of throw it back in their face [heterosexuals] ... That's the political aspect of it, but the aesthetic edge of it is that it is who we are, where we start from.

The butch/femme dynamic on and off stage is, however, far from unproblematic, and often comes under fierce attack as a relic of the past, a copycat, a crude stereotype. But as has been convincingly argued by Joan Nestle, among others, it is a dynamic with its own codes, symbols and meanings which are very different from the man/woman coupling it is supposedly imitating. And as Jewelle Gomez points out, 'Why should we accept the male/female dyad as the primary relationship on which all others are modelled?'[12] Furthermore, as Sue Ellen Case writes:

> the space of seduction, the butch/femme couple can, through their own agency, move through a field of symbols ... playfully inhabiting the camp space of irony and wit, free from biological determinism, elitist essentialism, and the heterosexist cleavage of sexual difference.[13]

While butch/femme is certainly *one of many* ways of representing lesbian sexuality on stage, what I think is more characteristic of lesbian theatre is an interplay of subject (desiring) and object (desired). These two positions are interchangeable, reversible – playfully occupied or abandoned at will, both within the sexual arena and outside it. This reciprocity, whether or not it is embodied in the butch/femme dynamic, challenges not only pre-conceived notions about lesbians but also the whole masculinity/

femininity dynamic, perceived and acted out by heterosexuals as a naturalized and not a constructed phenomenon.

## Androgyny

While Split Britches play with the butch/femme dynamic, Monique Wittig and Zande Zeig have gone in pursuit of androgyny both practically and theoretically. Zande Zeig toured with Monique Wittig's play *The Journey* in 1984. Her performance was celebrated by feminist critics for its unique combination of feminine and masculine gestures, and for being beyond those gestures. Zeig and Wittig extended their practical work and offered a class at New York University on the 'Dynamics of Language and the Semiotics of Gesture'. They experimented with 'a series of techniques specifically designed for learning the other sex class gesture system'. The students were encouraged to find their own impersonator – not a character created out of fictional information but 'oneself as the opposite sex'. They studied three systems of gesture, that of their own sex, that of the opposite sex, and neutral. They were then trained in using all three.

Zeig later articulated these ideas in her article 'The actor as activator'.[14] She views gestures as an aspect of women's oppression. There are no 'natural' gestures. People are so used to playing the man or the woman, they don't recognize gender as a social construction. 'The gestures appropriate to women are the gestures of slaves. It follows I suppose that the gestures appropriate to men are the gestures of slave masters. Neither is appropriate to a free human', she asserts. Gestures are like clothing, they can be put on and off. They are an essential theatre language and are particularly relevant to lesbians. Lesbians as social actors, as well as actors on stage, are forced to look at their physical selves in a political context. Zeig concludes that 'the task of the lesbian is to change the form of the actor's movement and gestures . . . through gestures, lesbians are able to radically influence the direction of contemporary theatre.'

In *Weldon Rising* by Phyllis Nagy, the writer describes Jaye, one of her two lesbian characters in the play, as 'thoroughly gorgeous', adding 'not at all coy or girlish, but not butch either'.

Androgynous maybe? While the writer didn't state it as such, the actress who played the part in the Royal Court production certainly combined feminine allure and masculine toughness in a truly androgynous way.[15]

## Fooling around

If there is one 'genre' that could be said to dominate lesbian theatre, it is pastiche. Most lesbian theatre companies from the first one ever, The Coventry Lesbian Theatre Group (1977–79), to Siren to Shameful Practice (Red Rag) and beyond, have appropriated dominant popular forms in order to subvert established notions of 'man', 'woman' and lesbian. One writer who has consistently used pastiche/comedy in her writing is Bryony Lavery, whose *Her Aching Heart* (1991) became something of a cult hit. The play is a two-hander and consists of a series of comic sketches that go back and forth in time between the present and the world of nineteenth-century melodrama. The two protagonists fancy each other madly but cannot express that desire because of class differences. Herein lies most of the play's humour. *Her Aching Heart* presents lesbian sexuality as a hilarious playground.

## Sex on stage

Andrea Weiss concludes her book *Lesbians in the Cinema* with the following sentence, 'The women start to make love, and shortly after that the film ends, the suggestion all the more powerful for its not being culminated on the screen'.[16] Would the representation of lesbian sex on stage also be more powerful if it were simply hinted at?

Searching for the moments I have found the most erotic in the theatre, the following ones stand out:

- a sensual femme, donning a veiled hat, black lace and velvet dress and high heels, deliciously conscious of her sexual power over the predominantly 'butchy' audience – the show was one of the first Siren gave in London

(Women's Arts Alliance, 1980) at a time when 'out' femmes were thin on the ground

- Lois Weaver, in *Little Women* by Split Britches, doing a 'strip show' in reverse, putting her clothes *on* (Drill Hall, 1990)
- Peggy Shaw, in *Anniversary* by Split Britches, taking off her 'butch costume' to reveal a strapless dress underneath (Drill Hall, 1991)
- Emily Claid, in 'Sweet Rage' of *Virginia Minx at Play*, having the self-inflicted knife wounds on her anorexic-looking body cleansed by a lover/mother/playmate figure (ICA, 1993)

Quite different from each other, these moments share the following similarities: none is sexually explicit, all are sexually charged, each one reverses expectations, all hold out a promise. What, though, of explicit sex on stage?

In Nagy's *Weldon Rising* the two lovers habitually torture each other. Jaye blackmails Tilly: 'No sex, no booze.' Their dynamic hints at sadomasochism: 'I love it when you're on your knees,' Jaye says to Tilly. Their exchange has a sexual charge, due primarily to Jaye's caustic wit, expressed in non-naturalistic form – heightened language as sex obviously works on stage!

However, at the very end of the play the two women strip and 'begin to make love'. while the gay male characters take action. The implications of this conclusion aside, the 'sex scene' was hugely unsuccessful on stage. The two actresses were rolling on the floor visibly trying to work out the logistics of where to put the various parts of their bodies to achieve 'authenticity'. Suddenly there was no mystery – just a mechanical reproduction of explicit sex, and cringe-making at that. Fumbling, awkward, unconvincing.

There was an explicit sex scene in *Foreign Lands*, too, which in the Finborough Theatre production was equally fumbling and awkward, stripping the two characters of any sexual charge they had so far communicated through looks and language. Whether this is due to the self-consciousness of the straight actresses and directors of those scenes or to a situation inherent in the writing of explicit sex on stage, I am not sure.

Certainly, as a spectator I found both the scenes ludicrous rather than erotic. As a playwright I can identify with the writer's desire to represent lesbian sex on stage. Potentially, it could have a transgressive rather than a voyeuristic effect. How though?

Is Richard Dyer, like Andrea Weiss, right in claiming that:

> Sexuality is on the whole better represented through symbolism. Colours, textures, objects, effects of light, the shape of things, all convey sexuality through evocation, resonance and association; they set off feelings about what sex is like more efficiently than just showing acts of sex.[17]

## Floor show

I believe that there are situations in live performance where explicit sexual gestures are exciting rather than embarrassing and embarrassed.

I would like to mention, first, one more performance of truly explicit sex which took place in a very different context from the above-mentioned plays.

The 'floor show', for that is what it was, took place in the Chain Reaction club in London some time in 1990. What we witnessed was meant to be an impromptu 'orgy'. Something between a performance and a spontaneous expression of lust, to which an audience was welcome.

A leather 'daddy' was holding the head of a blindfolded and feet-cuffed naked woman and whispering sweet or filthy nothings to her, while a femme wearing a braless body slip climbed on the table and started ritually fist-fucking her. The femme looked hard and cold and her movements were calculating and devoid of emotion or sexual energy. The blindfolded woman's body seemed tense rather than aroused. This went on for a while during which time I and most of the other women present in the room lost interest and carried on with our conversations, occasionally glancing at the music videos projected on the wall-hinged screen. Real-time action on 'stage' was obviously not working! Bar dykes leaning against the wall were looking utterly bored and obviously waiting for the pool table to be vacated. Elegant femmes discreetly wandered into the room, took one look, acted cool and walked out again.

The audience's attention was positively sagging. The daddy took action. She uncuffed and lifted the blindfolded woman, sat her on the edge of the table and well and truly fucked her for a few minutes, kissed her tenderly and whisked her off to the bar, to the cheers of the relieved punters – a painfully dull exhibition of 'raw sex' had come to a glorious end. At last.

## Queer notions

During June 1993 the Institute of Contemporary Arts (ICA) hosted a season of work on gender, *Bare Essentials*, part of which was 'Queer Notions'.

Emily Claid's show *Virginia Minx at Play* was one of the season's highlights. A blend of dance, theatre and live art performance, *Virginia Minx* was one of the most satisfying explicitly sexual lesbian performances. The show consisted of a number of cameos and personas inhabited by Claid, while her companion – in a long, slit-at-the-thigh black dress and red lipstick – played the saxophone and occasionally commented on or participated in the action.

*Virginia Minx* explores how masks of women determined by male desire can be subverted through the lesbian gaze. Emily Claid said of her characters, 'I want them not only to be sexual, but passionate and totally consuming in their way of being. They have a passionate hunger, eating life.'[18]

During 'Watch Me Witch You', a fierce tango, Virginia Minx performs a deliciously aggressive lesbian seduction. Not a split second of cringe-making moves here. The seduction and the performer's movements are explicitly sexual, playful and powerful. In 'Sweet Rage' a hooded cape-wearing figure fantasizes the ritual dismemberment of her enemies and culminates in orgiastic self-cutting and blood adornment. The most beautiful moment here is the one I have already described, where the figure is being 'cleansed and healed' by a mother/lover figure.

The 'Queer Notions' evening included Excessive Expression performing their theatre/dance piece 'Lesbian Dances'. Again, lesbian desire was unapologetically and defiantly expressed not only through the body but through language too. During a solo piece, Madeleine Dahm, the company's artistic director and central performer, moved back and forth through frantic posture impersonations of butch/femme, asking 'butch or femme?' with each posture, poignantly expressing the contradictions of butch/ femme within the same woman.

Marisa Carr, 'Performance Activist Extraordinaire', and her *Wendy Decades Odyssey* offered a classic example of queer desire on stage. One of the quotes used in Carr's programme was:

> We utilise sexually explicit words, pictures and performances to communicate our ideas and emotions. We denounce sexual censorship as anti art and inhuman, we empower ourselves by this attitude of sex positivism. And with this love of our sexual selves we have fun . . . [19]

Fun was certainly the name of the game in Carr's show. Coming out of her pink cunt-shaped Wendy House, cheekily holding a dildo and 'roaring' to live guitar music, she was fun personified. Moreover, *Wendy Decades Odyssey* combined taboo sexual images and fantasies with childlike innocence and charm, presenting female sexuality as both dark and playful.

## Performing desire

It appears, then, that lesbian sex can best be represented on stage either through heightened language (*Weldon Rising*) or through the body but in 'a performance' ('Queer Notions'). Sex on stage presented as 'real' inevitably appears false and contrived, as was the case with both *Weldon Rising* and *Foreign Lands* and the Chain Reaction floor show.

By contrast, in Emily Claid's *Victoria Minx Plays*, Excessive Expressions' *Lesbian Dances* and Marisa Carr's *Wendy Decades Odyssey*, the sex, no matter how explicit, was clearly being performed, re-presented for an audience. As a result it was not only more convincing but placed the spectator firmly in the position of a participator rather than a voyeur peeping through the fourth wall of the stage.

## *Endnote*

While the straight mind continues to perceive and represent lesbian sexuality in predictably limited ways, some of which seem hardly to have changed since a lesbian character first appeared on a western stage nearly 100 years ago, lesbians theatrically express our sexuality in a number of different ways: from 'zamis' to butch/femme to androgyny and beyond.

However, since the dominant theatre privileges heterosexual writers, the representation of lesbians by lesbians is currently being denied expression in contexts wider than our ghettos. It thus remains peripheral. Not until lesbians move from the 'margins to the centre', to use bell hooks's expression, will representations of lesbian desire by lesbians become part of the 'collective unconscious' and thus seriously contest heterosexual domination.

## *Notes*

1.  *Guardian*, 'Women', 10 September 1993.
2.  Michael Billington, *Guardian*, 9 January 1993.
3.  All quotes from Wedekind's Foreword to *Pandora's Box* in *The Lulu Plays*; John Calder, London, 1989, pp. 103–107.
4.  'Sick' is a rather odd choice of word at this critical point. I wonder whether Lillian Hellman meant it to carry a subtextual meaning or whether it was a slippage.
5.  Harriet Ellenberger, 'The dream is the bridge: in search of lesbian theatre', *Trivia 5*, fall 1984, pp. 17–59.
6.  In conversation with the writer, December 1992.
7.  *Foreign Lands* was reviewed by nearly all the major critics, none of whom even noticed the equation 'born evil: born lesbian'. It took a lesbian, Carol Woddis, to draw attention to the fact in her *What's On* review, 13 January 1993: '. . . yet again, lesbianism is seen to be equated with murderous evil'.
8.  Queer Bodies, ICA, London, 24 September 1993.
9.  Adrienne Rich, *Compulsory Heterosexuality and Lesbian Existence*. Onlywomen Press, London, 1981, p. 23.
10. Audre Lorde, 'Uses of the erotic: the erotic as power', in *Sister Outsider*. The Crossing Press, Trumansburg, NY, 1984, p. 59.
11. See 'Theatre of Moments', Nina Rapi interviews Split Britches, *Rouge*, issue 6, spring 1991.

12.    Quoted in JoAnn Loulan, *The Lesbian Erotic Dance: Butch, Femme Androgyny and Other Rhythms*. Spinster Book Company, San Francisco, 1990, p. 49.

13.    Sue Ellen Case, 'Towards a butch-femme aesthetic', in Lynda Hart (ed.), *Making a Spectacle: Feminist Essays on Contemporary Women's Theatre*, University of Michigan Press, Ann Arbor, 1989, pp. 282–99.

14.    All quotes from Zande Zeig, 'The actor as activator: deconstructing gender through gestures', *Women and Performance*, vol. 2, part 2, 1985, pp. 12–17.

15.    Even though she was described as 'butch' by *The Times* critic, 10 December 1992. 'Butchiness' is obviously in the eye of the beholder.

16.    Andrea Weiss, *Vampires and Violets: Lesbians in the Cinema*. Jonathan Cape, London, 1992, p. 161.

17.    Richard Dyer, *The Matter of Images: Essays on Representation*. Routledge, London and New York, 1993, p. 112.

18.    Emily Claid, interviewed by Ramsay Burt, Second Shift, spring 1993.

19.    The programme quote is credited to 'Vera: Veronica', in Andrea Juno and V. Vale (eds), *Angry Women*. Re/Search Publications, 1991, p. 23.

## Plays

Sarah Daniels, *Neaptide*. Methuen, London 1986.

Maro Green and Caroline Griffin, *More*, in Mary Remnant (ed.), *Plays by Women*, vol. 6. Methuen, London 1987.

Maro Green and Caroline Griffin, *Memorial Gardens*, unpublished.

Lillian Hellman, *The Children's Hour*, in *Five Plays of 1937*. Hamish Hamilton, London, 1937.

Karen Hope, *Foreign Lands*, unpublished.

Holly Hughes, *Dress Suits to Hire*. TDR, *Drama Review*, spring 1989.

Jackie Kay, *Chiaroscuro*, in Jill Davies (ed.), *Lesbian Plays*, vol. 1. Methuen, London, 1987.

Jackie Kay, *Twice Over*, in Philip Osment (ed.), *Gay Sweatshop: Four Plays and a Company*. Methuen, London, 1989.

Bryony Lavery, *Her Aching Heart*. Methuen, London, 1991.

Phyllis Nagy, *Weldon Rising*, in Annie Castledine (ed.), *Plays by Women*, vol. 10. Methuen, London, 1994.

Nina Rapi, *Ithaka*, in *Seven Plays by Women*. Aurora Metro, London, 1991.

Jacqueline Rudet, *The Basin*, in Yvonne Brewster (ed.), *Black Plays*, vol. 1. Methuen, London, 1987.
Jean-Paul Sartre, *In Camera and Other Plays*. Penguin, Harmondsworth, 1989.
Frank Wedekind, *The Lulu Plays*. John Calder, London, 1989.
Monique Wittig, *The Journey*, unpublished.


## Articles

Sue Ellen Case, 'Towards a butch/femme aesthetic', in Lynda Hart (ed.), *Making a Spectacle: Feminist Essays on Contemporary Women's Theatre*. The University of Michigan Press, Ann Arbor, 1989.
Kate Davy, 'Reading past the heterosexual imperative: *Dress Suits to Hire*', TDR, *Drama Review*, spring 1989.
Teresa De Lauretis, 'The technology of gender', in T. De Lauretis (ed.), *The Technology of Gender*. Macmillan, Basingstoke, 1989.
Teresa De Lauretis, 'Sexual indifference and lesbian representation', in Sue-Ellen Case (ed.), *Performing Feminisms*. The Johns Hopkins University Press, Baltimore, 1990.
Harriet Ellenberger, 'The dream is the bridge: in search of lesbian theatre', *Trivia 5*, fall 1984.
Diana Fuss, 'Inside out', in D. Fuss (ed.), *Inside/out: Lesbian Theories, Gay Theories*. Routledge, London, 1991.
Luce Irigaray, 'When the goods get together', in E. Marks and I. de Courtivron (eds), *New French Feminisms*. Harvester Press, London, 1981.
Audre Lorde, 'Uses of the erotic: the erotic as power', in *Sister Outsider*. The Crossing Press, Trumansburg, NY, 1984.
Monique Wittig, 'The straight mind', in *For Lesbians Only: A Separatist Anthology*. Onlywomen Press, London, 1988.
Monique Wittig, 'The point of view: universal or particular', *Feminist Issues*, fall 1983.
Zande Zeig, 'The actor as activator: deconstructing gender through gesture', *Women and Performance*, vol. 2, part 2, 1985.


## Books

Sue-Ellen Case (ed.), *Performing Feminisms: Feminist Critical Theory and Theatre*. The Johns Hopkins University Press, Baltimore, 1990.

# 65: 'That's Why You Are So Queer'

Richard Dyer, *The Matter of Images: Essays on Representation.* Routledge, London, 1993.

Lillian Faderman, *Odd Girls and Twilight Lovers: A History of Lesbian Life in Twentieth-Century America.* See especially Chapters 7 and 10. Penguin, Harmondsworth, 1992.

Marjorie Garber, *Vested Interests: Cross Dressing and Cultural Anxiety.* Routledge, London, 1992.

bell hooks, *Feminist Theory: From Margin to Centre.* South End Press, Boston, 1984.

bell hooks, *Yearning: Race, Gender and Cultural Politics.* Turnaround, London, 1991.

JoAnn Loulan, *The Lesbian Erotic Dance: Butch, Femme, Androgyny and Other Rhythms.* Spinsters Book Company, San Francisco, 1990.

Sally Munt (ed.), *New Lesbian Criticism.* Harvester Wheatsheaf, London, 1992.

Joan Nestle, *The Persistent Desire: A Femme Butch Reader.* Alyson Publications, Boston, 1992.

Adrienne Rich, *Compulsory Heterosexuality and Lesbian Existence.* Onlywomen Press, London, 1981.

Andrea Weiss, *Vampires and Violets: Lesbians in Cinema.* Jonathan Cape, London, 1988.

Chapter three

# Primary Intensities: Lesbian Poetry and the Reading of Difference

Liz Yorke

## Validating the lesbian body

It is, after all, always the meaning, the reading of difference that matters, and meaning is culturally engendered and sustained. Not to consider the body as some absolute (milk, blood, breasts, clitoris) for no 'body' is unmediated. Not body but the 'body' of psychosocial fabrications of difference. Or again, of sameness. Or again, of their relation.

Rachel Blau DuPlessis[1]

IN this essay I explore the re-visionary strategies of a number of women poets who are engaged in an attempt to construct a language which adequately re-visions the body, sexuality and libidinal trajectory of the lesbian woman. Coming to terms with lesbian sexuality involves the poets in the political effort of devising a pro-visional poetic strategy – as a means to make explicit what has been excluded from patriarchal discourses. This rethinking requires a major reorganization of sexual, linguistic and socio-symbolic systems; in addition it requires theorizing of the female body as a positivity rather than a lack. I will draw on Elizabeth Grosz's Irigarayan conceptualizations of the body as:

> structured, inscribed, constituted and given meaning socially and historically – a body that exists as such only through its socio-linguistic construction. She [Irigaray] renders the concept of 'pure' or 'natural' body meaningless. Power relations and systems of representations not only traverse the body and utilise its energies (as Kristeva claims) but actively constitute the body's very sensations, pleasures – the phenomenology of bodily experience.[2]

Recoding the lesbian body involves the poets in a strategic and transgressive effort to put in place new representations within language. Their effort is frequently directed towards countering the negative terms of Freudian and Lacanian accounts of the formation of a gendered identity. If gendered identity is not necessarily 'the result of biology, but of the social and psychical meaning of the body', then the way is open to reconceive of lesbian sexuality in terms other than the patriarchally given. Rather than seeing these poems as encoding a language of authentic female being, I shall analyse the fabrication of meaning that takes place within the mythical 'body' of a number of women's poems.

The language of poetry especially lends itself to the lesbian feminist poet's strategic and combative project, that is, the critique and revaluation of the coding of lesbian sexuality from different perspectives and locations within culture. Politically motivated lesbian poetry is interested in displacing inherited male models and myths through both a recoding of the relations between the self and 'the other' and a positive revaluing of a female body whose sexuality is lived in other terms – a poetry not necessarily concerned with the 'exclusion' of men as such, but rather, in Rich's words, with 'that primary presence of women to ourselves and each other first described in prose by Mary Daly, and which is the crucible of a new language'.[3]

As well as breaking through the cultural taboo against the depiction of an affirming lesbian sexuality in art, these poems render historically visible reconstructed representations which endeavour to treat the primary intensity of lesbian eroticism with respect and reverence. In effect, the poems offer a position for the lesbian woman subject with which it is possible in delight and/or in anguish to identify. The poet constructs a position or positions within language which offer lesbian women self-validating experiences. I see this poetry especially as offering a lesbian reader the validating experience of being able to recognize and realize her own position (or that of other women) as an identity in and through language. I use the term 'identity' in this special sense: identity is to be viewed as a desired position for the subject, constructed here so as to legitimate and validate particular lesbian viewpoints.

The poems included in this essay are chosen because they offer a legitimizing, cleansing, recuperative version of lesbian erotic life and its corresponding dimensions of joy and loss. Crucially, they embody a refusal to collaborate with the coercive, almost palpable, interlocking construct of heterosexual ideology, language and law which would deny and/or misrepresent the wholesome validity of the lesbian trajectory of desire, as well as attempting to delegitimate and harass the lesbian subject.

Luce Irigaray, the French feminist theorist, pays particular attention to the relation between mother and daughter, a relation inadequately theorized in either Freud or Lacan. She draws attention to the fact that, within western patriarchal cultures, women's relationships with their mothers and with other women are devalued. She argues that the little girl suffers 'narcissistic distress' because this primal 'carnal' relation to her mother is so censored, her own body is underestimated, even 'reviled' like her mother's (in Freudian and Lacanian terms), is castrated. She argues that:

> a woman, if she cannot in one way or another, recuperate her first object (i.e. make real the possibility of keeping her first earliest libidinal attachments by displacing them onto an/ Other), is always exiled from herself.[4]

How does she return from exile? How does a woman reclaim her 'self' and (as Irigaray puts it) re-mark, in language, her different economy of representation? Can she articulate an economy of desire that is not based on an assumption of the anatomical inferiority of the female and that will not concede anything to the hierarchy of values ordained within heterosexual phallocentric ideology? In particular, how does the lesbian poet put her relation to other women into words and inscribe the specificity of her desire within the symbolic? Is it possible to reconstitute herself as subject through the body, touch, words and gaze of the lesbian other – within and despite, the debilitating and destructive systems of patriarchy? Adrienne Rich, in her poem 'Origins and History of Consciousness' explores this struggle:

> It was simple to meet you, simple to take your eyes
> into mine, saying: these are eyes I have known
> from the first . . . It was simple to touch you
> against the hacked background, the grain of what we
> had been, the choices, years . . . It was even simple
> to take each other's lives in our hands, as bodies.
>
> What is not so simple: to wake from drowning
> from where the ocean beat inside us like an afterbirth
> into this common, acute particularity
> these two selves who walked half a lifetime untouching –
> to wake to something deceptively simple: a glass
> sweated with dew, a ring of the telephone, a scream
> of someone beaten up far down in the street
> causing each of us to listen to her own inward scream
>
> knowing the mind of the mugger and the mugged
> as any woman who stands to survive this city,
> this century, this life . . . [5]

Rich does not here imagine an ideal separatist world in which women may ecstatically rejoice in their discovery of one another.[6] Rather, she shows these women as actively struggling for survival, working together as lovers who trust each other. Lowered down an almost umbilical rope, they explore new ways of being in relationship. The metaphors of darkness and light point to a relationship in which contradictions and negativity are fully searched out and revealed. The women recognize each other, identify each other in the metaphoric darkness of the womb, and this new conception is for them an illumination. They are 'drenched in light' within the darkness. Their coming together is marked by joyful ecstasy – sexual, spiritual, mystic – as each identifies the other in the non-dualist patterns of language Rich has taken so much care to construct:

> Trusting, untrusting,
> we lowered ourselves into this, let ourselves
> downward hand over hand as on a rope that quivered
> over the unsearched . . . We did this. Conceived
> of each other, conceived each other in a darkness
> which I will remember as drenched in light.

Each woman is desired by and desires both the m/Other and her woman lover as Other. Each woman participates in the symbolic 'conception' of the other: they are 'mothers' *birthing* each other into language *through trust*. In Irigaray's words: 'We find ourselves as we entrust ourselves to each other.'[7] Yet, at the same time, both live in a world of darkness where the 'inward scream' is matched by the scream of 'someone beaten up far down in the street'.

In using these metaphors of conception Rich draws on the watery, oceanic, (heart)beating imagery of the womb/mother. The metaphors of conception, darkness and drowning – the suffocating panic of birth trauma – interconnect with metaphors of illumination, of awakening, of being 'drenched in light'. The women accept the mutual affirmation of the maternal gaze – and the associated pattern that inevitably accompanies this relation: the 'trusting, untrusting' that none the less enables the women to 'take each other's lives in our hands, as bodies'. The poet's use of 'us' indicates that both women simultaneously experience this return to the maternal oceanic space of womb/water as well as experiencing the exit from that space, the waking moment of rebirth. Their return is not, therefore, to some idyllic place of origin to re-establish contact and continuity with the mother but is, rather, conceived as a frightening rebirth or spiritual awakening – into a fuller understanding of the situation of women in patriarchy.

The poem itself is deceptively simple. Paradoxically, the

mutually returned gaze between herself and her lover, of 'eyes I have known from the first', may again be interpreted as signalling the woman's recuperation of the gaze exchanged between infant and mother. This symbolic desiring connection to the mother is recalled as difficult and dangerous. Yet the women 'conceive' of each other, recover each other from exile. This 'return' enables the women to become 'two selves' in relation. The lives of the women, together '*as bodies*' are present to each other, are able to revalue each other. The women are no longer represented as *object* to the male gaze, but as equally participating in a mirroring inter-relationship:

> We did this. Conceived
> of each other, conceived each other in a darkness
> which I remember as drenched in light.

The all-important adjunct 'of' differentiates active from passive mode, actor from acted upon, but the phrase 'each other' will not permit the patriarchal dualistic and hierarchical division into acting subject and acted on object: each conceives the other, is mother and daughter interchangeably, is both subject and object, is dark 'drenched' in light, reciprocally. As Irigaray puts it: 'Night and day are mingled in our gazes, our gestures, our bodies.'[8]

The mutuality and equality of this womanly mode of relating seem to be crucial to constructing an ideal, one which serves the utopian goal of building a 'gender/class/race-free' community for the social support and sexual and emotional enrichment of lesbian lives. At the same time and paradoxically, this seductive and inspiring utopian vision tends to deny, or seems to transcend, differences in economic power, class status and the experience of racial discrimination, not only within society, but also between one lesbian woman and another. It is necessary to be aware of the inbuilt contradictions of this position. It is also necessary to recognize that this effacement of the differences of race and class is a mid-1970s phenomenon which responded to the political urgencies of the time, those of forging an initial sense of solidarity between all women to set against the devastating fragmentation between women created by patriarchal social structures.

Today feminists face a somewhat different task, that of claiming and naming – sometimes celebrating, sometimes mourning – diversity and difference between women. Yet, the necessity for making this commitment to mutuality and equality – and creating a political and cultural context where such a relation may have a chance of being realized – remains important. We still have a political need to sustain and celebrate the woman–woman bond as between one subject and another subject, rather than conceding anything to the subject/object model typical of heterosexual patriarchy – spelt out for us by Simone de Beauvoir so long ago.

The 'I–I' of subject and subject in equal relationship may be seen as a radical calling into question of the hierarchical structures of the nuclear family – or of any extended patriarchal family situation where institutionalized and conventional heterosexual modes of relating still prevail. This challenge to the hierarchies of patriarchy underlies Rich's poetic (as it does that of Iragaray). But the ideal language that restores the object to speech and, in a sense, banishes the transcendent patriarchal 'I' to silence is the language of desire: that is, a language that escapes from repression, that emerges from the desire-laden unconscious, from the world of the dream. A dream from which, while patriarchy still exists, the woman must wake – to the reality of 'a scream of someone beaten up', that chilling sound that echoes her 'own inward scream'.

Lesbian feminist poets, writing from a position of otherness, as from a different psychic economy, have responded to this call, first voiced by Daly and Rich, to restructure language. The poets have especially tried to reorder the heterosexual codes that structure sexual difference – often in terms that are potentially disruptive to the social contract. In the transformed psychic economy proposed by lesbian poets, in their poetic representations of the woman's body, it is often and precisely the genital anatomical difference from the male which is celebrated and desired as an empowering source of pleasure, rather than being reviled as 'castrated'. In their diverse attempts to counter patriarchal heterosexual cultural codes, they have frequently tried to make real the possibility for a woman to keep in consciousness her deepest attachment in the transformed and transforming context of one woman's love for another.

To name publicly such lesbian attachment involves women in a difficult emotional and intellectual journey. In actual lived practice, the process of identification – through naming and claiming an identity, through revealing the lesbian trajectory of desire and thus bringing the unspoken to speech – is far from easy. Susan Griffin's poem 'The Woman Who Swims in Her Tears' explores the painful soul-searching and self-questioning that accompanied this lesbian relationship of the early 1970s. Rich, speaking of this poem and commenting on the difficulty of 'getting away' from male defined language, of naming for the first time, indicates the challenge and struggle it was, then, to find an appropriate language for lesbian sexuality: 'That poem has just never been written before; it condenses in one poem so much of a very long process that two women may go through in order to come together at all.'[9]

> The woman
> who slept beside the body of one
> other woman weeping
> the women who wept.
> the women whose tears wet
> each other's hair
> the woman who wrapped her legs
> around another woman's thigh
> and said I am afraid.
> the woman who put her head
> in the
> place between the shoulder and breast
> of the other woman and
> said, 'Am I wrong?'[10]

An impersonal voice tells of 'the woman', 'the other woman', 'the body of one other woman'. This voice, used to speak of this sexually intimate context, creates tension at different levels: privacy/revelation; proximity/distance; private/public space; concern/reluctance to intrude. There is tension, too, in the vague reference to other 'women'.

There may be an inclusive movement outwards to indicate a community of like women, but where, or how many, is not clearly defined. Who speaks? Why is there this distancing, this difficult, effortless repetition, this mode of anxiety, distress, self-questioning? These tensions gesture towards a struggle against muteness; a struggle to overcome the impediments to speech, the doubts, resistances, uncertainties; the struggle of dealing with raw conflict, of contradiction; and they indicate also the especially intense process of honestly bringing to language that which has been rigorously excluded from it:

> So much defiance needed for the possible. All the labour of feminism, casting away all the denials of female experience. The denial of what we know to be true. Unwrapping yards of bandages. Like the bandages wrapped around the dead. From our eyes. Ears. Hands. Skin. All we are complicit in hiding.[11]

To come out of hiding and cast away 'all the denials' requires validation of lesbian identity at the deepest levels. To accept and to claim an identity, a lesbian 'I', that culture has taught everyone to despise requires a major revaluation of both personal and cultural values. How is this defiant 'I' to be constructed so as to emerge from the silences of self-censorship and cultural exclusion?[12]

Drawing on Irigaray's account of the female psyche, I have suggested that the lesbian woman realizes the possibility of renewing her first earliest libidinal attachments by displacing them on to a lesbian Other.

To theorize this further, I must (briefly) refer to Lacan. In his earlier exposition, Lacan proposes two fields which together give birth to the subject: 'the subject in the field of the drive and the subject as he [she] appears in the field of the Other'.[13] The other, in articulating the chain of signifiers which govern 'whatever may be made present of the subject', thus plays an essential part in the construction of subjectivity in relation to the drive or libido.[14] Lacan stresses that the process of 'making oneself' necessitates 'loving oneself through the other'. By 'making oneself heard' and 'making oneself seen'[15] one is involved in 'subject making' – that is, working towards but never actually unifying the one, the one who is the (always divided) and constantly fading 'I' of apparent identity, appropriated out of and constituted within language.[16]

If we pursue the logic of Lacanian psychoanalysis to a point beyond Lacan's own emphasis, the reciprocal articulation of their desires of/for each other should play a part in the construction of the lesbian 'I'. I see the lesbian woman as learning to love and identify herself in the affirming field of meaning of the lesbian Other. I want to make the further suggestion that it is, at the deepest levels, the mirroring discourse of the lesbian lover which enables the lesbian subject to make her self, to identify herself so as to be seen and to be heard – to defiantly accept the costs and take the risks.

It is through receiving the deep acceptances of the reciprocal pleasures of lesbian love, that is, in the fullest dimensions of the physical, spiritual and sexual responses of her lover, that the lesbian woman is able to confirm the validity and integrity of her lesbian identity. In the context of poetry, this mirroring discourse may be seen as conveyed in the language of words or it may be conveyed in the gestural languages of the body or non-verbally, through the uses of sexually or emotionally charged images.

Olga Broumas's fine poem 'Innocence' is especially interesting in this respect.[17] This poem draws its inspiration from body spirituality being developed by feminist women of many different faiths who are exploring their spirituality and sexuality in theological terms.[18] In this poem it is in the 'mirroring' symmetrical relation between (unlike) lesbian lovers – that is, in the reciprocal relation between 'Love, Love' and their 'merging shadows', Queen and Jester – that the lesbian sexual relation is ecstatically celebrated. The poem specifically validates each woman's lesbian sexuality, each woman's lesbian body, as being in and of God, the women's bodies being created in the image of God.

The poem images God herself as participating in the love-making between the two women, the inventive and physically embodied hand of God appearing to produce extra pleasure. This manifest hand that is itself active in the sexual communion of the women, both is and is not, in and of them. She, God herself, is also imaged as around them, as the wind. This theology of the body dramatically counters fundamentalist (heterosexual and patriarchal) Christian pieties by representing religious ecstasy as of the body as well as the spirit and, by representing the sexuality of the lesbian women as not merely without sin but as divine and sacred in itself, as an aspect of God incarnate.

> God
> appears
>
> among us, elusive, the extra
> hand none of us – Love, Love, Jester, Queen –
> can quite locate, fix, or escape. Extra
> hand, extra
> pleasure. A hand
> with the glide of a tongue, a hand
> precise as an eyelid, a hand with a sense
> of smell, a hand that will dance
> to its liquid moan
> God's hand.
>
> loose on the four of us like a wind
> on the grassy hills of the South.

God is Love, physically embodied in, around and between these lesbian women – as they reciprocally give and receive the pleasures of sexual Love:

> Manita's Love
> opens herself to me, my sharp
> Jester's tongue, my
> cartwheels of pleasure. The Queen's own pearl
> at my fingertips, and Manita pealing
>
> my Jester's bells on our four
> small steeples, as Sunday dawns

In this playful and complex reworking of the idea of church bells ringing in celebration, the nipples? clitoral bodies? of the women, as it were, become the 'small steeples' of the church of Love where God herself is worshipped.[19] In mutual joy, the 'Jester's bells' ring out their sexual ecstasy for all to hear – 'as Sunday dawns'. In the closing lines of this challenging poem, God herself affirms and applauds the innocence of this spiritual/sexual relation by clapping with her one hand, that is, by making an 'audible' sign from an approving Other, as one who herself participates in creating their lesbian identity, and who signals her acceptance and recognition of their sexual pleasure. Broumas, in using this 'impossible' Zen figuration, the 'sound' of one hand that 'claps and claps', creates a paradox within her poem: the sound, like lesbian sexuality itself, is both there and not there. Lesbian sexuality has been one of the most deafening silences in history and, even now, when it is spoken out and celebrated, it is a voice that is frequently simply not heard. A wry twist, given the paradoxical hypocrisy of our cultural forms.

In the poem, this one hand seems to signal unconditional acceptance of lesbian sexuality, and is imaged by the poet as a part of God's creative 'making' of the lesbian sexual relation. This unconditional acceptance is also part of the poet's reconstruction of lesbian identity – in her creation of an affirming field of meaning for the lesbian reader, whether or not she is sexually active.

I want now to consider the specific position of black lesbian women. An affirming field of meaning is important to the white lesbian – but even if she suffers discrimination at work, at home, in social life, in religious life and elsewhere – she at least has access to 'skin privilege'. It must be even more important to the black lesbian woman who experiences, in addition to all the oppressive situations that can arise for the white lesbian, pernicious systematic racial and economic discrimination, sexual devaluation specific to black women and manifold overt and covert exclusions from certain fields of work, education and health care. There are no easy parallels to be drawn between black and white lesbian experience, though certain overlapping areas of oppression can be discerned.

It is also difficult to engage in any discussion of the dynamics of the bond between black mothers and their daughters according to white western models formulated by Freud, Lacan and white French feminists. The limitations of this body of theory begin to be acutely felt wherever child-rearing practice does not conform to the typical western patterns of the patriarchal nuclear family. Black women, as mothers, have a pivotal and powerful role in many black families, but the mother is rarely sole carer for the child as in the white middle-class pattern. Black family networks have taken very different forms. In America, the extended family systems of Africa could not survive in their old patterns through the centuries of slavery and then through sustained racial and economic oppression. In the situations typical of today, the black mother is of necessity called upon to work to support her family – the grandmother, aunt, sister, cousin or any significant other of the extended family or circle of friends may well be the one, or the one among many, to take care of her children. The child's relation to the mother is thus altered in important ways. The question arises: is Lacanian or post-Lacanian theory relevant in this changed context?

In her poem 'Black Mother Woman' Audre Lorde examines the nature of the conflict between herself and her own very powerful mother as a key figure in the relational process of self-definition.[20] The poet does not deny the difficulties of the relationship and it is clear that the political stance taken up by Audre Lorde is very different from that of her parents.

As daughter, the poet acknowledges the sharp edge of her mother's discipline: 'I cannot recall you gentle.'[21] Despite this, through the mother's pride, the daughter is able to recognize the love that is hidden in the silence of the not spoken, love which is conveyed to her in more subtle ways. The poet acknowledges both the centrality of her respect and love for her mother's 'aged spirit', as well as her sense of distance and difference from her. She bears witness to her mother's long-suffering acceptance of oppression, in these ambivalent lines:

> When strangers come and compliment me
> your aged spirit takes a bow
> jingling with pride
> but once you hid that secret
> in the center of furies
> hanging me
> with deep breasts and wiry hair
> with your own split flesh
> and long suffering eyes
> buried in myths of little worth.

In effect, the poet defines herself as other to her mother, in taking up
a position very different from any her mother might have chosen.
Yet, despite this, the daughter recognizes the 'core of love' that
enables the daughter to stand *as herself*:

> I have peeled away your anger
> down to the core of love
> and look mother
> I Am
> a dark temple where your true spirit rises
> beautiful
> and tough as chestnut
> stanchion against your nightmare of weakness
> and if my eyes conceal
> a squadron of conflicting rebellions
> I learned from you
> to define myself
> through your denials.

Alicia Ostriker has noted that 'this pattern of angry division
and visionary reunion is especially important, in fact almost
universal, among black and third-world women poets.'[22] She locates
its source to the 'ambivalence of maternal attachment, associated
with ambivalent views of the mother as a power figure'.[23] The
'magically strong' bond between mother and daughter gives rise to
these moving tributes to the black mother's strength and powerless-
ness. As a poet, Audre Lorde resists glossing over the anger, pain and
sense of difference experienced by black people: 'I have a duty to
speak the truth as I see it and to share not just my triumphs, not just
the things that felt good, but the pain, the intense, often unmitigat-
ing pain.'[24] This pain she experiences as the outcome of white
supremacist racism, and of sexism, heterosexism and homophobia –
some of which, most hurtfully, emerges from black culture itself.[25]
However, Lorde suggests that the courage to stand against all
oppressive definition must come from love: 'what was beautiful had
to serve the purpose of changing my life or I would have died.'[26]
Lorde affirms the necessity to feel deeply, to feel joy, to love deeply

as a crucial element of social protest: she bears witness to love above all:

> We define ourselves as lovers, as people who love each other all over again; we become new again. These poems insist that you can't separate loving from fighting, from dying, from hurting, but love is triumphant. It is powerful and strong, and I feel I grow a great deal in all of my emotions, especially in the capacity to love.
>
> The love expressed between women is particular and powerful, because we have had to love in order to live; love has been our survival.

In her poem 'Recreation' Audre Lorde affirms the possibility of identity re-creation through lesbian lovemaking: the lovers, 'moving through our word countries', affirm the 'coming-together' of each other's body – which is a poem.[27] This 'coming-together' is crucial to their creativity and writing, as to poetry, but is also crucial to the process of identifying each subjectivity to the other – through the signifying body of words. The categories – woman/poem/flesh; you/me; earth/body; outside/inside – fuse, boundaries between them collapse into each other and lose their categorical specificity; the poem creates a woman-identified locus/field/'country' where the erotic 'flesh' may 'blossom' into 'the poem you make of me':

> . . . as your body moves
> under my hands
> charged and waiting
> we cut the leash
> you create me against your thighs
> hilly with images
> moving through our word countries
> my body
> writes into your flesh
> the poem
> you make of me.
>
> Touching you I catch midnight

as moon fires set in my throat
I love you flesh into blossom
I made you
and take you made
into me.

Lorde, in her essay 'Uses of the erotic: the erotic as power',
sees the erotic as a powerful resource, one that is 'firmly rooted in the
power of our unexpressed or unrecognised feeling'.[28] As in the work
of Olga Broumas and Adrienne Rich, the deepest erotic passion of
love is not merely a sensual, but is also a spiritual, joy. For Lorde, the
erotic is 'a well of replenishing the provocative force' (p. 54) and a
source of 'power and information' (p. 53) – the sharing of its joys
being a provocative 'assertion of the lifeforce of women' (p. 55).
Lorde comments: 'Our erotic knowledge empowers us, becomes a
lens through which we scrutinize all aspects of our existence, forcing
us to evaluate those aspects honestly in terms of their relative
meaning within our lives' (p. 57). Representing the lesbian sexual
body, the sensual-emotional relationship, the material geography of
female pleasure in positive terms, becomes a political strategy – the
poet strives to generate a celebratory mode of writing in which this
empowering significance may be found.

Thus it is at this level of erotic sexual pleasure that lesbian
difference makes itself most clearly apparent. The lesbian libidinal
economy is neither identifiable by a man nor can it be seen as
referable to any masculine economy. Informing all of Adrienne
Rich's *The Dream of a Common Language* is her understanding of
the political – and spiritual – importance of this libidinal connection
between women at the level of the (textual) body:

I want to travel with you to every sacred mountain
smoking within like the sibyl stooped over her tripod
I want to reach for your hand as we scale the path,
to feel your arteries glowing in my clasp,
never failing to note the small, jewel-like flower
unfamiliar to us, nameless till we rename her[29]

Libidinal difference, the 'smoking within' of lesbian sexual desire, is at the heart of this poem: the lesbian desire for physical connection to the other woman; the wish 'to feel' the (arterial) pulsing life of her blood; her body; the wish 'to travel' together; to 'scale the path' together. Again, in representing the contiguities and reciprocities of the woman – woman relation, in making visible the lesbian libidinal difference from the heterosexual trajectory, the poet's words 'burn' with the energy of libidinal and spiritual commitment to the lesbian 'path' which is to be undertaken outside the libidinal economies of the masculine symbolic order. It is the bodily presence of each to the other that empowers the women to rename 'the small jewel-like flower' of Poem XI, a flower that recalls Lorde's image of 'flesh into blossom'[30], and Olga Broumas's exotic lines from her revised myth 'Leda and Her Swan': 'Scarlet/liturgies shake our room, amaryllis blooms/in your upper thighs, water lily/ on mine, fervent delta'.[31]

In 'The Floating Poem, Unnumbered', from Adrienne Rich's *The Dream of a Common Language*, the image of the vaginal 'rose-wet cave' takes on a value comparable to Lorde's 'blossom' and Broumas's 'amaryllis' or 'water lily' as a signifier of perfection, of the 'innocence and wisdom' of a sanctified and holy place. The 'Floating Poem', like Broumas's poem 'Innocence' is much influenced by the women's spirituality movement.[32] Its title (and possibly the title of her book) is taken from the zero card of the Tarot. This card, with no number and no specific place on the path, is, in effect, a floating card designated '0', which, according to Vicki Noble, 'represents innocence, without ideas of sin or transgression', and is 'free to speak the truth without punishment or censorship, because we trust in the absolute innocence of her motivation'.[33] The poem, like the card, is resonant with infinitely joyful, carefree spontaneity, just as in Broumas's poem 'Innocence', it finds the route to 'pure wisdom' – here, to the 'innocence and wisdom' of the body of woman:

> Whatever happens with us, your body
> will haunt mine – tender, delicate
> your lovemaking, like the half-curled frond
> of the fiddlehead fern in forests
> just washed by sun . . . [34]

This superbly erotic language of touch, tongue – of searching for and of reaching – which recognizes the tender mutuality of the women, names, validates and dignifies the lesbian sexual bodily relation. Rich not only makes available what was previously 'unspeakable', censored, unwritten, and named only in patriarchal terms, but also transforms the codes in which this relation is signified, as a vital part of her re-visionary poetic. Once published and public this poem again becomes a self-conscious and urgent breaking through of the cultural taboo against the depiction of lesbian sensuality/sexuality in art. This language functions to displace the homophobic messages of obscenity, of disgust that bombard the lesbian from masculinist (and pornographic) culture. Viewed unromantically as an artistic revaluation of an always-already socialized bodily relation, the poem renders historically visible a reconstructed representation concerned with treating the primary intensity of lesbian eroticism with respect and reverence. In this context, Lorde's vulnerable and courageous 'Love Poem', eventually published in 1971, is comparable in its strategy, a strategy Rich recognizes. She identifies (draws attention to) Lorde's poem, thus differentiating and confirming her position, and identifies with it – as a self-conscious choice. Rich comments in an interview, 'It was incredible. Like defiance. It was glorious.'[35]

> Speak earth and bless me with what is richest
> make sky flow honey out of my hips
> rigid as mountains
> spread over a valley
> carved out by the mouth of rain
>
> And I knew when I entered her I was
> high wind in her forests hollow
> fingers whispering sound
> honey flowed
> from the split cup
> impaled on a lance of tongues[36]

The warrior woman is an image very dear to Lorde, from which she derives the evocative symbolism of the mouth/tongue/

word/speech – imagery which is intrinsically linked to the warrior imagery of the lance/sword/knives. Often in her work, words and languages become 'weapons' which are employed in the fight for the survival of black integrity. Ancestral myths and images drawn from black African folklore form a vital part of Afro-American culture – and Audre Lorde powerfully develops this cultural project of reclamation in a feminist direction. Her use of these symbolic images gathers significance as we read, creating a symbolic network which resonates through many poems. In the poem 'Dahomey' for instance, we find the *fas* of the Nigerian god Shango spelled out by a woman: 'I speak/whatever language is needed/to sharpen the knives of my tongue.'[37] These images also link to Lorde's political desire to retain the concept of intrapsychic bisexuality:

> I have always wanted to be both man and woman, to incorporate the strongest and richest part of my mother and father within/into me – to share valleys and mountains upon my body the way the earth does in hills and peaks.[38]

These poets' refusal to submit to the coercive force of a condemnatory community, the challenge they offer to the pejorative clinical terminology of deviance, as well as their resistance to heterosexual ideology and practice, marks a particular choice – to identify publicly and defiantly as lesbian, despite that identity being socially stigmatized. Perhaps inevitably their challenge to heterosexual (medical or psychoanalytic) discursive practices finds as its locus or field the woman's erotic body, as the site of representation to be contested. These poets take responsibility for rewriting the codes informing lesbian social and sexual relations; for reformulating how 'the body', as locus in a network of relations, may be articulated. Thus, rather than accepting the conferred (despised) identity given within hostile but normative prescriptive discourses, the poets transform the codes, the categories: they change the rules. They offer another position for the lesbian subject to take up, to identify with, as a self-conscious cultural choice. Representing lesbians as normal rather than deviant; as sexually healthy rather than sexually 'sick'; as women whose behaviour is permissible rather than illegitimate –

the poems, in effect, protest the privileged status of much judge-mental prohibition concerning the lesbian and her 'unacceptable' erotic drives. Instead, they offer a legitimating, cleansing vision of her erotic life and its corresponding dimensions of joy and pain. The poets are involved in a process of producing, out of the erotic body's libidinal difference, social and political meanings unpoliced, uncen-sored, by a heterosexual patriarchy, validations which are woven into their poetry.

## Notes

1.  Rachel Blau DuPlessis, 'For the Etruscans' (1979), in Elaine Showalter (ed.), *The New Feminist Criticism: Essays on Women, Literature and Theory*. Virago, London, 1986, p. 273.
2.  Elizabeth Grosz, *Sexual Subversions: Three French Feminists*. Allen and Unwin, Sydney, 1989, p. 111.
3.  Adrienne Rich, *On Lies, Secrets and Silence: Selected Prose 1966–1978*. Virago, London, 1980, p. 250.
4.  Luce Irigaray, interviewed by Diane Adlam and Couze Venn, 'Women's exile', *Ideology and Consciousness*, no. 1, 1977, pp. 56–76.
5.  Adrienne Rich, 'Origins and History of Consciousness (1972–4)', in *The Dream of a Common Language: Poems 1974–1977*. W.W. Norton and Co., New York and London, 1978, p. 7.
6.  Nor does Rich collude with typically heterosexual patterns of femininity: the women she portrays are rarely passive or docile.
7.  Luce Irigaray, 'When our lips speak together', translated by Carolyn Burke, *Signs: Journal of Women and Culture and Society*, vol. 6, no. 1, 1980, pp. 66–79, p. 78. There is an intriguing similarity between these passages from Rich and Irigaray which, if it were not for the incompatibility of dates, would suggest a close influence. Alicia Ostriker tells us in her book, *Writing Like a Woman* (University of Michigan Press, Ann Arbor, 1983), that Rich was, by 1973, 'assuming an influential position in an intellectual movement which includes not only such Anglo-American writers as Millett, Greer, Daly, Piercy and Olsen, but the contemporary French feminists Hélène Cixous, Monique Wittig, Luce Irigaray and Marguerite Duras' (p. 110).
8.  *Ibid.*, p. 78.
9.  Elly Bulkin, 'An interview with Adrienne Rich', *Conditions Two*, vol. 1, no. 2, October 1977, pp. 53–66, p. 57.

10.   Susan Griffin, 'The Woman Who Swims in Her Tears', in *Made from This Earth: Selections from Her Writings*. The Women's Press, London, 1982, p.274.

11.   Susan Griffin, 'Notes on the writing of poetry', *Made from This Earth*, p. 226.

12.   Olga Broumas's poem 'Rumplestiltskin' is a wonderful example of revaluation through one woman's lesbian love for another. Olga Broumas, *Beginning with O*. Yale University Press, New Haven and London, 1977, p. 64.

13.   Jacques Lacan, 'From love to the libido', in Jacques-Alain Miller (ed.), *The Four Fundamental Concepts of Psychoanalysis*, trans. Alan Sheridan, Penguin, Harmondsworth, 1979, p. 199.

14.   Jacques Lacan, 'The subject and the other: Aphanisis', *ibid.*, p. 203.

15.   Jacques Lacan, 'From love to the libido', *ibid.*, pp. 194–95.

16.   Jacques Lacan, 'The subject and the other: Aphanisis', *ibid.*, p. 218. Lacan writes: 'Hence the division of the subject: when the subject appears somewhere as meaning, he is manifested elsewhere as "fading", as disappearance.'

17.   Olga Broumas, 'Innocence', in *Beginning with O*, p. 45.

18.   Readers interested in following this up might look at Linda Hurcombe, *Sex and God: Varieties of Women's Religious Experience*. Routledge and Kegan Paul, New York and London, 1987. See also Charlene Spretnak (ed.), *The Politics of Women's Spirituality: Essays on the Rise of Spiritual Power Within the Feminist Movement*. Anchor Press, New York, 1982.

19.   How far these 'small steeples' may be seen as phallic is a difficult question. I imagine a more conical design, volcano shape, wide at the base and squat! Short steeples surely can be imagined as breast-shaped, even if rather sharp! This seems to me to be an appropriation of imagery traditionally considered as male, re-inscribing it in female terms. (What male would like his organ to be described as 'small'?) But perhaps it is also useful to place this image in the context of Cixous's account of bisexuality: 'bisexuality: that is, each one's location in self (*repérage en soi*) of the presence – variously manifest and insistent according to each person, male or female – of both sexes, non-exclusion either of the difference or of one sex, and, from this "self-permission", multiplication of the effects of the inscription of desire, over all parts of my body and the other body.' Hélène Cixous, 'The laugh of the Medusa', in Elaine Marks and Isabelle de Courtivron (eds), *New French Feminisms: An Anthology*. Harvester Press, Brighton, 1981, p. 254. That is to argue that female specificity is not bound to traditional ideas of 'the feminine' and nor does is exclude characteristics currently considered as masculine. Openness and receptiveness to the other means that the psyche is

not exclusively female. This is to posit a female specificity that is, paradoxically, both/and rather than either/or.

20. Audre Lorde, 'Black Mother Woman', in *Chosen Poems: Old and New*. W.W. Norton, New York and London, 1982, p. 52.
21. I see Lorde as creating 'patterns for relating across our human differences as equals' in this poem. See Audre Lorde, 'Age, race, class and sex: women redefining difference', in *Sister Outsider: Essays and Speeches by Audre Lorde*. The Crossing Press, Trumansburg, NY, 1984, p. 115.
22. Alicia Suskin Ostriker, *Stealing the Language: The Emergence of Women's Poetry in America*. The Women's Press, London, 1987, p. 188.
23. *Ibid.*, p. 186.
24. Audre Lorde, 'My words will be there', in Mari Swans (ed.), *Black Women Writers: Arguments and Interviews*. Pluto Press, London and Sydney, 1983, p. 261.
25. For an example of this see Johari M. Kunjufu, 'Ceremony', in Erlene Stetson (ed.), *Black Sister: Poetry by Black American Women 1746–1980*. University of Indiana Press, Bloomington, 1981, p. 192.
26. Audre Lorde, *Black Women Writers*, p. 264.
27. Audre Lorde, 'Recreation', in *The Black Unicorn: Poems*. W.W. Norton, New York and London, 1978, p. 81.
28. Audre Lorde, 'Uses of the erotic: the erotic as power', in *Sister Outsider*, pp. 53–59, p. 53.
29. Adrienne Rich, 'Poem XI' from 'The Twenty-one Love Poems', in *The Dream of a Common Language*, p. 30.
30. Audre Lorde, 'Recreation', in *The Black Unicorn*, p. 81.
31. Olga Broumas, 'Leda and Her Swan', in *Beginning with O*, p. 6.
32. Rich was researching *Of Woman Born* and reading many of the founding texts of the women's spirituality movement at this time. See especially her chapter 'The Primacy of the Mother'.
33. Vicki Noble, *Motherpeace: A Way to the Goddess through Myth, Art and Tarot*. Harper and Row, San Francisco, 1983, pp. 25, 27. However, Sally Gearheart and Susan Rennie, *A Feminist Tarot*, Persephone Press, Mass., 1981, first came out in 1976 and could have been influential. Rich was later to distance herself from more individualist manifestations of the spirituality movement in her interview with Margaret Packwood in *Spare Rib*, February 1981, p. 14.
34. Adrienne Rich, 'Floating Poem' in 'The Twenty-one Love Poems', *The Dream of a Common Language*, p. 32.
35. Elly Bulkin, 'An interview: Audre Lorde and Adrienne Rich', in *Sister Outsider*, p. 98.

36.    Audre Lorde, 'Love Poem', in *Chosen Poems – Old and New*. W.W. Norton, New York and London, 1978, p. 77.
37.    Audre Lorde, 'Dahomey', in *The Black Unicorn*, p. 11.
38.    Audre Lorde, *Zami: A New Spelling of My Name*. Sheba Feminist Publishers, London, 1982, from the prologue.

# Part Three
# In or Out (of the Mainstream)

Chapter four

# Lesbian Journalism: Mainstream and Alternative Press

**Veronica Groocock**

IN 1967 subscribers to Britain's first lesbian magazine, *Arena Three*, learned that an eminent psychiatrist had given the magazine his seal of approval. A letter from Dr D. J. West in the October 1967 issue stated that he was working on a revised edition of his best-selling paperback, *Homosexuality*, and would list *A3* (as the magazine was then known) as 'one of the reputable publications'. In an era where the existence of lesbianism was ridiculed and often denied, such recognition from the medical 'establishment' was something of a watershed. The word 'homosexuality' had always been associated in the public's mind with men; with the passing of the Sexual Offences Act earlier that year, *male* homosexuality had been placed firmly on the public agenda. Women simply did not figure in the equation (Queen Victoria, after all, questioned the very notion of sex between women).

Paradoxically, the 'swinging 60s' were rabidly heterosexist, and sexual permissiveness was not deemed to extend to individuals who identified as lesbian or gay. Social outlets were limited to a few pubs and clubs, and opportunities for meaningful discourse were virtually non-existent. Not surprisingly, therefore, most lesbians and gays chose to remain in the closet. Consequently, for lesbians across the UK, as well as overseas, *A3* represented a lifeline.

Throughout the 1960s the mainstream media mirrored the public mood by ignoring the issue, and so lesbianism continued to be relegated to the minority of small-scale, *samizdat* publications, a situation that changed only with the advent of the women's movement in the early 1970s. From the restraint and partial self-censorship of those tentative, pre-feminist years, lesbians found a new voice and it was louder, bolder, more articulate and far-reaching than ever before.

The late 1980s and 1990s have seen further massive shifts in perspective. Lesbian issues are no longer confined to the 'alternative' press but have made important inroads into the national media, where they are being debated in top-selling women's magazines. How significant a trend is this? Is it a mark of wider social acceptance – or simply a passing journalistic fad, a way of spicing up heterosexuality? A fashionable ploy catering for a fickle public or a genuine move towards greater social and sexual parity? These are some of the questions I shall address. My aim is to show some of the ways in which lesbianism has been depicted in both 'alternative' and mainstream journalism, and to trace its progress from the early 1960s until the 1990s. I shall give particular attention to early lesbian, gay and feminist publications in view of their unique and pioneering role in lesbian herstory.

For young lesbians and gays in the 1990s it would be easy to underestimate the hard-won gains of the gay liberation and feminist movements. Before these movements there were no helplines, no visible signs of an organized subculture. The concept of lesbian and gay pride, of a joyous coming-out on any mass scale, had not yet been born, let alone addressed. Gay women, if acknowledged at all, were barely tolerated. In its concern to preserve the heterosexual status quo, society decreed that boats must not be rocked, horses must not be frightened.

The emphasis was on discretion and the suppression of one's innermost feelings. This was the received wisdom and it was reflected in the *Sunday Telegraph*'s reply to a request from *A3*'s co-founder, Esme Langley, for advertising space:

Dear Miss Langley,
Thank you for your order for a classified advertisement. We agree that we have carried advertisements for you before, and we do not object to doing so again. However, we would like you to re-think this copy. We find it rather bald, and likely to cause unnecessary offence to some of our readers. Can it be altered, please?

The 'offending' advert read, simply: 'Homosexual women read *Arena 3*' – scarcely the stuff of revolution. (*A3* generally used the term 'homosexual woman' or 'female homosexual' rather than 'lesbian'.)
This was Langley's indignant rejoinder:

Statistically, many thousands of *Sunday Telegraph* readers must be either homosexual, or sensibly heterosexual. We wonder how many of them are 'offended' or astonished by the attitude displayed in the above letter. It is the kind of twisted thinking that we must tackle collectively, unless the views and wishes of sane and responsible people are to go on being smothered in favour of twilight fantasy and embattled ignorance.

And she urged readers to write to the newspaper's editor 'in no uncertain terms' (October 1967).
Another equally powerful reminder of those heterosexist times is the fact that only single women were eligible to subscribe to *A3*. A married woman had to have her husband's permission, as indicated in this letter from Miss T.Q. of Newcastle, headlined 'Point of Honour':

I wrote some time last year wishing to become a subscriber, but couldn't fill in the form as although I am known as a single person, in fact I was once married.
So, rather than fill in forms dishonestly, I set about looking for my Husband who I hadn't heard of in 16 years. So in the past 12 months, I have found him and won a divorce petition against him, and have now become a single person by law.

Therefore, I am once again applying for two forms so that I and my friend who has been with me for over 10 years may now subscribe.

The climate of repression was such that for many years most letters were signed with initials rather than names. (This also applied for some time to *A3*'s successor, *Sappho*.) There were, however, a few honourable exceptions, such as the writer Naomi Jacob, who wrote of her close friendship with Radclyffe Hall and Una Troubridge: 'two of my greatest friends . . . I only wish that [they] were here that they might read your magazine with me. I thought the last number was exceedingly good and most interesting' (written in May 1964, shortly before her death).

Another correspondent was writer Mary Renault. 'Dear Esme,' she writes, 'It was extremely nice of you to send me *Arena 3* and I've enjoyed reading it. I admire the high and decent plane on which you are consistently keeping the whole issue . . .' She goes on to say that although she feels no *personal* need of such a periodical (however good):

> I do realise how wonderful it must be for those Lesbians who live in isolation, shame and guilt; but I don't think it can ever be sufficiently plugged that most of the persecution gregarious Lesbians complain of is due to the fact that they are prepared to accept a lower standard of character and behaviour in Lesbian associates than in heterosexual friends, rather than push out boldly among their fellow-humans like people with nothing to be ashamed of. (July 1970)

The implication here seems to be that all lesbian oppression is self-inflicted, and the remaining paragraphs represent a plea for greater openness, less self-consciousness.

On the opposite page is a letter from a Manchester woman, recounting her feelings of unrequited attraction towards a close friend:

> I decided to stop chasing a hopeless situation and do something constructive . . . Through your personal

announcements I contacted various women and . . . am now living with one of the girls I met. We are terribly happy and now I feel for the first time in my life I am completely myself, and regret the wasted years trying to live a life unfulfilled for me.

My only heartache is that I have had to leave my two boys with their father, as he doesn't know why I have left them . . . The only explanation I can offer to him is that I don't love him any more. I dare not reveal my true reasons in case I jeopardise my chances of having access to my sons. (July 1970)

The issue of married lesbians was a highly contentious one, regarded by many readers as a contradiction in terms. To be a 'true' lesbian ruled out any semblance of heterosexuality and, indeed, all permutations within the sexual spectrum. Bisexuality was rarely discussed. Married women who professed to have lesbian feelings were frequently stigmatized and treated with scepticism, even contempt, as another reader indicates:

As for Mrs R., well, words fail me, for after so many years of marriage she finds out *now* that she has Lesbian tendencies? Never in this world can I believe that pifle . . . I would advise her to think again and ponder on just what a real Lesbian is, looks like, feels like and acts like, then perhaps she will tuck the kids in bed as usual and sleep happily with her husband, knowing that she just hasn't got what it takes to qualify for the title LESBIAN. (March 1969)

'Madam Chairman' (alias Esme Langley) replies: 'it is a popular myth that if a girl will only get married and have some children, all that "schoolgirl crush nonsense" will magically come to a sudden stop . . . ' And she reminds readers that Sappho herself was a wife and mother.

In another issue a married reader castigates the smug, judgemental attitudes of some unmarried lesbians:

The tragedy of (married) unions is obvious: they haven't only themselves to think about. There is another person – and often children – to consider. Suppose a husband still loves his wife? What then? Someone must suffer deeply. It isn't an unsubtle cleavage between 'true, selfless love' and a dogmatic 'Mine's true blue, yours is black and dirty.' (July 1970)

Besides the 'Free Speech' section from which these letters were taken, the magazine carried book and film reviews, the occasional poem or short story, and extracts from the British and American mainstream press. One item in the former was a question-and-answer piece about lesbianism: 'Is it caused by T.B. or cancer? Is it hereditary or is it due to lack of love during childhood? Is the lesbian the forerunner of a new biological type? Can lesbians get married and have children?'

Below this *A3* printed a photograph of a 'gay wedding', headlined 'Homophile America', featuring two women in cowboy hats at a 'Gay-In' (*Los Angeles Advocate*). The juxtaposition of these two items pinpointed the ideological gulf in understanding of lesbianism between Britain and the States at that time.

There were, however, some British mainstream publications which ran enlightened, sensitively written features on lesbian issues. One notable success was 'Lesbians – Have you really tried to understand them?', an informative, well-researched three pages written by Mick Brown (a self-styled 'heterosexual guy') for *Nineteen*, a popular magazine aimed at the teenage market (7 March 1969). The article elicited hundreds of letters from all over Britain enquiring about clubs and social groups.

Another, published in *Vanity Fair* (circa 1970) and titled 'Love without a Man', featured two lesbians 'talking frankly about themselves' to novelist Nicola Thorne. Thorne concludes: 'It is dangerous to generalise about any minority group because there are so many different types of people within it, and this certainly applies to lesbians.' *A3* received occasional interview requests from provincial newspaper journalists, including women's page editors.

In the absence of any viable support network, social isolation was one of the main problems lesbians faced in the pre-feminist, pre-gay liberation years. Subscribers to *A3* could make contact with other women via the classified advertisements section, and various social groups were also listed. Probably the best known of these was Kenric, founded in 1964 (by *A3* staff) and still in existence today.

Other more short-lived groups and clubs emerged, among them Southampton's first gay club 'for femmes only', and the (London-based) SM Group which, despite its name, had no connections with whips, chains or black leather. Indeed, it represented the very peak of respectability:

> As the group meets at a private flat, not a public place, the tenants – us – rely on the commonsense of their guests in the matter of dress, etc., to preserve good relations with landlord and neighbours. (March 1970)

This sense of restraint is conveyed in a reader's letter in the same issue expressing ambivalence about the idea of a sex manual for lesbians:

> I agree . . . that a sex manual for 'lesbians' would be a useful asset to one's library, but personally I find natural instinct, love and sensible adaptation of heterosexual books . . . really all that is necessary.
> A sex manual serialised in *A3* would only attract the prurient type of reader. Let people find out for themselves. Love will always find a way.

Such sentiments are imbued with a kind of pastoral innocence, which must be adjudged in the context of a more carefree, pre-AIDS era where there was no such thing as unsafe sex.

There was also a sense in which lesbian sexuality was seen, even by lesbians themselves, as secondary, as merely an offshoot to heterosexuality. This was reflected in the sometimes high moral tone of letters such as the above, and in the sparse media coverage allotted to lesbian issues in general at that time. Lesbians had yet to be released from the roots of their oppression. The negative, pejorative images associated with lesbianism needed to be replaced by positive, life-enhancing ones.

This was a process which began to evolve in America, with Stonewall and the gay liberation movement, and gradually filtered through to the UK. In its section on News from the US, *A3* ran a piece headed 'The Birth of Gay Power' (from the *DOB New York Chapter Newsletter*):

> On July 2, 1969, a new chapter was written in the history of the homophile movement. Outraged at politically-inspired raids on the Stonewall Inn and other gay bars, 400 male and female homosexuals rioted in the streets of Greenwich village . . . Homosexuals have traditionally been passive in the face of persecution, have traditionally declined to fight their tormentors. But this time the US homophile groups responded . . . A Gay Liberation Front has been formed. (October/November 1969)

It marked the dawning of an era of radical change in which the internalized anger of years of repression and injustice turned outwards into a collective, burgeoning mood of pride and celebration. This turning point in lesbian and gay history coincided, in the early 1970s, with the beginnings of the UK women's movement which produced a plethora of publications, some of them lesbian-feminist, others with a strong lesbian perspective.

Of those in the first category, the best known was *Sappho*, launched in April 1972 out of the trail-blazing ashes of *A3* which had folded the previous year. A more radical successor to *A3*, *Sappho* styled itself a monthly lesbian feminist publication 'by homosexual women for all women'. It was run as a collective, with Jackie Forster as co-ordinating editor backed by a dedicated core of women volunteers. Like its predecessor, *Sappho* was self-supporting, relying on donations and goodwill from readers and subscribers instead of grants. Among its aims and objects were:

- to encourage social groups everywhere to relieve the loneliness of the lesbian and to publish information about existing groups
- to accept articles, stories, poems, etc. from all those with an intelligent interest and empathy for lesbians and feminists

Women subscribers received an accompanying sheet of 'contact' advertisements, also detailing speakers and events at forthcoming *Sappho* meetings (in a London pub). The first issue, funded with capital of a single donation of £25, sold 50 copies and acquired about 15 subscribers. Five years later, the magazine expanded from 14 to 36 pages and sold an average of 1,000 copies a month at 40p.

Most of the magazine's content was generated by readers and encompassed a corresponding diversity of topics: personalized stories of lesbian identity, relationships and careers; a series on 'remarkable women' (Radclyffe Hall, Glenda Jackson, Norwegian activist Kim Friele, former MP Maureen Colquhoun); overseas news (especially from Scandinavia); poems; the occasional short story or competition; hints on car maintenance.

There was a strong emphasis on women's health issues, like self-examination ('Happiness is knowing your own cervix'), and an early series by 'Speculum' ('a beautiful, married, qualified nurse and midwife') on vaginal infections and other 'internal' affairs.

Regular features included Heteracetera (readers' letters), book and record reviews, Amazon (the resident lesbian gossip), The Adventures of Sandy (cartoon strip), a crossword and The Spike (pages of listings). Conveying *Sappho*'s constant struggle for survival was a regular exhortation to readers to 'Help Us Please – The Teapot [sketched] Is Almost Empty: Stamps and Money Required Now.'

There was the occasional quiz (Amazon's 'Just how sexy do you think you are?') or questionnaire (*Sappho*'s mini-survey of lesbian sexuality, 'Sextionnaire', filled in by '50 women of all sexes').

Through the 1970s the magazine broadened its editorial coverage, mirroring the new climate of lesbian feminism and giving more space to politics, conferences, action. The May 1973 issue, reporting on CHE's (Campaign for Homosexual Equality) first national conference in Morecambe, included the following observation: 'Women in CHE – or rather the lack of them – moved the conference to vote for a Woo-Women drive this year.' *Sappho* advertised itself as 'the only lesbian magazine in Europe' until the editor of its opposite number in Berlin wrote in to assert prior claim.

Its back cover continued to bear the women's symbol encircled with 'Lesbian Feminist Voice'.

As well as acting as a valuable and stimulating source of contact for isolated lesbians in the UK and overseas, *Sappho* instigated and sponsored a number of campaigning groups, including the Gay Teachers group, Action for Lesbian Parents and a Dry Group for Lesbians with drinking problems. It recorded and celebrated some of the major feminist and gay milestones: the birth of the The Women's Press and Sisterwrite bookshop, the first birthday of Lesbian Line, the fiftieth issue of *Gay News* (GN).

Unlike *Gay News*, *Sappho* was never the subject of a court case, although for most of their existence both publications were banned from public libraries. Britain's first regular gay newspaper, *GN* was launched in June 1972, just two months after *Sappho*. It grew out of the Gay Liberation Front and, like *Sappho*, began as a collective. In the ensuing decade, however, *GN* acquired a more hierarchical structure, headed by Denis Lemon as editor, backed by a team of mainly male contributors.

One early accusation levelled at *GN* was that it was too male-oriented, a situation which altered in June 1977 with the appointment of Alison Hennegan as Assistant Features Editor. Her arrival coincided with the furore over Mrs Mary Whitehouse's charge of blasphemous libel which brought Denis Lemon and *GN* to the dock at the Old Bailey. (They were found guilty. Lemon was sentenced to nine months' imprisonment suspended for 18 months and fined £500; *GN* was fined £1,000. They appealed, both to the House of Lords and to the European Commission of Human Rights, but lost in each case.)

Although Hennegan was the first female editorial staff member, women such as Jackie Forster, Marsaili Cameron and myself were among its freelance contributors. As well as regular book reviews, I wrote several features, including a series on 'live-in' relationships called 'Together': 'a series which explores, through interviews, the pleasures, pressures, frustrations, habits, changes and challenges which result from gay people living together'. Each interview was conducted in question and answer format and illustrated with pictures of couples with pet dog, cat or teddy bear in a state of cosy domesticity. As I recall, lesbians were considerably more cautious than gay men about the prospect of coming out, even to a gay newspaper, and requests for interviewees elicited about three male partnerships to every female one.

By 1980, despite the increasing numbers of women involved in its production, *GN* had seen a diminishing of lesbian material, and it was only a buy-out by marketing director Robert Palmer in 1982 that promised improved coverage for women. A new, collectively run feature section called 'The Visible Lesbian' was introduced which aimed to redress the balance between the perspectives of lesbians and gay men. In so doing, however, it provoked some deeply misogynistic letters. The newspaper continued through a volatile period of struggles and power bids until its final collapse on 15 April 1983.

In terms of 'alternative' coverage of lesbian and gay issues, *Sappho* and *Gay News* were the longest survivors. There has been no comparable lesbian successor to *Sappho* since its demise in 1981. From the first soundings of gay liberation, other gay publications of various political dimensions have appeared (albeit briefly), only to prioritize male gay issues. Among them were *Come Together* (affiliated to the Gay Liberation Front (GLF)), *Gay Left* and its lesbian-feminist counterpart *Lesbian Left*, the bi-monthly *Out* (published by CHE) and the popular if less radical or 'right-on' *Lunch*, 'an independent homosexual monthly magazine for men and women'.

*Lunch*'s lesbian content was mostly limited to interviews with 'high-profile' women like Jill Johnston, the abrasive American lesbian columnist for the *New Yorker*, who believed that the only way to true liberation for women was to become lesbian: 'Women don't have penis-envy. Men have womb-envy' (November 1973).

There was the occasional male interviewee, such as the Samaritans' founder, Chad Varah, whose patronizing allusions to lesbians would not have passed muster in the 1990s. On 'counselling lesbians':

> The biggest single group of people I do counselling interviews with are lesbians. I'm happy that this should be so because they – the ones that come to me, anyway – appear to be lovable and admirable people, easy to help if you really like

and understand them . . . well, not that any man can claim to understand a woman. (August 1973)

Because of the predominantly masculine perspective of such publications, many lesbians chose to ally themselves with radical feminist magazines such as *Red Rag, Scarlet Women, Outwrite* and – most of all – *Spare Rib* (*SR*). Launched in July 1972 with a budget of £2,000 and a 20,000 print run, *Spare Rib* acted as a potent, creative and influential voice for the women's liberation movement in Britain, reflecting the interests and concerns of women across the social spectrum. Initial publicity proclaimed that '*Spare Rib* will be the first magazine to approach women as individuals in their own right'.

Its declared aim was to reach *all* women although, in the early issues, lesbian topics were noticeably absent. This was partly in deference to the mainstream media, sizeable sections of which had taken a vociferously anti-feminist line. There was a wish to avoid obvious areas of controversy, and lesbianism was clearly a contentious issue.

Later, lesbianism was more frequently in the ascendant, and there was an attempt – as with the magazine as a whole – to achieve a balance between personalized accounts and factual information. Certain topics of necessity 'belonged' in both areas: lesbian mothers and their custody battles, for instance, were probably the most pertinent example of the women's liberation maxim 'the personal is political'. There were reports of campaigns, conferences, even a poem ('The trial of a lesbian mother') about the emotional ordeal experienced in court over the custody of a daughter (June 1981).

There was a strong focus on stories of coming out (mother to daughter, daughter to mother, as a lesbian school student) and personal identity ('How did we get this way?' by Sue Cartledge and Susan Hemmings, September 1979).

Anniversaries and other landmarks were recorded and celebrated: five years of Lesbian Line, ten years of GLF, annual women's liberation conferences. Campaigns which in retrospect seem relatively trivial were closely monitored, such as the 'unfair dismissal' charge by the young office worker (Louise Boychuk) sacked from a City stockbroker's for wearing a 'Lesbians Ignite' badge (January 1977).

Eschewing the 'personality cult' approach of most traditional women's magazines, *SR*'s interviews with prominent lesbian women were centred on their work and ideas: Dr Charlotte Wolff on bisexuality; Adrienne Rich (radical femininist/writer/poet); Jeanette Winterson and Anna Livia (novelists); and, following the closure of *Sappho* in December 1981, editor Jackie Forster.

*SR*'s original objective of reaching *all* women posed inevitable problems, proving that it simply was not possible to please all women all the time. In the same issue as the Forster interview, the editorial featured an anonymous reader's letter complaining about excessive (*sic*) coverage of lesbian issues – and its response:

> A whisper – which is all *Spare Rib* has really given to lesbians over the years – can seem like a shout when all around is silent. No other nationally distributed magazine gives lesbians any kind of voice of their own – just the passing curious mention or derogatory comment. So when the word appears in *Spare Rib* it probably stands out a mile . . . (March 1982)

More than a decade later *Everywoman* magazine elicits the opposite complaint on its letters page, 'Hersay':

> Where are the lesbians? . . . Save the odd token article you conveniently ignore gay women. I am 19, lesbian and live in London. Why, in 1993, should I have to search so hard to find a lesbian voice? We exist. The vast majority of us hold feminist beliefs . . .
> Women, gay and straight, must stick together to show the patriarchy our common power, so give us gay women a voice. (October 1993)

Lesbian feminism, clearly, is not dead after all.

Despite its chequered history and eventual decline, for most of its 21 years *Spare Rib* successfully straddled the barriers between mainstream and 'alternative' press, like some feisty feminist colossus making bold inroads into white, middle-class heterosexist society.

Its distribution sources included the larger retailers as well as smaller, specialist outlets such as feminist bookshops or women's groups. (Rosie Boycott, one of the original collective, made a radical career leap from the frontiers of feminism to the editorship of *Esquire*, one of Britain's leading men's magazines.)

Throughout the 1970s lesbianism was appropriated by feminism. It was radical, political, with connotations – fostered by the mainstream media – of butch, boiler-suited, man-hating fanatics. Such stereotypical images were reinforced in the 1980s by the often negative media portrayal of the women at Greenham Common. Lesbians have been in the frontline of the feminist backlash and, for the tabloids in particular, the Greenham 'wimmin' represented a convenient 'stick' with which to attack lesbianism.

However, there have always been mainstream publications which treated lesbian issues in a positive and non-sensationalist manner. In April 1983 *Cosmopolitan* published a feature on 'Women who love women':[1] 'What makes a woman become a lesbian? Is she discriminated against socially and professionally? Can she be sexually fulfilled?' A cross-section of 'gay women' were interviewed and the article began as follows: 'After 24 years of marriage, three children and no inkling that she harboured erotic feelings towards women, Marilyn fell in love with 23-year-old Wendy . . . '

Three years later a first-person account, 'Why I'm glad to be gay', appeared: 'I love the sameness of our bodies, the likeness of our minds and it's worth facing the hurdles.'[2] Conclusion? Lesbianism is 'an alternative lifestyle that can be fulfilling. Women are clever, romantic figures. Sex with the right one can be a tender, thoughtful experience.' All of which, despite the writer's sympathetic tone, made it sound as though women were some rare, freakish, endangered species instead of the majority of the population.

*Cosmo*'s editor at the time was Linda Kelsey, who went on to edit *She*, a magazine whose reputation for innovative, quirky journalism was probably not unconnected with its lesbian origins. Joan Werner Laurie, editor of *She* in the 1950s, was the lover of writer and broadcaster Nancy Spain (both women died in a plane crash in 1964). It was, however, a history of which Kelsey had been largely unaware. When she was brought in with 'a whole new brief', all links with the *She* of the past had been broken, but she admits that those links are still remembered, mostly with affection though occasionally with acrimony. In July 1993 someone from corporate advertising had declared: 'I am not having our products advertised in that *lesbian* magazine.' Kelsey was deeply shocked and 'couldn't understand where this was coming from' – until a colleague enlightened her.

Back in the mid-1960s *She* published a three-page feature on homosexuality, headlined 'Should men marry men?' This focused exclusively on gay men, apart from passing allusions to Sappho (the poet) and same-sex relationships. Despite the writer's non-judgemental perspective, there was the (then) almost *de rigeur* use of the word 'normal' to indicate heterosexuality, and the outmoded 'deviate', suggesting some kind of aberration or psychiatric disorder.

Three decades later *She*, *Cosmo* and other mainstream publications respond to lesbian issues rather differently. There is a sense in which lesbianism is a *given*, an accepted part of mainstream culture, not confined to the closet but bursting out of it, not marginalized out of existence but integrated and absorbed into the social fabric. It is a subject that has become ripe for critique, and methods of critique vary.

*She* takes a pragmatic approach. 'Women who leave their husbands for another woman': this was the coverline for the May 1991 issue featuring Cathy and Liz, 'who fell in love – and are still counting the cost five years on'.[3] The four-page feature centres on the ongoing problems each woman faces in relating to her former husband and children as they attempt to come to terms with the new status quo. The women's dialogue is juxtaposed with comments from a female counsellor.

This type of 'pop psychology' approach reflects the growing demand, especially among women, for counselling and therapy. Unlike the more authoritarian stance of traditional psychiatry, it is a client-centred approach where society's prejudice, not lesbianism, is seen as the problem. *She* subsequently focused on Diana and Nicola, who 'felt their once-exciting relationship was becoming just like those they'd had with men' (June 1992). Through sessions with a couples counsellor both women were enabled to see how in their own relationship they had been repeating old, destructive patterns from childhood (oddly, the accompanying photograph 'repeated' the same models as the May 1991 article).

With its long tradition of progressive journalism the *Guardian* has provided consistent, sympathetic and informed coverage of lesbian and gay topics. It was there at the birth of Gay Lib in 1971, with the late Jill Tweedie's cogently argued, torch-carrying 'Gay's the Word' feature ('Though they may still have their residual worries – society does not change overnight and conditioning clings like a bad smell – for them, on the whole, at last, gay is good').[4] Five years later Eleanor Stephens, of Action for Lesbian Parents, wrote about a mother's right to care for her child whatever her sexuality.[5] The piece marked an historic decision by three Appeal Court judges to give custody of eleven-year-old twins to their lesbian mother. Until then custody in such cases had always gone to the father.

Throughout the 1970s and 1980s the *Guardian* continued to foreground lesbian concerns, and it is there as we approach the millennium, still treating lesbian issues seriously but perhaps less earnestly than before. Both the Women's and Style pages have reflected and recorded the theme of lesbians as 'radical chic'. A lighthearted assessment of the changing politics of lesbian fashion, headlined 'Gay abandon', opens with: 'Move over rad les fems – here come les femmes fatales'.[6] Coining the term 'lesbo-erotica' to denote the growing presence of overtly lesbian images in mainstream magazines, the writer cites Vivienne Westwood's 'female harlequins kissing across the pages of the glossies' and 'nubile nude vixens' in a 'chic to chic' clinch on the front of the *Tatler*. The trend away from dungarees and badges stating 'I'm not badly dressed – I'm just anti-fashion' into a new 'designer dyke' age is seen as auguring well for lesbians, whose past dress code was 'a little tyrannical and not a lot of fun'. And there is the inevitable reference to Madonna. 'In sectors of today's media,' the writer concludes, 'women are portrayed as being more in control of their sexuality and their image, as opposed to being controlled by them.'

The 1990s has witnessed a spate of mainstream articles in which lesbianism is depicted as stylish, fashionable, *fun*. The most unlikely publications appear to have been competing for coverage, even the *Sunday Telegraph* ('Are designer dykes becoming "fashion accessories"?' 11 July 1993).

A few days earlier the *Evening Standard* had proclaimed lesbianism to be 'currently at the very acme of the fashionable world'.[7] Writer Louise Guinness cited as role models Martina Navratilova, kd lang and Jeanette Winterson – 'all attractive, successful, positive women who are lesbians not because they hate men but because they love women'. This jettisoning of the man-hating image may be one crucial clue as to why lesbianism appears to have gained a tacit acceptance.

The previous month the *Evening Standard* published a piece about the sauna where London's lesbians are 'bright, chic and glamorous'. Such atypical content from one of Britain's most reactionary newspapers prompted one male reader to call for an end to 'the sequence of glossy promotions of female homosexuality . . . sick souls can buy a top-shelf magazine if it's titillation they are after'.[8]

Despite the objectionable nature of such views, it could be argued that the portrayal of lesbianism as some kind of fashion accessory carries an intrinsic risk of diluting its power, of trivializing it and relegating it to a cheap media bandwagon. For a broader, all-encompassing view it is necessary to turn to the current lesbian and gay press, which has expanded considerably since the years of *Sappho* and *Gay News*.

The diversity of styles and images to be found within the gay community is reflected in the sheer range of titles available. The best-known of these is the *Pink Paper*, a free weekly newspaper 'for lesbians and gay men'. Since its launch in 1988 it has evolved into a highly professional publication with a clear but varied format and a reasonably even balance between news and features. Lesbian input has increased to a certain extent since the early weeks, which may be due in part to the appointment of Alison Gregory as editor (in 1993).

Pre-dating the *Pink* is *Gay Times*, which first appeared in the early 1980s: a monthly glossy magazine 'incorporating *Gay News*', though very different in format and style from its predecessor. In most issues articles relating to gay men tend to outnumber lesbian ones, and the prolific arts reviews, even where they feature lesbian themes, are frequently accompanied by male bylines. However, despite the heavily masculine perspective (in the classifieds, three pages of Men's Personals as against two single *adverts* under Women's Personals), there is usually at least one major item per issue that is virtually guaranteed to attract lesbian readers (for example, interviews with Navratilova and Pam St Clement, July 1993; fag hags, January 1993; interviews with Lillian Faderman and Sandra Bernhard, September 1992).

More recent titles include the quarterly *Body Politic* (feminism, masculinity, cultural politics), edited by a woman (Elsie Owusu) and featuring more raunch than reportage with topics such as 'Queer heterosexuality: the new politics of sexual diversity', cross-dressing, lesbians who want sex with gay men, and 'Down with vanilla-sexism' (co-written by Owusu and her male deputy editor, Mick Cooper), and *Rouge* (liberté, égalité, sexualité), edited by a man and with a strong socialist slant. An eclectic mix of the serious and trivial, there is a concerted attempt at parity of lesbian input: lesbian activism in Australia; lesbian lobbying in Prague; the musings of a female to male transsexual on femininity, masculinity and gender identity; women's sex shops; lesbian and gay parenting (focusing on a lesbian couple); lesbians and AIDS; a short story by Sarah Schulman.

Despite any initial idealistic notions, however, lesbian topics tend to be less well represented in 'mixed' magazines. For this reason, just as some lesbians in the 1970s opted for 'rad fem' publications in preference to gay ones, some of their 1990s counterparts identify more with publications such as *Bad Attitude* ('Radical Women's Newspaper') or the US-based *Off Our Backs*. And the emergence of any new *lesbian* publication is always an encouraging and empowering event. Three titles, all very contrasting in style and format, are *Lesbian London*, *Quim* and *Shebang*.

*Lesbian London*, launched in January 1992, is a 16-page monthly containing a lengthy section on London-based groups, events and actions, plus news and feature pages, an arts and culture spread, readers' letters and an astrology column. This is an informative, readable magazine with no hidden agenda, no murky subtext.

*Quim* ('For Dykes of All Sexual Persuasions') is slick, sexy and heavily into SM. About as subtle as a dildo in a bedding centre, it makes *Gay Times* look like the *Church Times*. It has been described as 'an orgasm with no foreplay' and 'cliterature with a nasty after-taste of testosterone' (*Lesbian London*, February 1993).

*Shebang*, a bi-monthly, is the younger 'sister' of the *Pink Paper* (they share the same publisher: Gay Community Press). Styling itself 'The Dyke Active Ingredient', *Shebang* is a mixture of sex, health, informed comment and interviews, and gives plenty of space to pictures and graphics – a kind of lesbian hybrid, trying to be all things to all dykes and sometimes succeeding. Lesbian terrorists, post-feminist lesbian sex, breast cancer, clubbing, women silk spinners in China: all these, and more, featured in issue 5 (August 1993).

The previous issue (issue 4) embraced bisexuality, the Canadian film *Forbidden Love*, cervical cancer, Sarah Schulman, Riot Grrrls . . . and five women's memories of schoolgirl crushes. The latter was subsequently reproduced on the *Guardian* women's page, illustrating the increasing interaction between 'alternative' and mainstream media.

This interaction was further highlighted in Jane Solanas's castigation of the media's relentless promotion of the 'lipstick lesbian', which she sees as a trite euphemism for the 'economically powerful lesbian' (*Shebang*, issue 5). 'Unfortunately,' Solanas observes, 'the phrase has stuck, spilled over into the gay media and captured the imagination of the lesbian community – always fond of a good political dust-up no matter what the cost.' It's an invention that has 'triggered off the tired old debate about butch and femme roles'[9] – sentiments scathingly endorsed (in the same issue) by American writer and academic Mary Daly, who regards such a superficial definition of lesbianism as 'contra-feminism' and opines that women 'seem to be starving for radical feminism, or lesbian feminism and philosophy'.[10]

Whether and to what extent this is the case is a moot point. Daly provides us with no evidence for her assertion. Certainly, it is in America that the new cultish image of lesbianism appears to be most evident: 'Want to get ahead? Get a girlfriend. Why lesbians are big news in the US'.[11] The new activism of American lesbians in response to the Aids crisis has accorded them a greater, more defiant visibility, the writers claim. There is no equivalent movement in the UK, only 'a wall of silence', and the writers berate Britain for 'an absence of home-grown lesbian images, positive or otherwise'.

In terms of 'out' celebrities, this would seem to be true. The mainstream theatre in particular lacks lesbian role models. While there is no shortage of 'out' gay *male* actors in British theatre it is much harder for female actors to come out as lesbian as they are allotted parts very much on the basis of their physical appearance, and their career advancement depends to a large degree on conforming to stereotypical images of femininity. As long as this is the prevailing belief there will continue to be a dearth of 'coming-out' interviews with British women actors who happen to be lesbian.

Few lesbian women anywhere appear to be as comfortable or confident about their image, as self-possessed, as snug inside their own skin, as Martina Navratilova or kd lang. The *Vanity Fair* cover featuring scantily clad Cindy Crawford shaving pinstripe-suited kd lang was one highly visible instance of 'lesbian chic'. Inside, more gender-bending pictures illustrated a nine-page interview, reinforcing lang's reputation as a sassy, classy, exciting role model. She talks about her rural upbringing, her love of motorbikes ('I love the feel of them . . . the aloneness . . . the romance'), being lesbian ('I find women more enticing, both emotionally and sexually'), and coming out:

> I didn't try to dispel lesbian rumors . . . I just lived my life. There was a part of me that really didn't think it was important to make an announcement. But to the gay community, saying 'I'm a lesbian' is dispelling any doubt.[12]

There is no pretence, no sham, about kd lang. In media terms, it's a case of 'what you see is what you get'. Torie Osborn, executive director of the National Gay and Lesbian Task Force, sums up her appeal:

> She's absolutely herself, and when you see her onstage you see a living example of how, when you step out of the closet, you become more whole and are able to be more powerful. She's come out with grace and ease – no loss in sales. She counters the mythology.[13]

Other famous 'upfront' lesbians exploit fetishistic fantasies of lesbianism and are, in turn, exploited by the media in such a way that they almost become legends before their time. Take Sandra Bernhard, for instance. *Cosmopolitan*'s provocative coverline, 'The world's most delicious lesbian on love, SEX and men' (September 1993) is accurate but misleading. It promises more than it delivers. The word 'sex' on the cover of any magazine is a guaranteed selling point, as editor Marcelle d'Argy Smith admits, but Bernhard's raunchy autobiographical ramblings contained nothing about lesbianism, and lesbianism is what most readers will have been led to expect. They are warned – but only on the inside pages – that the woman is, indeed, 'strictly tease'.

However, as I have already indicated, there is more to media lesbianism than the hyping of a few flamboyant female icons, influential though they undoubtedly are. A women-only sex survey by the *Sunday Mirror* magazine (11 July 1993) posed questions such as: 'When you make love with a man, do you ever fantasise about having sex with a woman?' and 'Have you ever wondered what it would be like to stroke a woman's breasts?'

Women readers were assured that being attracted to another woman was perfectly natural: 'Studies indicate that all women have a tiny amount of lesbian in their make-up.' In the absence of quoted sources for this statement, one is tempted to speculate on just how 'tiny' this lesbian component may be – could it be a deliberately conservative estimate, in order to avoid the risk of a mass lesbian uprising which would overthrow society as we know it?

Other women's magazines have published surveys with more specific findings. *New Woman* (1991) found that at least one in ten women had had a lesbian relationship and a significant number of others would consider doing so. According to *Elle* (March 1992), one-sixth of heterosexual women said they would like to try sex with another woman.

*Company*, a magazine with a reputation for 'sexy' journalism, tackled the subject of 'Women who leave men for other women' (July 1993). Six months earlier *New Woman* had posed the question: 'Do lesbians have more fun?' (January 1993). Writer Joy Legatte concludes that 'Eve and Eve' have no secret formula, no built-in guarantee of lasting bliss, and are subject to the same kinds of pressures as heterosexual couples.

The influence of women's magazines must not be underestimated. In the autumn of 1993 the combined monthly circulation of *New Woman*, *She* and *Cosmopolitan* was 1,004,808 (267,371, 260,000, and 477,437 respectively).

*New Woman* publishes regular lesbian features every three or four issues. Editor Gill Hudson attributes the apparent media trend to her influence. Although she is heterosexual she has several lesbian friends, who have heightened her awareness of lesbianism. This, coupled with the results of the 1991 sex survey, triggered off her interest in the subject:

> Traditionally, everyone has been more cautious about covering lesbian issues in young women's magazines, in case advertisers were offended . . . My concern as an editor is to reflect what is going on 'out there'. If a minimum of one in 10 has had some sort of lesbian activity in life, it is our duty to cover it.

Freelance journalist Beverly Kemp has contributed several articles on lesbian issues to *New Woman* and other 'glossy' magazines. Although encountering very little homophobic reaction from editors, when she offered an 'If your daughter was a lesbian' piece to one of the more traditional weeklies, the commissioning editor 'dropped the phone in horror'. Another magazine commissioned a piece on lesbian mothers which Kemp wrote and submitted, but she was not prepared to write an additional paragraph allaying readers' fears about lesbian mothers and consequently withdrew the piece.

Interestingly, often it is *readers* who are judgemental. Kemp cites two of the 'younger' women's magazines which published articles on lesbian mothers (circa 1992–93), producing 'an avalanche' of hostile letters pleading 'Please don't run anything like that again'. The apparent subtext, Kemp surmises, is: 'Lesbianism is fine as long as "they" do not choose to have a child.'

However, Kemp has found reader response to be 'very positive' in the main. She has written (and published) several articles of the 'Women who leave men for other women' type. It is the kind of feature that generates sackfuls of mail, the gist of many letters being 'My God, I thought I was the only one'. An astonishing pointer, observes Kemp, to the sheer numbers of closeted women 'out there'.

Gill Hudson recalls a former stint as editor of *Company*, when it seemed that only one subject could save it: Sex. 'No one was doing sex at all, because of AIDS. As soon as we did one sex supplement, it was a complete sell-out. Sex came back in and changed the face of women's publishing.'

Hudson welcomes the new media prominence given to lesbian issues, seeing it as 'almost inevitable'. Prejudice has been 'slowly eroding', and it's as if lesbianism is 'the last straw to break the camel's back. It's been a very long time coming'. She has no fears that it might be a case of 'all style and no substance':

> There is so much debate about sexuality . . . In Soho now you have gay consumers, there are gay insurance firms and gay travel agents, and once it is established in a structure like that you don't backtrack. It is not a case of concepts floating around: people are going and *living* it.

She feels that it is time lesbianism had a more glamorous image, and compares the erstwhile worthy *Spare Rib* with the 'sparky' *Quim*, and praises *Vanity Fair* ('To have kd lang on the front cover, giving it style in the way that gay men have had style for a lot longer . . . ').

The magazine's readers are aged 25 to 35. Most are in a relationship, though not settled with children:

> One of the philosophies at *New Woman* is that we don't *assume* things about readers. You can be who you want: a hundred per cent housewife, Chair of British Airways, or whatever. The crux is: 'What would make you happy?' If you are unhappy with heterosexual relationships you may be happier with a gay one. The right thing is to give the options, the information, and let people make up their own minds.

> If we are dong a relationship piece, we put 'partner', not husband or boyfriend, because often it can relate just as much to a female partner.
>
> I don't think all the readers will 'turn gay' if we run a gay or lesbian feature. It's as good as anything else in the magazine and generates as much interest . . . It's just part of the magazine. I don't want to make a big deal about it.

Nevertheless, sex sells and, in the perennial search for fresh, more erotic variations on the theme, magazine editors appear to have singled out lesbianism as a *cause célèbre*. But does its popularity as a subject for debate signify a wider social sanctioning of lesbian lifestyles, a genuine opening up of the issues – or, instead, the need to satisfy a sexually voracious, voyeuristic public? *She*'s editor, Linda Kelsey, believes there is 'a growing appetite for discussion of all things sexual':

> People seem to have developed an insatiable curiosity for anything to do with sex . . . My personal view is that lesbianism is not really accepted and gay men have a far easier time of it than gay women.
>
> I guess authors like Jeanette Winterson, who have come out very openly as gay, have made it to a degree more acceptable, but my feeling is that if there is more coverage it is more to do with fashion, style and kd lang than any great leaps forward for lesbians.

It was Winterson who, back in the mid-1980s, posed nude for a magazine's centre spread, a move which seems to have enhanced rather than harmed her 'street cred' as one of Britain's best and brightest lesbian role models. She later wrote about the experience in *Marie Claire* (November 1990):

> At first I was amused, then aghast, but I agreed. I have always admired Gloria Steinem for her stint as a bunny girl (the best weapons are the ones you take from the enemy), and I

thought that on a humbler scale I might have something to add to the endless Page Three debate . . .

One of the 'younger' women's magazines, *Marie Claire* has frequently covered lesbian issues since its launch in 1988. There was 'Why I'm a lesbian' in the 'Real Lives' series, which described the empowering and liberating feeling of coming out.[14] Paradoxically, the writer chose to remain anonymous. This is a gauge of the powerful homophobic fears and taboos which lie just below the surface of our society.

Two lesbian couples were the subject of a sensitively written feature on gay parenting, complete with photographs (*Marie Claire*, September 1991). There was no hint of secrecy, no concealment. Instead, readers witnessed open, smiling faces and absorbed positive images of stable, warm, loving family relationships.

'When your lover turns out to be gay' headlined interviews with four heterosexuals whose partners became involved in a same-sex relationship.[15] These dealt with issues of rejection, jealousy and self-doubt. One male interviewee admitted finding 'something quite erotic' about his female lover having a girlfriend. 'Looking at lesbian lovers is one of the classic male fantasies. I suspect that, deep down, a bit of me is turned on by it.'

In terms of the *presentation* of lesbian issues in the printed media, it is not always easy to ascertain to what extent they may be pandering (albeit subconsciously) to men's erotic fantasies. In their analysis of representations of lesbian sex, Jenny and Celia Kitzinger highlight the practical difficulties of defining a 'lesbian gaze' 'as opposed to adopting a male gaze and utilising the conventions of male pornography. Simply claiming that they are "by women, for women" doesn't solve the problem.'[16]

Although they are focusing specifically on lesbian erotica (they cite *Quim*, which they regard as a lesbian porn magazine), their arguments are equally applicable to the 'fun' images of lang, Bernhard or Winterson. In radical feminist terms these images may not be deemed 'politically correct' but they have become a signifi-cant part of contemporary lesbian culture.

Lesbian chic, then, is *in* and widely represented, but why

now? Why not ten, fifteen years ago? *Cosmopolitan* editor Marcelle d'Argy Smith agrees with Linda Kelsey that the timing was just right:

> There was a point, just before AIDS, when the most stylish thing in the world to be was a gay man. It was the 'pink' economy, particularly in the States, and as women are breaking through to all levels and can earn a great deal of money, it seemed only natural – a kind of following-on [from gay men] – that it would happen.
>
> Gay men have had an awful lot of press coverage. It was only a matter of time and it only took a few people out there, a few strong women – like Sandra Bernhard – to say 'I'm gay and I'm terrific' before everyone else felt they could stand up and be counted.
>
> We wouldn't run a feature on (say) the 10 best lesbians, or '10 women you never knew were lesbians'. That's not our function. Our function, our philosophy, is to encourage women to be the best they can, to be confident and happy. It is to illuminate difficulties and point out solutions, so in the course of writing about women some of them are going to be gay but that's not why we're writing about them.

Like Linda Kelsey, she doubts whether the media's obsessive curiosity about lesbianism points to more enlightened attitudes in society generally:

> I don't think that if you scratch the surface there's a genuine, wholesale acceptance, of a gay lifestyle. People are very prejudiced, but at least *outwardly* there's more acceptance . . . and there's always wonderful speculation about people's sex lives. After a while a woman is meant to get married and reproduce and therefore be sexless in a way. Somehow 'My wife left me for a woman' is *dreadful*, the final insult . . . [d'Argy Smith's husband left her for another man – 'I was relieved. I thought, "Thank God it's not another woman." ']

Sex is part of woman's power base . . . Most women (still) derive their power second-hand, from men. To watch a woman go all the way up to the top, without *need* of that, on her talent, strength, guts, is very inspirational whether or not you are, or want to be, a lesbian.

It's on your own terms. Therefore, there are sighs of admiration. You think 'kd lang, Madonna – wow!' They've even taken on sex to a point where – it's *sexual*: it doesn't have to be the romantic stuff the rest of us have pulped into us. It seems to me to be about sex and power, and it's much spicier . . . I think power is very attractive on the whole.

She criticizes some lesbians for their 'sense-of-humour failure'. *Cosmo* had published American humorist Cynthia Heimel's piece called 'I wish I were a lesbian' (August 1993), which evoked a spate of furious letters from lesbians saying 'How dare you?' and 'You don't understand'. Defending her decision to publish it, d'Argy Smith said:

We're not in the world, we're certainly not in the magazine business, to deride or poke fun so I'm a bit saddened that they haven't by now cottoned on to our intent, which is to embrace all women . . .

One of the reasons we don't do more [on lesbianism] is the difficulty of pinning people down and finding stories. As it is, *Cosmo* uses a lot of pseudonyms. In fact, Bea (Campbell) wrote a piece for us called 'Why gay women don't come out' – because they tend not to come out in the way that men do, and they are definitely bottom of the socially acceptable 'pile'. It seems to me that on a social level a fourth-rate man is [considered] better than a first-rate woman.

For lesbians the process of self-affirmation and empowerment has been slower (than for gay men), but 'I'm sure women *like* other women and I think most of us, even if we're not physically gay, we're emotionally pretty damn gay, all of us.'

It would be interesting to conduct a survey on 'emotional lesbianism' (lesbian psychiatrist Dr Charlotte Woolf used the term 'homo-emotionalism' in the early 1970s), and to discover what proportion of women consider themselves in those terms. However, this is well beyond the scope of this essay and entails many complex questions about lesbian identity ('what is a lesbian?'). My principal aim has been to chart some of the changes in the media's depiction of lesbian images and issues, and to assess the value and significance (if any) of those changes. While it is true to say that lesbianism has always defied rigid categorization, stereotypes have become fewer and styles more varied, flexible and colourful as the debate, in both 'alternative' and mainstream media, has opened up.

It would be all too easy to dismiss the 1990s vogue for 'designer dykes' or 'lipstick lesbians' as a myth or ploy concocted by a male-dominated media to sell newspapers. There may indeed be some element of escapism in this particular image, a reaction against the 'right-on' earnestness of lesbian feminism, a way of putting back the 'sex' into sexual politics. However, I believe that in the process it has helped remove any remaining stigma attached to lesbianism, making society less inclined to regard dykes as victims or objects of ridicule. Lesbianism has developed an increasing profile in the world and, clearly, that is here to stay. Lesbians are everywhere. They are not about to backtrack, to revert to the illusory shelter of the closet. We are highly visible. We are powerful, not in the tokenist (post-feminist?) sense in which Marcelle d'Argy Smith describes it, but in our sheer *numbers*.

Our influence is clearly seeping into many areas of British social life. Bridging the gap between mainstream and 'alternative' media, *Time Out* and the now-defunct *City Limits* have for many years run a weekly 'Out' section on lesbian and gay events and groups. The women's 'glossies' cited in this essay may be seen as both moulding and reflecting public opinion, as throwing down a gauntlet of sisterhood to the lesbian community. In an age dominated by the cult of the personality we need more role models: not only celebrities or cult figures like Bernhard, but 'ordinary' women who are successful in their chosen sphere, who have other stories to tell, other aspects to their lives besides the perennial sex/relationship problems. Only time will reveal the extent to which mainstream publications demonstrate a genuine, serious commitment to lesbian women's lives.

## Notes

1.   Candace Lyle, 'Women who love women', *Cosmopolitan*, April 1983.
2.   Kate Bergman, 'Why I'm glad to be gay', *Cosmopolitan*, September 1986.
3.   Trudy Culross, 'Leaving your husband for another woman', *She*, May 1991.
4.   Jill Tweedie, 'Gay's the word', *Guardian*, 12 April 1971.
5.   Eleanor Stephens, 'Must a loving mother love men?', *Guardian*, 12 November 1976.
6.   Toni Nealie, 'Gay abandon', *Guardian*, 18 April 1990.
7.   Louise Guinness, 'The love that has learned to laugh', *Evening Standard*, 6 July 1993.
8.   *Evening Standard*, 8 July 1993.
9.   Jane Solanas, 'Well, frankly . . . ', *Shebang*, August 1993.
10.  'Meeting Mary' (Mary Daly talks to Tanya Dewhurst), *Shebang*, August 1993.
11.  Katharine Viner and Justine Hankins, 'Want to get ahead? Get a girlfriend. Why lesbians are big news in the US', *Guardian*, 8 July 1993.
12.  Leslie Bennetts, 'kd lang cuts it close,' *Vanity Fair*, August 1993.
13.  *Ibid.*
14.  'First Person: "Why I'm a lesbian" (One woman tells her story to Marina Cantacuzino)', *Marie Claire*, October 1989.
15.  Adam LeBor, 'When your lover turns out to be gay', *Marie Claire*, June 1989.
16.  Jenny and Celia Kitzinger, 'Doing it: representations of lesbian sex', in Gabriele Griffin (ed.), *Outwrite: Lesbianism and Popular Culture*. Pluto Press, London, 1993.

Chapter five

# Screened Out: Lesbians and Television

**Rose Collis**

THERE is a memorable scene in the movie *Network* where
TV station executive Diane Christiansen (Faye Dunaway) is having
sex with colleague Max Schumacher (William Holden). Her mind,
however, is not firmly on the job:

> What's bugging me now is my daytime programming, I'm
> thinking of doing a homosexual soap opera. You know, *The
> Dykes*, the heart rending saga of a woman hopelessly in love
> with her husband's mistress. What do you think?

Well, what *do* you think? A populist drama series about lesbians,
watched daily by millions – good joke, isn't it? Presumably,
*Network* writer Paddy Chayefsky knew this would pass as the most
outrageous and unlikely idea that TV bosses could come up with.
And, of course, he was right; until a wealthy, powerful, 'out' dyke
takes over a channel or network (don't hold your breath), television
will play its part in keeping lesbians out of the mainstream. Unless
you count Nancy Spain's appearance on *Juke Box Jury* and *What's
My Line?* (and there are many who do), in television's first 50 years,
lesbians were only seen as an 'issue' – a 'subject' up for analysis, not

represented as a positive way of life. With a few exceptions, this remained the case until the mid 1980s.

## Test cards

The first major programme to appear was typical of the format and tone adopted by producers for nigh-on 20 years. *This Week: Lesbians* was a po-faced dissection of lesbianism with a clutch of 'experts' giving their opinions: a Harley Street doctor was asked 'What do lesbians do?' and 'Can it be cured?'. A better attempt, in the best traditions of the 'mission to explain' topical programme, was *The Important Thing Is Love*. It avoided using shots of dark, dingy discos and put across a positive image of the subtle emotional differences in women's relationships, avoiding judgemental commentary. *Man Alive: The Women* was much more negative and voyeuristic in its approach. In typical *Man Alive* style, reporter Angela Huth probed away at interviewees, some of whom were clearly very unhappy, and she didn't discourage the women from piling on the agony. More positive (but, significantly, used far less) was footage of other women having a round-table discussion in the Gateways club in Chelsea.

*Gay Life* was a groundbreaking series which failed to please the lesbian and gay audience it was supposed to be aimed at. Some of its problems could be attributed to its bias towards representation of gay men, and to the fact that it appeared to be gearing itself too much to a heterosexual audience, despite its claim to be 'for London gays'. The producers rounded up all the usual suspects: relationships, police entrapment, discrimination at work, lesbian custody, gay politics, all shoved out at 11.30 p.m. on Sunday nights. A second series was mooted and, aware of the gender imbalance, the producers vowed to get lesbians more involved on the production side next time. Despite encouraging ratings and viewer response, there was no 'next time'. However, it had at least served its purpose in showing TV bosses that a regular programme for lesbians and gay men would not mean the end of their careers or their channels.

# Today, we're discussing . . .

A great deal of television time has been devoted to defending or 'explaining' lesbians as an 'issue'. Studio discussion, or 'live debate', shows the world over are notoriously cost-effective – a good way of filling air time cheaply. And any producer worth their salt knows that having a live discussion on homosexuality makes the hours whizz by, whether it's outing or lesbian mothers or gays in the Church. Of course, the structure of these programmes means that there is always an equal number of homophobes and bigots participating. This does not, however, mean an equal amount of time given to the different viewpoints, and lesbians and gay men usually find themselves forced on to the defensive. And, of course, sometimes the presenters don't help – the goddess Oprah being a notable exception. Whether it's been Miriam Stoppard on *Where There's Life*, Mike Scott on *The Time, The Place* or Robert Kilroy-Silk of *Kilroy*, they fail to disguise the problems they themselves have in accepting lesbians and gay men. For instance, Stoppard's liberal veneer was stripped away when confronted with the fact that people know they are gay as young as nine. Her face registered extreme shock and she was soon spouting, 'We have sex to keep the race going, don't we?' Even if you dispense with the presenter, the results are little better. *Just Sex* was a series about many aspects of sex and sexuality and, inevitably, included a slot on 'What is normal?' This consisted of two separate groups of men and women, with equal numbers of straights and gays, having rather sterile discussions, intercut with interesting clips taken from early pro-grammes on homosexuality. While the women's group stuck to talking about lesbianism, some of the straight men in the other group were keen to stray off the subject of male homosexuality and, virtually unchallenged, voiced their attitudes to lesbians: 'frustrated women' who needed 'a good dicking'.

There have been rare occasions when we've been able to complain about our representation. Even then, the balance always seems to be tilted towards the opposition as in one edition of *Biteback*, a frail attempt by the BBC to give its viewers a right to reply, hindered by the brittle presence of Sue Lawley. Perhaps she has never been able to forgive or forget the night in 1988 when, about to read the BBC evening news, she suddenly found several lesbians chained to her desk, screaming 'Stop Clause 28'. Whatever the reason, she makes no attempt to hide her homophobia and when a group of lesbians and gay men took part in the programme to grill BBC1 Controller, Alan Yentob, about poor representation, she controlled the 'debate' from start to finish. She interrupted one lesbian participant with the far-from-neutral 'What percentage of the population are you?' and, most infuriatingly, the programme's producers had invited two regulars from Rent-a-Bigot to attack the BBC for showing *too much* homosexuality. It has to be said that these 'topical debate' programmes are probably the least effective in improving lesbian representation and visibility on or off television. Whether it be the presenters, the producers or the prejudiced prats who get so much air time, they will always work against us.

## Coming out to you, live

But even when we spot a lesbian being used for dramatic effect, she's usually in the act of Coming Out. Sometimes this takes one scene, occasionally it's the basis of a whole episode. And, of course, there's an endless variety of characters she can come out to: parents, husbands, colleagues – or just herself. *Emmerdale*, the first British soap to feature a main lesbian character, used this device several times. By the early 1990s, the long-running tale of life in a farming community was in danger of being put out to grass and so its producers made a desperate attempt to go for a younger audience. Suddenly, storylines were full of steamy affairs and illicit liaisons – and we all know there's nothing more steamy or illicit than a lesbian, don't we? And so, at the drop of a hat, they unveiled Zoe Tate (Leah Bracknell), vet and daughter of Emmerdale's baddie, alcoholic Frank Tate (Norman Bowler). First she came out to her ex-boyfriend, then to her father in a scene which contained every negative response imaginable from a parent: 'You were such a lovely little girl . . . you haven't found the right man . . . you can't be . . . I'm devastated.' But credibility went belly-up when, within a minute of being so devastated, Frank told her 'It was brave of you . . . I'll always be proud of you.' It's a certainty that, if Zoe is not written out, she'll never be seen having an affair – illicit, steamy or any other kind – unlike a couple seen in 'The Ties That Bind', an episode of the popular, gritty hospital drama *Casualty*.

Businesswoman Olivia Purcell (Amanda Redman) is brought in with a broken wrist, accompanied by her husband. One of her colleagues, Louise (Trevyn McDowell) arrives at her bedside, full of concern. The husband makes references to Olivia's many 'late nights at the office'. It's soon obvious that she's been putting in some overtime with Louise but hasn't told the husband. The distraught Louise comes out to a friendly nurse: 'I'm not going to go round pretending I'm invisible. Too many gay women do that.' Well, three cheers for Louise. She then outs them both to Olivia's husband who spits 'What have you done to her?' and exits. Unfortunately, Olivia is not pleased and feels sorry for her spouse. But the out and proud Louise has the last word: 'You've got to stop messing about with people's feelings,' she tells her lover. The message is loud and clear: pretending makes no one happy, least of all yourself.

The one-off drama *Nocturne* has a similar theme, though it featured an unusual way of finding that happiness. Marguerite Tyler (Lisa Eichhorn), a woman in her thirties, inherits her childhood home when her mother dies. The house is full of memories of her uptight, repressed parent and Marguerite's beloved tutor, Miss Carpenter (Jackie Ekers). When two young lesbians, on the run from reform school, fall through her french windows, the past and present collide. Marguerite remembers that her mother dismissed the tutor after giving her a passionate kiss. Then, over a sumptuous dinner, she and her guests play mind games, full of sexual tension which, ultimately, free Marguerite from her own 'prison'. After spending a drunken night with her, the two obnoxious visitors make off with the family silver but she couldn't give a damn: in the end, they've given her more than they've taken.

Towards the end of its long and illustrious run, the ground-breaking cop drama *Hill Street Blues* teamed Lucy Bates (Betty Thomas) with a female partner, Kate MacBride (Lindsay Crouse). After they arrest a hooker involved in a robbery, the woman alleges that MacBride made a pass at her. Of course, it's a ploy to get the cops to drop the charges, but the allegations are investigated.

Initially, Bates vehemently defends her partner: 'The percentage of lesbian cops is damn low!' But then MacBride takes her to one side and advises her to stop defending her 'on the grounds I'm not a lesbian'. Bates feels deceived, then awkward and doubtful about her partner's innocence. Eventually, she overcomes her doubts and they nail the villains. They remain partners but MacBride has been faced with the fact that, as a lesbian, she is 'not like other cops'.

The comic side of coming out was nicely captured in the short satirical play, *Came Out, It Rained, Went Back in Again*. Jane Horrocks played an L-plate lesbian, freshly out and about on the urban gay scene. She finds it all too cliquish or depressing, complaining that with so many discos and marches 'you have to be fit to be gay', and dreams of a lifestyle to fit her fantasies. A mere ten minutes of television but a nice change from all the angst we usually see.

# Crimes and Msdemeanours

So much for coming out. But television has also been full of lesbian characters more concerned with *getting* out. The lesbian-as-criminal device has been plundered time and again, providing some of the most infamous television portrayals of dykes. The Villainess, The Murderess, The Crim. And, of course, those guilty of crimes against morality. An early example was seen in *Police Woman*, the popular series starring Angie Dickinson as a tough, gun-totin' female detective – the generic forebear of *Cagney and Lacey* (US) and *The Gentle Touch* (UK). One episode had our Angie on the trail of three lesbians who were systematically murdering residents of a retirement home. There were protests against its broadcast but it went ahead anyway.

The women's prison drama *Within These Walls* revealed the startling notion that (gasp) lesbian relationships took place behind bars as well as in them. Typically, it was the hatchet-faced assistant governor, Martha Parrish (Sonia Graham) – the series' resident Wicked Witch of the West – who had 'tendencies'. In one episode she was shown to have formed a close attachment to a prisoner, Joan Harrison (Susan Brown). It appeared to be strictly non-physical as

Harrison, about to be transferred to another prison, tells 'Spooky', 'I'll never know whether you fancied me.' However, unable to contemplate life without Martha (and in the good old mainstream tradition that says the only good dyke is a dead one), she throws herself off the prison roof. In the surprisingly cult Australian series *Prisoner: Cell Block H* (nickname: Within These Wobbly Walls), there was always at least one lesbian character from episode 1 through to 692. First off we had the Chiselled-in-Stone Butch, Frankie Doyle (Carol Burns), the eternal outsider in society looking for a little love (usually with an eternally straight woman) and the undisputed star of the first nineteen episodes. Frankie died with her boots on, shot while on the run – her last words: 'Bloody bastards!' Next up was the foolish but cuddly Judy Bryant (Betty Bobbitt), who followed her wayward, drug-pusher girlfriend Sharon Gilmore (Margot Knight) into prison because she couldn't bear for them to be parted. Sharon cheated on her and then (here comes that tradition again) was murdered by a male officer. Judy's character was probably the most multi-dimensional: disinherited by her American family because she was lesbian, she settled in Australia. She had a daughter, later adopted, and later still reconciled with her. Her trips in and out of prison showed the problems female ex-offenders had to deal with on the outside and she was always full of good intentions, if not wisdom. Of course she had no sex life to speak of; instead, she was a bit like everyone's kindly (albeit butch) aunt.

Bobbit told *Gay Times* (April 1990), 'I always felt for Judy because she was a victim of her love.' However, the nature of that love was toned down once the series was sold to the American market; she wasn't even allowed an onscreen kiss. As if this wasn't enough, the storyliners really lost the plot with the character of Joan 'The Freak' Ferguson (Maggie Kirkpatrick), a sadistic, predatory officer with a fondness for conducting intimate body searches on the prisoners whilst wearing leather gloves. Every negative lesbian stereotype imaginable appeared to go into the making of 'The Freak' – in which case, we're probably lucky she didn't end up spit-roasting babies or starting World War Three.

But then there's never been anything as popular as a predator in a uniform. The short play *Girl*, set in the British Women's Royal Army Corps, featured Corporal Chrissie Harvey (Myra Frances), a khakied Casanova who gave a whole new meaning to the phrase 'fatigue duty'. One of the many privates who paraded through her bed was the naive but besotted Jackie Smithers (Alison Steadman). It was Jackie who ends up in trouble, on the receiving end of a dishonourable discharge because she was pregnant. Hurt by Chrissie's philandering, she went out with a man who then raped her. 'I'm a proper swine', Chrissie once told her in bed. True. But she was also responsible for one of the best all-female kisses ever seen on television – the rotter.

And speaking of rotters, it seems nearly everyone, at one time or another, thought Vita Sackville-West was a 'proper swine': sons, husbands, lovers, mother. She might well have wanted to be remembered for her writing but fate and history have conspired against her and her claims to fame can be summed up thus: Sissinghurst and Violet Trefusis. *Portrait of a Marriage*, the four-part series about one of the most famous lesbian relationships this century, sealed it. A lavish production, based on Nigel Nicolson's book about the Vita/Violet affair, it pulled no punches in its depiction of the passionate, physical side of the relationship, even down to the infamous scene where Vita, inflamed with jealousy, sexually assaults Violet. 'I'd much rather not have these scenes,' director Stephen Whittaker told the *Sunday Telegraph* (5 November 1989), but he must have been as aware as anyone that to delete the sexual core of the relationship would have rendered the whole series dull and void. It has to be said that all four protagonists – Vita, Violet and their respective husbands – emerge with little credit. Harold Nicolson is depicted as concerned that his wife's openness will wreck his diplomatic career and reveal his own homosexuality. Apart from this 'crime', Vita was also damned for abandoning her sons and the drama leaves you in no doubt that leaving Violet and returning to the domestic fold was the right thing to do. The Nicolson career and dynasty were safe – but at what cost?

Light years away from such opulent melodrama was the drama series *Rides*, about an all-women cab company, with a sideline in motorbike dispatch deliveries. This franchise is run by the resident butch'n'femme lesbian couple, George (Nicola Cowper) and Sasha (Charlotte Avery). Sasha is bright, blonde and ambitious;

George is insecure, an ex-con and devoted to Sasha. Faced with the prospect of losing her love to someone more wealthy and successful, George sets out to woo her back with expensive presents. To do so, she does some extra-curricular work involving stolen cars and ends up getting arrested. But this disaster seems to bring Sasha to her senses and, after spending a 'second honeymoon' in Brighton, you imagine they are destined for a happy ending. Get real – TV dykes don't have happy endings, remember? George is sent off to crash in a multiple pile-up, ending up head-first in a canal. She is last seen in a wheelchair, neckbrace and all, with no one (including us) sure if she'll walk again. Maybe crippling her was a way of demonstrating that she and Sasha were really committed to one another, but did it have to be so *extreme*?

Now *this* is extreme: of the 41 women currently on death row in America, at least 17 are lesbians. *Aileen Wournos: The Selling of A Serial Killer* was a documentary about the most infamous of them – branded as 'the first-ever female serial killer' as the result of collaboration between the different factions who would profit if this label stuck. Wournos had been working as a prostitute since she was 15; her father had sexually abused her. When a client, Richard Mallory, brutally raped her and threatened to kill her, she shot him. She subsequently killed six other men in similar circumstances but her plea of self-defence was ignored and she was portrayed in court as 'a man-hater, preying on an innocent man'. The documentary successfully revealed how the police, film companies (15 of them), Wournos's lawyer and a born-again Christian woman who adopted her all took turns at exploiting the 'man-hating lesbian' and (particularly distressing) how her own lover made a deal with the police to get herself off the hook and (allegedly) helped them secure a movie deal *before* Wournos went on trial. Although it was never stated outright, the film intimated that because Wournos was a lesbian, it was easier to sell an unsympathetic image of her to the juries and the public.

If the subject of 'lesbians who kill' is a sensitive area, so too is that of female-to-female abuse. *Unspeakable Acts* attempted to tackle this but, although with the very best of intentions, in a rather muddled and unhelpful way. The problem was that it lumped

together harrowing accounts of sexual violence in lesbian relationships alongside mother-to-daughter sexual abuse in childhood –
very different situations and best explored in separate programmes.

## Outside interference

What television has accurately represented (though not
always with total sympathy) are the problems lesbians face when
other people perceive their sexuality as a problem: friends, family,
neighbours, employers, colleagues, or jut plain old 'society' itself. In
the TV movie *A Question of Love* it was the ex-husband and eldest
son of Linda Rae (Gena Rowlands) who thought it was wrong for
the youngest boy to live with his mother and her partner and child.
Despite a dignified battle, she loses custody of him. Unusually,
though, the film's sympathies were solidly with her. Parents, not
children, caused the problems in *Heartbeat*, set in a maternity
hospital and the first US television drama to have a regular lesbian
character (though, of course, she was never allowed to kiss
onscreen): Marilyn McGrath (Gail Strickland), Marilyn and her
lover, Patty, were constantly struggling to get their families to accept
their relationship. The series itself struggled offscreen, with right-
wingers and fundamentalists demanding that the plug be pulled.
They didn't succeed but the show's consistently low ratings soon
stopped its pulse. It was a combination of parents *and* fundamentalists (a lethal brew) that wreaked havoc on the newly out Jess
(Charlotte Coleman), teenage heroine of the three-part drama
*Oranges Are Not the Only Fruit*. Adopted as a baby by two leading
lights of a tight-knit Lancashire Pentecostal community, Jess's
'unnatural passion' for her friend, Melanie, is punished by physical
abuse, public damnation, exorcism and enforced separation. Despite this, Jess recovers to love another day and escape from the
fanatics. This adaption drew rave reviews, optimum media coverage
and swept off with a mantelpiece-worth of awards. It was also
hailed as a breakthrough in positive lesbian representation. Now the
fuss has died down, it's hard to see why. Perhaps the fact that 1990
was a particularly poor year for British television drama meant that
the BBC had to milk its only half-decent offering for all it was worth.

Whatever the reason for its uncanny success, it still managed to turn the feisty young dyke of the novel into an insipid, uninspiring shadow. You feel sympathy for her treatment at the hands of the fundamentalists but its ultimate message seemed to be a paeon to Oxbridge, rather than her sexuality.

Midwife Veronica Pickles found herself with problems after she appeared on *World in Action: Coming Out*, which covered Jimmy Saville's live radio programme with the Milton Keynes Campaign for Homosexual Equality. Not only were some of the participants unhappy with the way they had been represented, Pickles's employers, Buckinghamshire Health Authority, withdrew her place on a health visitor's training course because of the 'adverse publicity'. Although she won her fight to be reinstated, her experience, captured on film, was a fierce reminder of the worst results of coming out. *Breaking the Silence* was a documentary which, despite some fiendishly horrible music and too many tedious shots filmed out of a train carriage, was a powerful portrait of lesbians' fight to keep their children. The mothers and their children talked about their experiences at the hands of former male partners and the High Court: in one case, a court order forbade one of the women to have any contact with her lover.

*The Women of Brewster Place*, a four-hour mini-series adapted from Gloria Naylor's novel about the lives of a group of black women, included a lesbian couple, one of whom can see nothing but the problems involved in being out. Lorraine (Lonette McKee) complains to her lover (Paula Kelly) that she doesn't like hanging out with her camp gay male friends: 'I'm just the same as everybody else!' she protests. Her lover reminds her they are most definitely *not* – but that doesn't mean they should be ashamed or sorry for what they are.

The character of Kim (Jane Lapotaire) in the play *The Other Woman*, wasn't ashamed either. A talented but poor artist (of course), unkempt, stroppy, feminist and uncomfortably honest, she is first seen attempting to stop her younger, airhead girlfriend, Niki (Lynne Frederick), from getting married. Kim's complex, haphazard lifestyle also involves Robin (Michael Gambon), a businessman with whom she sometimes (reluctantly) sleeps in return for living and studio space; and Rose (Rosalind Adams), a prostitute and Kim's occasional model and bedpartner. They play itself was as much about Kim's struggle to survive as an uncompromising artist as anything else but her lesbian feminism also pitted her against her immediate world. This character was slammed not only by lesbian viewers, who complained it was a rehash of old stereotypes, but also by the play's author, Watson Gould, who branded it a 'slimy production' (*Radio Times*, June 1976). But time has proved them wrong: both play and characters have remained memorable and well written and, considering when they were seen, remarkably bold compared with much of the drama produced in the 1990s.

## Changing channels (or, 'let's see what's on the other side')

One problem that some lesbians had with the character of Kim in *The Other Woman* was the ease with which she switched from women to men, even though it was made clear that she overwhelmingly preferred women. Oddly enough, though, switch-hitters pop up on TV with increasing regularity – with mixed results. In the drama series *Fox*, Joey Fox (Larry Lamb) was one of five brothers, good old-fashioned South London lads. Cab driver Joey gets off with kooky designer Bette (Maggie Steed), who introduces him to the delights of saunas and jasmine tea. However, he is not so delighted when he finds her in bed enjoying some sex 'n' spliffs with two girlfriends. His manhood is obviously so threatened by this that he can't have sex with her anymore. Later, his mature student brother tells him 'You're out of your depth with her.' But, it seems, it's not just the sex: the intimation is that a working-class boy will not be happy with a weirdo middle-class trendy. Bette's bisexuality is seen as another trait of her class, something that the working classes have nothing to do with, reinforcing the notion of being lesbian or gay as specific to certain social types.

One of the most famous and costly kisses – the first between two women ever on American network television – was seen on *L A Law*. The unveiling of CJ Lamb's (Amanda Donohoe) bisexuality was woven into an episode that dealt primarily with a defendant who had multiple personalities (geddit?). The object of her affections was her colleague Abby (Michele Green): 'You have a big fan in me, Abby,' she tells her after going out for dinner one night. Then came The Kiss. We're not sure if America quaked, though advertisers did and took their custom elsewhere, and a confused Abby scuttled off home. At the office, CJ explains, 'I'm flexible', but wants to know (as do we) why Abby kissed her back. She puts it down to curiosity and they agree to stay 'just good friends'. In a later episode, though, Abby invites CJ to dinner on a 'sort of' date, after which Michele Green promptly left the show – allegedly because the producers wanted Abby and CJ to pair off. *Capital City*, a short-lived drama series about yuppy wheelers and dealers in the City of London, featured its own brief 'lesbian love shocker', as the tabloids billed it. Sirkka Nieminen (Joanna Kanska), recovering from an abortion, has a night out with a friend, Yolande (Pia Henderson). As usual, there's the quick jump from a passionate kiss to post-sex cuddling and, although they are later seen holding hands on the Embankment, it's clear that Sirkka usually bats for the other team.

In *The Life and Loves of a She-Devil*, Ruth Beaswell (Julie T. Wallace) hard-done-by housewife, transforms herself into an avenging amazon, stopping at nothing to wreak revenge on the glamorous novelist who has stolen her husband away. She regularly switches identities and, as Lily Latimer, she becomes a nurse at a retirement home. There she strikes up a friendship with fellow misfit, Nurse Hopkins (Miriam Margoyles). When Hopkins announces she is leaving to work in an asylum, she gives Ruth/Lily a kiss. Ruth/Lily then says she will join her. 'When will you come?' asks Hopkins. 'Imminently, I should think,' quips Ruth. In their new room at the asylum, Hopkins suggests they push their beds together to be 'a bit warmer'. She becomes Ruth's partner in crime and ultimate beneficiary. Ruth doesn't give up her plan of regaining her husband but she stays with Hopkins until the last phase of her complex plot and, at least, Hopkins is much better off after their relationship. The role of Nurse Hopkins was expanded for television and, in adaptation, it is clear that for both women it was the most affirming and rewarding relationship they had.

Another successful adaptation of a novel, *The Rainbow*, similarly gave its lesbian relationship a larger, more positive portrayal than originally written. In D.H. Lawrence's novel the love affair between Ursula Brangwen (Imogen Stubbs) and her teacher, Winifred Inger (Kate Buffery) was in a chapter entitled 'Shame'. But in this adaption shame has nothing to do with it. In contrast to Ursula's male suitor, Skrebensky, Winifred doesn't try to pin her down and encourages her to widen her horizons, even if it means they separate. Their relationship blossoms when Skrebensky goes off to the Boer War and the two women spend idyllic days and nights together at Winifred's cottage, in scenes full of tender eroticism, including a naked moonlight swim. 'I don't ever want to leave this room – or you', Ursula tells her lover. But, realizing that Winifred might not be as fearless and bold as she'd imagined, she introduces her to her Uncle Tom Brangwen. Soon, he has proposed marriage, as Ursula had hoped. However, her split with Winifred is devoid of the scorn and callousness displayed by Lawrence. Instead, Winifred sadly tells her, 'I came to your bed last night because that's where I wanted to be – and want to be. My desire for you is greater than any living thing – but I know these things are limited.' It's not their love that is limited, of course, but Winifred knows that their chances of being allowed to love openly in a small, tight-knit community are virtually nil and so, for Ursula, her one happy relationship ends.

A two-part drama about the life of Colette (imaginatively entitled *Colette*) also showed that the main lesbian relationship of the celebrated French writer was her happiest and least constricting. After being exploited by her caddish husband, Willy, Colette (Macha Meril) leaves him and joins a dance/mime troupe. In one piece, 'The Dream of Egypt', she passionately kisses her offstage lover, Missy (Anouk Ferjac), who is in male drag, which causes an uproar in the theatre. The two live happily together and, after Colette's disastrous, denigrating marriage, Missy gives her a sense of her own worth and talent. When she observes 'Whatever I do, you never object,' Missy replies, 'Because I am on your side.' Ever the aristocratic gentleman, Missy gracefully bows out when it is obvious her lover has fallen for Henri de Jouvenal.

One of the strangest but most touching examples of lesbian love in a cold climate was seen in *Playing for Time*, the harrowing drama based on the memoirs of Fania Fenelon, a survivor of Auschwitz who had played in the women's 'orchestra' there.

Portrayed by Vanessa Redgrave, Fenelon is seen as the oracle of wisdom that the women turn to for advice or opinion. One night, amidst the horror, a young woman asks her what she thinks about Misha, one of the violinists: 'I think of her all day – I don't understand what is happening to me.' When Fenelon says it is obvious she loves her, the young woman is shocked. But Fenelon says 'Why not? Don't despise yourself – to feel at all may be a blessing.' Fenelon is also suspected of having a female admirer; unfortunately, it happens to be Mandel, SS Kommander of the women in Auschwitz . . .

## Peek viewing: just passing through

Some enchanted evening, you may see a stranger and think: 'That's a dyke'. Then you blink, and she's gone. This is the case as far as mainstream television dramas are concerned, anyway. Take *May We Borrow Your Husband?*, a particularly nasty piece of television drama, full of fear and loathing of all kinds, with the most vicious saved for the gay characters. Apart from the two predatory gay men who steal away a newlywed groom from under the nose of his näive bride, there are also 'the German ladies', fellow inmates of the upmarket Antibes hotel. Though only cameos, they are obvious symbols of the prevailing decadence that surrounded the innocent newlyweds. The Deutches Dykes (played by Nathalie Varallo and Agneta Antonsson) are dressed in tweeds and nasty brown leather trouser suits, usually smoking cheroots. They are last seen playing backgammon together, giving each other affectionate slaps on their leather-clad thighs, between shots of the virginal heroine – the inference being that, if the bitchy queens can get the groom, *just imagine what could happen to the bride!*

Happily, there were no such predatory overtones in the superb adaptation of Olivia Manning's *Fortunes Of War* trilogy, set in Eastern Europe and the Middle East during World War Two. Harriet Pringle (Emma Thompson), one of a group of British refugees stranded when war breaks out, becomes estranged from her lecturer husband, Guy (Kenneth Branagh). She decides to get an evacuee boat home, then changes her mind and hitches a lift to Syria from two women Army lorry drivers, Mortimer (Clare Oberman) and Phil (Erin Donovan). They are not major characters but they play a pivotal role in Harriet's story. On the way to Damascus, they stop for a seaside walk at sunset; Harriet watches them from the lorry. Ever so casually, they take each other's hand and continue walking – a wonderful contrast to all television's tortured 'coming out' scenes. It's just a gorgeous moment of tenderness and it is obvious that Harriet envies their love. Back in the lorry, they joke about 'the road to Damascus' and Harriet asks Mortimer, 'Have you ever seen a light from heaven?'; she quietly replies, 'You might say that . . . '. Once again, Harriet looks at Phil with envy. A fleeting, but golden, moment.

This image of a lesbian couple free from sensationalism or 'danger' could easily have served as a pointer to producers of British soaps who have, amid great publicity, introduced gay male couples as major characters but always kept lesbians offscreen or, at best, in peripheral roles. *Emmerdale* may prove to be an exception, but at the time of writing there is no guarantee that Zoe Tate or, indeed, the series itself will survive. *Brookside* (considered the 'alternative' soap) and *EastEnders* both made clumsy attempts to include regular gay male characters but in both cases most of their storylines were to do with (predictably) coming out or (even more predictably) life-threatening illnesses: AIDS and multiple sclerosis. No happy endings there. For the lesbian characters, there weren't even any really happy beginnings. In 1986, Barbara Black (Brenda Elder), the ex-wife of one of *Brookside*'s newer residents, was revealed to be a lesbian, living with her children and her lover. Unfortunately, the writers also had her working in an inefficient, badly organized women's co-operative, thus reinforcing the 'loony lefty lesbian' stereotype the tabloid press has become so fond of. This character was not retained and we have not seen her like again.

*Brookside* finally introduced a lesbian storyline into the winter 1993-94 episodes. Disappointingly, it chose to focus on a character who most easily fitted a classic lesbian stereotype, in a situation that was certain to end in tears. Beth Jordache (sensitively portrayed by Anna Friel) is an eighteen-year-old student who has been raped by her father when she was fourteen. Unable to endure more of his physical abuse, Beth and her mother murder him and bury him in their garden. Their friend, the window cleaner, Sinbad, obligingly lays a nice patio over dastardly, decaying Dad. Shortly after this, Beth begins to have an affair with another neighbour, Peter Harrison, who, it turns out, has once been charged with raping a former *Brookside* resident. After this, Beth declares that she has had enough of men and begins to spend more time with her best friend, Margaret Clemence (Nicola Stephenson). Two teenage girls, both fed up with men – well, you just *know* what's coming next . . .

Beth's love for Margaret is eventually revealed after each has thought the other was after Margaret's flatmate, the well-meaning but nerdy Keith Rooney (Kirk Smith). Beth's jealousy of the time Keith and Margaret spend together does not go unnoticed by several people, including the chirpy Sinbad, who all assume it is Keith she fancies. When Beth eventually reveals the truth to Sinbad, he is a little shocked but supportive, although he assures her it is 'just a crush' and 'it'll pass'. But it doesn't and Beth decides to tell Margaret the truth – in phases. At first, she tells her she's in love with another woman and Margaret, not knowing it's her, does not reject her friend. On Christmas Eve, Beth lets down her guard and attempts to kiss a horrified Margaret, who then flees to the haven of her mother's house in another city. Beth, hurt and embarrassed, wants to salvage their friendship but Margaret is wary and confused. In a tacky incident, she ends up going to bed with Keith after a New Year's Eve party – presumably just to check that her heterosexuality is intact and to prove to Beth and herself that she doesn't share her friend's feelings. Right from the outset it is clear that a happy ending for Beth and Margaret is never on the cards and so it proved, although Beth was allowed to begin an affair with one of her female lecturers. Unfortunately, this coincided with a suspiciously high number of Beth-free episodes.

Similarly, *EastEnders*, after establishing a gay male couple, gave us the merest glimpse of a lesbian character then jerked her away out of sight before we got too excited. A storyline that ran from December 1985 to February 1986 involved the increasing infirmity of Albert Square's oldest resident, Lou Beale, and her living arrangements with her family. A social worker, Ruth Lyons, helps their GP, Dr Legge, sort the problems out and, eventually, there is speculation that they are having a relationship. It is only once Ruth's services are no longer needed that Dr Legge reveals that she lives with another woman – and – hey presto, she is never seen again. A BBC spokeswoman told *City Limits* (6 October 1988) that her disappearance was completely in accordance with other social workers' appearances in the series: 'the Square has had five or six different ones – they get transferred, you see.' OK, but why not have a lesbian character who's a little less transient?

## Gay for a laugh

It's one of the best-kept secrets that lesbians have a sense of humour, far keener and more enduring that we're ever given credit for. Mercifully, we have been spared the extreme stereotypes of gay men seen so often in comedy – the John Inman/Larry Grayson camp-as-a-row-of-tents figure. In fact, as far as television comedy goes, lesbians have often come out more positively. One of the most surprising examples was the unstated but obvious lesbian Cissie (Catherine Rabbett) featured in the 'Upstairs, Downstairs' comedy series, *You Rang M'Lud*. Resplendent in classic, monocled Radclyffe Hall drag, Cissie is wealthy but radical: she helps transform her father's factory into a workers' co-operative. Another 'goodie' is Helen Cooper (Ingrid Lacey) in the hilarious *Drop the Dead Donkey*, the topical satire set in a TV newsroom. Helen is the new assistant editor, a feisty gal who stands up to the smarmy, sexist boss. She eventually has to come out to George (Jeff Rawle), the downtrodden news editor, because he has been making overtures towards her. The laugh is that George has such low self-esteem he thinks that Helen is pretending to be a dyke just to shake him off. 'How do I convince you?' she asks him, 'Throw Sally to the ground and stick my tongue down her throat?' At the time of writing, though, we've yet to see if Helen's sexuality is ever mentioned again, for laughs or otherwise.

Now, you would think a sitcom about four women sharing a house together might have just a hint of lesbian undertone but the rampant heterosexuality of the *Golden Girls* was never in any doubt – even though, ironically, its camp, exaggerated portrayals has made it such a hit with gay men. During its seven-year run, lesbianism had one episode and then a one-liner in the very last show: when Sophia (Estelle Getty) stumbles on Rose (Betty White) and Blanche (Rue McClanahan) in a farewell embrace, she quips 'Hey! What is this, Wimbledon?' Ironically, the other episode in question was the very one which clinched the series a thoroughly deserved Emmy award for the best TV comedy. In it, a friend of Dorothy's (nice little gay in-joke there) is coming to stay. But Dorothy (Bea Arthur) is worried about whether or not Jean (Lois Nettleton), whose partner, Pat, died a year ago, will get on with her eccentric housemates. Dorothy's mother, Sophia, twigs that she is really worried because Jean is a dyke – something she's known since they were at college. The comedy proper starts when Jean arrives but, though the episode is screamingly funny (certainly one of the best ever), you're not really sure who ends up having the last laugh. However, the funniest moment is actually when the man-hungry Blanche is mortified to discover that Jean has fallen in love with the naive Rose: 'To think Jean would prefer Rose to me!' After Jean tells a shocked Rose that 'I'm quite fond of you,' she decides to leave the next morning. Meanwhile, the others are worried that, having shared a room for a night, Jean will have forced herself on Rose. In the end, Jean's feelings for Rose are quickly dismissed: 'I just got very confused,' she explains and, to everyone's relief, they agree to be 'just good friends'. It's a shame that a series which was such a breakthrough in portraying older women as sexually active beings should cop out and reduce its sole lesbian character to one for whom 'friendship is enough'.

*Roseanne* went one better and introduced a regular lesbian character, in the form of Sandra Bernhard as Roseanne's friend, Nancy, but even this ended in an almost unforgivable U-turn. Initially, Nancy is married to macho bonehead Arnie (Tom Arnold). Then, after becoming a partner in the diner owned by Roseanne (Roseanne Arnold) and her sister Jackie, Nancy announces that her new lover is called Marla (Morgan Fairchild). At first they think she is just kidding, then Jackie gets worried that Nancy might 'start checking me out' – how many times have you heard *that* from a straight woman? In subsequent episodes Marla and Nancy are accepted, albeit with some awkwardness from Dan (John Goodman). Just when you think . . . suddenly, Nancy is all done with Marla, talking about having a baby and eyeing up sleazy businessman Roger (Tim Curry) as a potential father. 'I am a people person,' she explains to a confused Roseanne. 'Oh *no*', groaned lesbians the world over. So the joke was still on us . . .

## Do not adjust your sex

This is a blank screen: lesbians don't have proper sex – not on television, anyway. (And, no, the scene where Vita Sackville-West raped Violet Trefusis in *Portrait of a Marriage* definitely does *not* count.)

## Putting ourselves in the picture

The harsh fact has to be faced: mainstream television, especially in America, will never properly put lesbians in the picture; the heady brew of closetry within Hollywood and other centres of the entertainment industry, pressure from ultra-right movements and prestigious advertisers will always conspire against it. However, the late 1980s and early 1990s have brought us one or two positive developments that have forged the way forward into television's second century. The first was the introduction of cable television, particularly in America and some European countries; the second was the creation of Britain's Channel 4 in 1982, with its charter commitment to providing quality 'minority' programming. These have provided lesbians with the first real opportunities to create the images and cover the issues that have either been previously botched or (more commonly) not even attempted.

Right from the start, Channel 4's intention was true, if not its aim. On the first day of broadcasting it put out *One in Ten*, a well-intentioned but hopelessly misguided 'gay entertainment'. It was branded 'vile sexist crap' by some of those who took part; others complained about the way women were used in it, and when a group of performers were being filmed in London's 'Heaven' nightclub, singing a twee little ditty about how we were all 'free to be you to be me . . . to love and be loved as we choose' (if only), they were booed off stage. Despite this rather unfortunate start, Channel 4 tentatively attempted to keep its commitment to lesbian and gay programming. Predictably, this usually meant commissioning lesbian or gay documentaries. Younger lesbians were the focus of *Veronica 4 Rose*, a worthy but visually dull film which did little for its contributors. Curiously, when Channel 4 boss Jeremy Isaacs left the company, he included this film in his farewell 'Best Of . . .' season. *Framed Youth* was a livelier affair, produced by 26 lesbians and gay men (including someone called Rose Collis), most of whom had no previous film experience, and on a budget which was supposed to be merely development money. However, commissioning editor Alan Fountain was so impressed by this 'pilot' that he decided it was good enough to broadcast as it was. His decision was vindicated when the film scooped the British Film Institute's prestigious Grierson Award for Best Documentary of 1984. Unusually for a mixed project, both the editorial and technical input and the representation of lesbians was high, and the film's visual style and energy remain refreshing.

One of the few lesbian-produced dramas commissioned by Channel 4 was *Domestic Bliss*, a comic tale about a small, diverse group of women friends all struggling to deal with their chaotic domestic lives. The central characters were a lesbian couple, Diana (Penny Nice), a doctor, and her partner, Emma (Mandy More), and Emma's slightly bolshy daughter, Jenny (Martha Parsey). House-proud Diana is struggling to deal with the practical repercussions of living in a 'pretend' family while Emma has her own problems with ex husband, James (John Gillet).

Unfortunately, it was a painfully weak piece which didn't do much to dispel the myth about lesbians not having a sense of humour. In the meantime, Channel 4 was still testing the waters to see if a regular lesbian and gay slot was feasible. *Six of Hearts* was a series of documentaries which combined music, comedy and drama, three of them focused on lesbians. *More than a Journey* was the coming-out story of Paola, a Greek-Cypriot holiday rep, and *Waitng for the Green Light* was basically an embarrassing audition tape for actress Carol Prior. Equally unsuccessful was *Tides of Laughter*, a fictional story set in the 1950s about two women entertainers, the double act in an 'end of pier' show. After discovering the secret of their landlady's late 'friend' (a woman, of course), it dawns on them that they, too, are like her. This might have worked better if the story hadn't been intercut with interviews with real variety performers.

By 1989, Channel 4 had decided the time had come to chance its arm and commission the first lesbian and gay magazine programme, *Out on Tuesday*. After two series it was moved and became *Out on Wednesday* and, by the time of its demise, it was just plain old *Out*. Encouragingly, all the senior editorial personnel, including the two producers and the series' editor, were lesbians. In its time this slot covered everything from lesbian sex to the popularity of Country and Western music with dykes. Interestingly, some gay male viewers complained that it was too biased towards lesbians – presumably because they (like everyone else) were just not used to seeing so many on the television and felt as though they were being excluded. After some initial hoo-ha the series settled down to comfortable ratings – and predictability. Unfortunately, *Out* suffered because it was being forced to be too many different genres: current affairs documentary, arts magazine, campaigning/consumer programme – and, on top of all that, dangerously *sexy*. It also suffered from a reliance on too many items full of 'talking heads', no 'live' input and, occasionally, too many nods towards urban trendiness.

The main problem, however, was Channel 4's tendency to confine lesbian or gay programmes to 'seasons' or, alternatively, to squeeze them into the *Out* slot. They gave *Torch Song Trilogy* its TV premier, but only as part of a *Summer's Out* film and documentary season which went out when most of its intended audience were soaking up the sun in Sitges or Lesbos. *Women Like Us*, a breakthrough documentary about the lives and experiences of older lesbians in Britain, was originally commissioned for the Sunday evening slot, *People to People*. When this was cancelled, the programme was shunted into the *Out* series and, for reasons of continuity, so was its successor, *Women Like That*. True, they were given repeat screenings outside of the series – but in the television wastelands of the 'after midnight' schedule.

After three years the production team of *Out* had already split, with one half putting together a mixed bag of documentaries, drama and topical items for *Saturday Night Out*, BBC2's one and only token gesture towards catering specifically for lesbians and gay men. Encouragingly, though, one of its highlights was a humorous reportage piece on Martina Navratilova and her devoted lesbian fans. Back at Channel 4 it was time for a rethink: *Out* was – well – out. However, a successor series was commissioned for 1994.

Cable has yet to make any significant impact in Britain, but elsewhere it has provided a few opportunities for lesbians to produce programmes over which they have complete control. *Two in Twenty* was perhaps the best programme so far and showed what could be possible if you turned each television genre on its head and geared it towards dykes. The world's first lesbian soap opera was made over a three-year period by a group of Boston-based dykes and broadcast on the city's cable station under the spoof name *WCLT*. The programmes dealt with all the aspects of lesbian life imaginable: coming out, monogamy and non-monogamy, racism, child custody, careers and communal living – complete with queuing for the bathroom. It was all handled with wit, warmth and awareness. As if this wasn't enough, the episodes had their own 'a word from our sponsors' breaks, station announcements, public information messages and adverts: 'Carte Lez – don't come out without one'. The programme was shown to rapturous audiences the world over but the rigours of producing it – with time, equipment and money loaned or donated – have meant that it has yet to be continued.

The New York-based Gay Cable Network (GCN) has been producing lesbian and gay programmes since 1982, including the game show *Be My Guest* and *Pride and Progress*, which covered politics. It also put out *The 10% Show*, a news show which was also broadcast in many other major cities, including Los Angeles, Chicago and San Francisco. It almost goes without saying that San Francisco has its own regular cable show for lesbians and gay men; it's called *Lavender Lounge*, complete with adverts for gay stores and services. The best offering, though, is New York's *In the Life*, the first lesbian and gay series on public service television. It's a lively mixture of comedy, music, interviews and current affairs which benefits enormously from going out in front of a live audience – it exudes a pleasantly warm, affirming feeling.

Cable TV in Berlin shows what is currently the world's only regular lesbian slot, *Lesbische TV*. Its offerings have included an interview with the women who run the city's brothel for lesbians and diverse vox pops. In Holland, there is *Zo op Zondag* (Out on Sunday), a lesbian and gay magazine series. As the name suggests, it is remarkably similar to the British *Out* programmes in style and content, even right down to the title sequence and the filming of such items where two dykes discuss seduction techniques over dinner. Holland is also the home of *The Theo and Thea Show*, a madcap programme supposedly aimed at children. One show featured a tea-party with several lesbian and gay couples joining in the fun. Theo and Thea, dressed like overgrown kids complete with false buck-teeth, talk about 'homosexuality' while eating a messy tea. They consider their dog Trudy: 'Is she a lesbian? I often see her sniffing at Tess [another dog]', then they get the couples to snog for the cameras. Try to imagine Julian Clary and Sandra Bernhard presenting an edition of *Blue Peter* or *Sesame Street* and you'll start to get the picture . . .

The growth of public access television throughout the world and, in Britain, the continued (though sporadic) commitment of Channel 4 are positive developments in the battle to get dykes on the box. What doesn't bode so well for the future, however, is the continuing paranoia/homophobia/resistance (whatever you call it, it's all the same) of major networks, especially in America. Here we are, in the 1990s and no US company would co-finance the adaption of *Tales of the City* with Channel 4 (who else?) unless the lesbian and gay content was watered down or even eradicated altogether – screened out. We've come a long way in the last decade but we're still light years away from the time when a TV executive will say, in all seriousness, 'I'm thinking of doing a homosexual soap opera. You know, *The Dykes*.'

## Notes

An A–Z guide to the programmes featured in this chapter, with production details (where possible) (Produced in UK unless otherwise stated). The following abbreviations are used: ad., adaptation by; d., director; ed., editor; w., writer; pr., producer.

*Biteback*, BBC1, 1993.
*Breaking the Silence*, d. Melanie Chait, Lucia Films for Channel 4, 1984.
*Brookside*, pr. Phil Redmond, Mersey TV for Channel 4, 1986.
*Came Out, It Rained, Went Back in Again*, w. Claire Dowie, BBC2, 1991.
*Capital City*, Thames TV, 1990.
*Casualty*, w. Stephen Wyatt, BBC1, 1993.
*Colette* (France), w. Chantal Remy and Gerard Poiton-Weber, d, TFI/Tele-Hachette-RAI 2, 1985.
*Domestic Bliss*, w. Gillian Slovo, d. Joy Chamberlain, Newsreel Collective for Channel 4, 1984.
*Drop the Dead Donkey*, w. Andy Hamilton and Guy Jenkin, d. Liddy Oldroyd, Hat Trick Productions for Channel 4, 1993.
*Eastenders*, pr. Julia Smith, BBC1, 1985–86.
*Emmerdale*, w. Bill Lyons, d. Mervyn Cumming, Yorkshire TV, 1993.
*Fortunes of War*, ad. Alan Plater, d. James Cellan Jones, BBC1, 1987.
*Fox*, w. Trevor Preston, d. Jim Goddard, Euston Films for Thames, 1980.
*Framed Youth*, Lesbian and Gay Youth Video Project for Channel 4, 1984.
Gay Cable Network (US), New York, 1982.
*Gay Life*, ed. Jane Hewland, pr. Michael Atwell, LWT, 1981.
*Girl*, w. James Robson, d. Peter Gill, BBC, 1974.
*Golden Girls* (US), w. Jeffrey Duteil, pr. Susan Harris, Touchstone Pictures, 1986.
*Heartbeat* (US), pr. Alison Hoch, ABC, 1988.
*Hill Street Blues* (US), w. Jeffrey Lewis, David Milch and Walon Green, MTM, 1988.
*The Important Thing Is Love*, d. Brigid Segrave, ATV, 1971.
*In the Life* (US) Public Service Broadcasting.
*Just Sex*, d. Sarah Boston, pr. Gina Newson, 51 Per Cent Prods for Channel 4, 1984.
*LA Law* (US), pr. Steven Bochco, 20th Century Fox TV, 1991.
*Lésbische TV* (Germany), 1993.
*The Life and Loves of a She-Devil*, ad. Ted Whitehead, d. Philip Saville, BBC1, 1986.
*May We Borrow Your Husband?*, ad. Dirk Bogarde, d. Bob Mahoney, Yorkshire TV, 1986.

*Man Alive: The Women*, rep. Angela Huth, d. Adam Clapham, BBC, 1967.

*Nocturne*, w. Tash Fairbanks, d. Joy Chamberlain, Maya Vision for Channel 4, 1990.

*One in Ten*, d. Ken Howard, Kinesis Films for Channel 4, 1983.

*Oranges Are Not the Only Fruit*, w. Jeanette Winterson, d. Beeban Kidron, BBC2, 1990.

*The Other Woman*, w. Watson Gould, d. Michael Simpson, BBC, 1976.

*Out on Tuesday*, Abseil/Fulcrum for Channel 4, 1989.

*Out on Wednesday*, Abseil/Fulcrum for Channel 4, 1990.

*Out*, pr. Cheryl Farthing/Richard Kwietnowski, Alfalfa for Channel 4, 1991–2.

*Out on Sunday* (*Zo op Zondag*) (Netherlands), 1993.

*Playing for Time* (US), w. Arthur Miller, d. Daniel Mann, Syzygy Productions, 1980.

*Police Woman* (US), ABC, 1974.

*Portrait of a Marriage*, w. Penelope Mortimer, d. Stephen Whittaker, BBC2, 1989.

*Prisoner: Cell Block H* (Aus), Reg Grundy TV, 1979–86.

*A Question of Love* (US), w. William Binn, d. Jerry Thorpe, Viacom, 1978.

*The Rainbow*, adapt. Anne Devlin, d. Stuart Burge, BBC1, 1988.

*Rides*, w. Carole Hayman, d. Andrew Morgan, Warner Sisters for BBC1, 1993.

*Roseanne* (US), w. Betsy Borus and David Raether, Viacom, 1993.

*Saturday Night Out*, BBC2, 1992.

*Six of Hearts*, d. Paul Oremland/Caroline Mylon, Kinesis Films for Channel 4, 1986.

*The Theo and Thea Show* (Netherlands), 1993.

*This Week*, Bryan Magee, Associated Rediffusion, 1965.

*Tides of Laughter*, w. Howard Wakeling, d. Paul Oremland, Kinesis Films for Channel 4, 1986.

*True Stories: Aileen Wournos – The Selling of a Serial Killer*, d. Nick Broomfield, Lafayette Films for Channel 4, 1992.

*Two in Twenty* (US), Laurel Chiten/Cheryl Qamar/Debra Granik, 1988.

*Unspeakable Acts*, Frances Allan/Open Space CPU, BBC2, 1993.

*Veronica 4 Rose*, d. Melanie Chait, Lucia Films for Channel 4.

*Where There's Life*, pr. Gwyneth Hughes, Yorkshire TV, 1986.

*Women Like Us*, d. Clio Co-op for Channel 4.

*Women Like That*, Clio Co-op for Alfalfa.

*World in Action, Coming Out*, pr. Peter Carr, Granada, 1975.

*Within These Walls*, w. Tony Parker, d. Tony Wharmby, LWT, 1974.
*The Women of Brewster Place* (US), d. Donna Deitch, ABC, 1988.
*You Rang, M'Lud*, w. Jimmy Perry and David Croft, d. Roy Gould, BBC1, 1992.

Chapter six

# Twisting the Dials: Lesbians on British Radio

**Sheridan Nye, Nicola Godwin and Belinda Hollowes**

## Why radio?

RADIO may lack the glamour of film or television, but it is undoubtedly an essential part of everyday life for millions of people. As an instant, easily accessible means of *communication* it has no equal and here lies its potential for lesbians – both as listeners and as programme-makers.

It would be pre-emptive to construct a theory of a 'lesbian radio genre', as lesbians have hardly developed a large enough body of material from which significant patterns could usefully emerge. Lesbians are rarely heard on radio, and those who are heard are often lone voices from within the heterosexual mainstream. Without the benefit (or hindrance) of a sense of history of our involvement in radio, each lesbian's contribution has tended to be an isolated event, passing by largely unnoticed by wider lesbian culture.

However, what has also been overlooked is the enthusiasm

and sheer numbers of lesbian radio listeners who regularly tune in to a variety of programmes, and who are not hearing much that reflects their own lifestyles, concerns and cultures. Data reflecting lesbians' consumer tastes is hard to come by in relation to *any* product, let alone the media, and to estimate the time lesbians spend listening to radio is notoriously difficult.

*Literature* is one area of cultural production where lesbians have become part of a niche market. Books by and for lesbians, particularly crime and non-fiction, are established favourites of lesbian readers, and similarities between the acts of reading and listening may give clues to a corresponding popularity of radio. Both activities are usually solitary, personal experiences and both media convey their message by making an 'appeal to the imagination'.[1] Where radio is markedly different from literature, and from all other media, is in not demanding the *visual* attention of the audience, so freeing the listener to perform other tasks. This freedom, and the easy portability of most modern receiving equipment, has allowed radio into the home, the car, the workplace, the school, garden and park, in fact almost anywhere an adequate signal can be picked up.

Communication via radio depends on sounds, music and above all *voices*, with the presenter/performer seeming to address the listener personally wherever she goes. On daytime radio the ubiquitous male 'jock' DJ exploits these characteristics by 'chatting' to the theoretical housewife as she moves around the home. This sense of one-to-one intimacy that radio effortlessly commands is also heard on night time phone-in programmes where listeners are invited to share their innermost personal problems – which many willingly do.

It is difficult to confirm the extent to which radio is a popular accompaniment to our own daily routines without adequate research material on lesbians' lifestyles. A clue may be found in the findings of a survey recently completed by One in Ten radio production group. Preliminary results show that around 60 per cent of lesbians questioned (all over 25 years old) listen regularly to BBC Radio 4.[2]

Before considering how lesbian programme makers could tap into this potential audience it is worth taking a look at lesbians' relationship with radio over the past forty years or so.

# Lesbians in radio history

Before the launch of the first independent stations in 1973 the BBC essentially *was* British radio. In its very early days, before World War Two, the Corporation's output was dominated by the rather staid and paternalistic ideals of its first Director General, the dedicated Calvinist, John Reith. His over-zealous interpretation of the BBC's public service remit, to educate and culturally uplift the nation, proved unpopular with the majority of the public, and by the end of the war many were eagerly tuning in to American-style music and entertainment from rival stations on the Continent.

Ironically, the BBC's reverence for 'high culture', which continued long after Reith's retirement, ensured that radio drama would often set out to challenge its audience, both aesthetically and intellectually. This occasionally involved challenging pre-conceptions and prejudices as well, and consequently fictional lesbians were featuring on British radio long before lesbianism was considered to be in any way an 'acceptable' lifestyle. In the 1950s several such programmes were broadcast, including *Corrick's House*, a play about a teacher/schoolgirl relationship, and a reading of Sappho's poetry on the Third Programme. In 1952 even *The Archers* explored the lesbian relationship theme (an affair between Christine Archer and an older woman).

Unfortunately, radio's transient nature means that, once broadcast, lesbian material is unlikely to pass into lesbian folklore. Radio listening is often a matter of a 'chance hearing' and individual radio programmes rarely get much in the way of pre-publicity, whereas books and videos can be reviewed, reread and passed around among friends. Sadly, there are no records of most early lesbian material as only a percentage of radio broadcasts are ever selected for preservation in archives.

Some of the earliest references to lesbianism were almost certainly made on *Woman's Hour* (The first radio feature about

*male* homosexuality was broadcast on the programme sometime in
the late 1940s, although no record is available). From its launch in
1946 *Woman's Hour* continued the BBC tradition of daytime radio
as a 'companion' for the housewife. Anne Karpf describes early
programmes as seeming sometimes 'like a soothing lozenge'.[3] In
fact, the programme's producers were keen to broaden this role at
least as early as 1957; in the foreword to *The Woman's Hour Book*
the programme editor, Joanna Scott-Moncrieff, claims: 'With the
passing of the years the number of minutes from Woman's Hour
devoted entirely to practical, domestic matters has gradually been
reduced.'[4] The menopause and wages for home makers were among
the subjects aired on the earliest programmes.

There was no assumption that the housewife's lot was a
blissfully happy one, either. In 1952, among talks on 'The Christian
ideal of marriage' and 'Spotlight on a well-dressed woman', Moya
Woodside questioned young women's idealistic expectations of
their husbands in 'The ideals and realities of marriage'. In a frank
admission of women's dissatisfaction with their lot, Scott-Moncrieff
set out the aims of the programme:

> to lift the load of loneliness borne by women facing
> misfortune and to help them realise in time of trouble that
> they are not alone, that others are having to keep a home
> running, despite the despair and discouragement of unalter-
> able circumstances.[5]

BBC records may not tell us enough about lesbianism on
early broadcasts of *Woman's Hour*, but one particular lesbian was
appearing on the programme throughout the 1950s and 1960s, as
well as on other popular radio series such as *My Word!*, *Any
Questions?* and *In Town Tonight*. Nancy Spain was a flamboyant
society lesbian, writer, journalist and broadcaster. Although not
'out' in the 1990s sense (she never referred to her lesbianism on air
or in any of her newspaper articles), it was widely known that she
shared a house with her long-term lover, the editor of *She* magazine,
Joan Werner-Laurie. Spain openly refers to 'Jonnie' as 'my partner'
in her 1961 autobiography *A Funny Thing Happened on the Way*.[6]

As a popular gossip columnist she was often found at the social gatherings of the rich and famous, invariably wearing men's trousers and shirt or a suit. She was close friends with Noel Coward, Ginette Spanier and Marlene Dietrich and was admirably suited for her speciality on *Woman's Hour* – the celebrity interview. Her former producer, Sally Thomson, says: 'She loved celebrities . . . She'd treat them like equals . . . and she'd persuade them to give some little nugget which hadn't been given to anyone else.'[7]

At the height of her fame Spain allowed the tabloid press to speculate on a possible marriage between herself and fellow broadcaster Gilbert Harding, although it seems unlikely that this was ever more than a private joke between them.[8] By the 1960s she was finding the transition from radio to television uncomfortable and her fame declined. Tragically, shortly after confiding to a friend that she thought she would probably die in an air crash, both she and Jonnie were killed while travelling on a chartered flight to the Ascot races in 1964.

One of the most popular radio plays to feature a lesbian couple as central characters was broadcast in April 1975 as part of Radio 4's 'Monday Play' series. Although a simple portrayal of a relationship, *Now She Laughs, Now She Cries* challenged contemporary mores by presenting lesbians in a positive and realistic light, while exploring negative social attitudes. The BBC, overly anxious not to offend its regular audience, broadcast an announcement before the play warning of its unsuitability for 'family listening'. As it turned out the response was pronounced and enthusiastic and the author, Jill Hyem, received hundreds of letters from delighted lesbians who felt they had been accurately represented for the first time. Ironically several listeners wrote to the *Radio Times* to complain that the warning itself was offensive and unnecessary, including a vicar who condemned the caveat and declared: 'this was the best play about love I have ever heard'[9].

While the portrayal of lesbians in drama can present a rare opportunity for the lesbian listener/viewer to experience complex, well-rounded characterizations within mainstream culture, the temptation to succumb to stereotyping as a form of shorthand has overwhelmed many writers and producers. The caricature butch and unhappy lesbian in film has been well documented,[10] but stereotyping on radio is not such an easy option. In their survey of lesbian and gay portrayal on television and radio,[11] Lorraine Trenchard and Mark Finch comment: 'Lesbian and gay stereotyping seems dependent on a *visual* checklist – the overtly masculine or the limp-wristed' (emphasis added). Their survey showed that, of 688 hours of British radio monitored during the week 12–18 August 1985, only 0.32 per cent mentioned either lesbians or gay men. Lesbians were mentioned only once during the monitoring period – an insulting remark made during a drama, *Bilgewater*, serialized on *Woman's Hour*.

Portrayal of lesbians in drama is always controversial because its unavoidable by-product is a contribution to mainstream society's perception of lesbians. In the United States the portrayal of a bisexual, ice-pick-wielding murderer in the film *Basic Instinct* attracted condemnation from the Gay and Lesbian Alliance Against Defamation (GLAD). Claiming the film would create an unflattering image of lesbians and bisexual women as homicidal maniacs, GLAD expressed a very real fear of the effects of negative 'PR'.

In contrast, coverage of lesbian issues within radio news and current affairs is sporadic, but often surprisingly fair. In part this demonstrates the advantage radio can offer as a *live* medium for lesbians to express their views directly to the public. Access to live broadcasting is far easier on radio than on television, particularly on local radio where the 'phone-in' discussion programme is a cheap and popular format; as dependably 'controversial' subject-matter, lesbians are often invited to face inquisition by the curious public. The publishing and social group Sappho appeared on numerous such programmes during the 1970s and 1980s, discussing subjects ranging from artificial insemination and lesbian motherhood to general equality issues. Jackie Forster, a Sappho founder member, claims she was usually treated fairly in the debates and often felt that the presenters were 'on our side'.

The passage of Clause 28[12] through Parliament in 1988 caused a flurry of interest in lesbian and gay issues, particularly on BBC radio. On *Woman's Hour* Ann Taylor brought a rational perspective to the issue of gay sex education in schools, contrasting the views of Conservative MP David Wiltshire on 'pretend' families with the contented family life of a lesbian couple and their five-year-old child. *Third Ear* on Radio 3 examined the threat of 'backdoor censorship' posed by the clause, and *File on Four* investigated the potential increase in incidences of 'gay bashing'. All these programmes betrayed an undercurrent of liberalism in allowing both sides of the debate to air their views, while focusing on the negative effects of the clause. Phone-ins on Radio London's *Robbie Vincent* show and Radio 4's *Call Nick Ross* opened the floor to gay men, lesbians and homophobes alike.

Obviously, access to radio is not always enough to guarantee a fair hearing. In 1972 Sappho complained to *Woman's Hour* after one of its members, a lesbian mother, was invited on the programme only to find that her co-guest was a psychiatrist. At the time it was considered appropriate in the media to 'qualify' the opinions of lesbians and gay men with comment from the medical profession. Sappho were among the first to challenge this and was rewarded by *Woman's Hour* capitulation when the group refused to appear on any future programme if a psychiatrist was also invited.

Undoubtedly there have been occasions over the years when newsworthy lesbians have not been represented at all. In April 1993 the lesbian and gay 'March on Washington' was reported neither on BBC radio nor on television despite being the largest civil rights march ever held in the United States, and despite wide coverage in the British press and on satellite television. It is possible that the complaints which followed, made by various lesbian and gay organizations including Outrage and the BBC's own lesbian and gay group, affected the BBC's coverage of the serial-killer story which dominated newspaper headlines during June 1993. In something of a departure for the BBC, both television and radio broadcast interviews with community activists and gay men in pubs and clubs during the hunt for the killer of five gay men in London.

While this may be an indication of a new willingness to listen to the gay community, *Woman's Hour* is probably the only programme to have addressed lesbian representation head-on by allocating a producer with particular responsibility for lesbian issues. This clearly had some bearing on a discussion in 1993 on the Child Support Act which featured lesbian mothers as participants. In March of the same year a feature on lesbian crime fiction included readings by some prominent authors, including Mary Wings.

Women make up just over half of Radio 4's weekly audience of nine million, and *Woman's Hour* itself commands a daily audience of 600,000, so the programme's reputation of being almost a part of the national fabric is hardly surprising. This explains the outrage felt by the tabloid press at *Woman's Hour's* positive attitude towards lesbians. In an article in the *Daily Mail* headlined 'BBC Lesbians' Hour'[13] a former presenter, Jean Metcalfe, described the programme as having 'an obsession with being politically correct'. She continued, 'there's so much militancy at the BBC. They keep going on and on about feminism and gay issues'. The current programme editor Sally Feldman responded, 'We have always evoked criticism from one corner or another. It is an established tradition of *Woman's Hour* to go ahead and talk frankly about any subject. We have a duty to do that.'

A national radio station that has frequently covered lesbian and gay issues, often with little or no comment from the press, is Radio 5. Launched in August 1990 as a repository for the sport, youth and schools programming previously broadcast on Radios 3 and 4, Radio 5 has struggled with its ungainly remit to establish a coherent identity, and was recently described by one journalist as a: 'jerry-built shambles'[14]. However, the influence of gay-positive producers at the station has inspired confidence in gay programming for teenagers, and Radio 5 has included young lesbian and gay participants in several of its programmes, including a *Guardian* award-winning feature on safe sex. Caroline Raphael, editor of youth programmes on Radio 5, chose to appoint some of her producers from theatrical rather than broadcasting backgrounds in the interests of encouraging originality in her section. As a consequence new people were brought in who were either gay themselves or who were used to working on gay and lesbian productions.

In 1991 one such producer, Anne Edyvean, directed a dramatization by Sarah Daniels of Nancy Garden's novel *Annie on My Mind* (Virago Upstart series, 1988), which told the tale of schoolgirl love in the face of condemnation at home and school. Although not sexually explicit, the novel was notable for alluding to teenage lesbian sex while managing to avoid moral condemnation by the tabloid press. Says Anne Edyvean, the producer, 'I don't really know why the tabloids didn't pick up on us. In fact we got good reviews in both the *Daily Telegraph* and the *Times Educational Supplement.'*

While local authorities dared not be seen 'promoting' homosexuality, fearing the uncertain consequences of contravening Clause 28, Radio 5 fulfilled a valuable role in bringing lesbian and gay life to Britain's teenagers. This makes the announcement that the station is to close in April 1994, to make way for 24-hour news and sport, all the more tragic.[15]

# Radio – up for grabs in the 1990s?

Both the commercial and public-service sectors of the radio industry have experienced radical change over the last decade. Some of these changes, while doing little for job security in the industry, do offer possibilities for new and exciting programming as competition between rival broadcasters hots up.

## A brief history

Commercial radio officially began in 1973[16] with the launch of the first Independent Local Radio (ILR)[17] stations, Capital Radio and the London Broadcasting Company. Since then various interested parties have lobbied government to encourage the growth of the commercial sector and to open up the industry to outside investment. In 1993 there were over 50 ILR and two INR (Independent National Radio) stations[18] – consequently commercial radio's audience share has increased from 14 per cent of total listening time in 1976 to 38 per cent today.[19]

However, in investment terms, Britain's commercial sector is still under-developed in comparison with other European countries, particularly France and Spain. In Coopers & Lybrand Deloitte's report on investment opportunities in European radio the UK market is assessed as having 'a great potential for growth' which 'could show an excellent return [on investment]'.[20] This implies that there could be an explosion in the number of independent radio stations in Britain – if commercial radio can attract sufficient audiences and advertising revenue, and if more frequencies become available (a factor still controlled by the BBC).

Traditionally programming on commercial radio has tended to be somewhat bland. Dominated by 'pop and prattle' formats and phone-in request shows, ILR has been obliged to stick to its own proven formula to guarantee its advertising revenue (the influence of ILR and pirate radio on listeners' tastes has in turn persuaded the BBC to adopt popular formats, particularly on Radio 1 and local stations). During the early 1980s ILR was lambasted by several commentators for its condescending attitude towards its women listeners. In 1983 a damning Local Radio Workshop report on commercial radio in London described male presenters' behaviour towards women guests: 'They frequently interrupted women, interpreted and redefined what women were saying and were sometimes blatantly obstructive.'[21] Baehr and Ryan quote an Essex radio employee: 'We call our average listener Doreen. Doreen isn't stupid but she's only listening with half an ear and doesn't necessarily understand "long words".'[22] Fortunately these attitudes have become as outdated as they are offensive. It is debatable which has had the most effect, public criticism or changing attitudes in society, but in the late 1980s and early 1990s ILR has noticeably taken on a more urbane presentation style, particularly on inner-city stations.

As the recession bites, commercial stations are fighting for less available income from advertisers who are themselves feeling the pinch. It is difficult to predict the effect this will have on programming. On the one hand, in this highly competitive environment, programme commissioners can no longer afford to take the moral high ground on questions of sexuality in programming, especially if they think they can smell a lucrative market. Advertisers' discovery of the 'pink pound' is a phenomenon of the recent recession, but the proportion made up of lesbians' disposable income has yet to be investigated and so the feasibility of, for instance, a lesbian-oriented radio series remains untested.

On the other hand, difficult market conditions in the industry encourage takeovers, and ownership of ILR stations is increasingly concentrated in the hands of relatively few major players.[23] As the links between stations grow it becomes convenient to syndicate more programmes nationally (for instance the *Network Chart Show*) and the consequent need to attract national advertising pressurizes stations to keep their programming at the conservative end of the scale. In their drive to deliver maximum audiences to advertisers, ILR may leave lesbian, gay and progressive women's programming out in the cold. This is often proving to be the case as many stations are choosing to concentrate on local news and events, these being cheaper to produce than speech-based features.

An exception that proves the rule is the 1992 Sony award-winner for best new station, Wear FM. Commended by the judges for its 'verve, style and wit' the Humberside station includes a regular lesbian and gay programme, *Gay 2 Gay*. If *Gay 2 Gay* sometimes sounds like a camp version of Radio 1's *Steve Wright Show*, with the 'Gay 2 Gay Gang' providing a backdrop of frivolous gay banter, the host, Michael Lumsdon, is unrepentant: '*Gay 2 Gay* is definitely not a political programme ramming gay rights down people's throats. I think you can get the message across in a less confrontational way through entertainment.'[24]

While Conservative governments have smiled on the growth of ILR, the BBC's immunity to market forces has long been a target for reform. The BBC is accountable to Parliament by virtue of its Royal Charter which comes up for renewal in 1996. The government, taking advantage of the impending renewal date, has brought the whole ethos of public-service broadcasting into question and tightened the screw on the Corporation's finances. It has employed various methods in the attack, including reducing the Corporation's licence fee income and indirectly forcing it to reduce staffing levels by insisting that independent companies make a proportion of its programmes (under the requirements of the 1990 Broadcasting Act, BBC Television must commission 25 per cent of its output from independent production companies).

Under pressure to justify the licence fee, Director General John Birt has been forced to re-evaluate the Corporation's role and to review programming policy. In his 1992 policy document *Extending Choice*, Birt sets out the BBC's objectives for radio: 'to assign priority to those networks and services which are truly distinctive and unlikely ever to be matched in the commercial marketplace.'[25] Significantly for potential lesbian programme makers, under the heading 'A clear public purpose for the BBC' another stated aim is 'to take risks with innovative programming'.[26] In the summer of 1992 BBC Network Radio pre-empted an expected statutory requirement for radio by announcing it would be working towards a voluntary target of 10 per cent independent production by 1996. These two factors, 'distinctive' programming and the opening up of production to outsiders with the necessary skills and ideas, have already resulted in more out lesbians on BBC radio.

The first independent production on Radio 4 was also BBC Radio's first lesbian and gay programme. *A Sunday Outing*[27] this was a two-hour live magazine programme broadcast of St Valentine's Day 1993 from Broadcasting House in London and the Flamingo Club in Blackpool. Produced by Outcast Media Productions (an offshoot of an informal networking group for lesbians and gay men working in the media called 'First Tuesday'), *A Sunday Outing* was promoted as 'taking the lesbian and gay community into the heart of the establishment', but was allocated a Sunday afternoon slot where, by Radio 4's own admission, there were 'no listeners left to lose'. Under pressure to address straight Radio 4 listeners as well as a general lesbian and gay audience, Outcast stuck to familiar themes – coming out, homosexuality and religion, the existence or otherwise of the gay community – interspersed with vaudeville cabaret. In the event the programme suffered somewhat from its own self-consciousness as the first gay and lesbian enterprise on national radio. Described by the *Independent* as a 'tranquil affair', the programme failed to generate much enthusiasm among gay or straight listeners, although it was a success in technical terms considering the ambitious scale of the event.

Despite *A Sunday Outing*'s lukewarm reception BBC Radio, encouraged by the lack of any serious backlash against its first lesbian and gay production, went on to commission two other gay magazine programmes. *Loud and Proud* was a series of six half-hour shows on Radio 1, 'for young lesbians, gay men and their friends'. Broadcast during August and September 1993, and made by Outspoken Production Company from Manchester, the series used an eclectic mix of news, opinion, music and celebrities to attract both gay and straight listeners. Under John Birt's *Extending Choice* regime Radio 1 has to distinguish itself from commercial stations which also rely predominantly on pop music. *Loud and Proud* fitted the bill by virtue of its lesbian and gay remit and its even balance of music and speech-based features. In contrast with *A Sunday Outing*, *Loud and Proud* managed to breathe new life into well-worn subjects by the inspired use of celebrities to present features, including Terry Christian on homophobia, Neneh Cherry on bisexuality and Margi Clarke on sex.

Although lesbians and gay men appeared on the programme, there were objections that the presenter of the first national radio lesbian and gay series was a straight woman. Club DJ Paulette is a popular performer in gay clubs in Manchester and London and was invited to anchor the programme by Outspoken. *Loud and Proud* producer Mark Ovenden explained in the *Pink Paper*: 'We asked Paulette to do the show because she epitomises everything about the way we want to make lesbian and gay issues more acceptable to the straight community.'[28] While this stance against ghettoization may have been successful in not alienating straight listeners, it raises the question of how 'acceptable' lesbians can be – or would ever wish to be.

While both *A Sunday Outing* and *Loud and Proud* sought to fit in with the established order, another BBC lesbian and gay magazine series, *Gay and Lesbian London*, has been spared scrutiny and allowed simply to reflect the interests of London's gay and lesbian community. *Gay and Lesbian London*, on the Corporation's local station, Greater London Radio, is a weekly hour of news and pop music similar to *Loud and Proud* but with more emphasis on news and events. As a community access (rather than independent) production, all staff and presenters are volunteers and the programme is put together on a less-than-generous weekly budget of £90. The BBC recently showed its commitment to the show by moving it to GLR's FM frequency. (GLR's medium-wave frequency is likely to be reallocated by the Radio Authority to ILR in the near future.) Roving reporter Rebecca Sandles believes the project is benefiting from the way lesbians and gay men are 'taken more seriously these days'.

*Gay and Lesbian London*'s success highlights how lesbians and gay men living in inner-cities form *geographical* audiences sharing common interests and so are ideally suited to local radio 'special interest' programming. The *commercial viability* of this gay, urban audience was demonstrated recently by the success of *G-Spot* on Brighton Festival Radio. The two-hour weekly magazine programme comfortably financed itself with on-air adverts made by the G-Spot production group itself for various local lesbian and gay businesses.

Community radio is the third sector of the radio industry, created according to Lewis, 'as a response to the failure of local radio in Britain'.[29] Until the mid-1980s it was left to pirate stations to fill the gap for genuinely community-based broadcasting. The pirates were popular among black, Greek and Asian communities, with many running as thriving small businesses. This entrepreneurial spirit struck a chord with some Conservative MPs and it seemed likely that some stations would be legalized, particularly as the cost of trying to close them down was proving excessive. The government finally launched the community radio 'experiment' in 1985, at the culmination of a nationwide campaign led by the Local Radio Workshop. Despite the short notice for preparing the necessary paperwork the Home Office received 286 applications for just 21 licences (including one from an early incarnation of Spectrum Radio, see below). However, the project was suddenly postponed shortly after the applications were submitted, amid rumours that the government was having second thoughts about its policy on political reporting. In a naive oversight the licence regulations made no provision to ensure that community stations remained impartial in their news and current affairs coverage. Belatedly the government realized that, in an election year, unregulated, politically partisan broadcasts could provoke popular revolt, or at least motivate more inner-city residents to register to vote, and so the 'experiment' was hastily shelved.

In 1989 the community radio project was rejuvenated, the process carried through and licences issued. (The issue of political balance was addressed in the 1990 Broadcasting Act which requires community radio stations to demonstrate editorial impartiality – only outside contributors are permitted to express political views, within the bounds of existing legislation, and the right of reply must be honoured.) Currently there are only six community radio stations on the air in Britain, most of which are based in London, but with an expected increase in the number of available frequencies on the FM band there could be as many as 300 by the end of the decade.

Community radio has spawned Britain's longest running gay radio programme, *G.A.Y.*, broadcast on the west London station Spectrum 558.[30] *G.A.Y.* started in August 1992 and is one of a number of programme 'strands' on Spectrum, most of which target London's ethnic communities. Effervescent club DJ Jeremy Joseph hosts and produces the programme, blending the latest in club-music with celebrity interviews (Debbie Harry and Jason Donovan have both been guests), phone-ins and discussions. Interestingly, response to the phone-ins suggests the audience is probably made up of equal numbers of men and women – nearly as many lesbians as gay men phone in to the programme to express their points of view during discussion slots. Although this could mean simply that lesbians are more inclined to phone in to radio programmes, it may be that club culture can reach across gender boundaries in a way that more serious, issue-based programming can not.

Despite its community-service remit Spectrum is an unashamedly commercial enterprise. By the end of its first six months of broadcasting *G.A.Y.* had conclusively demonstrated its commercial viability by virtue of the enthusiastic response of London's lesbians and gay men and by the amount of advertising time bought up by lesbian and gay businesses. Joseph's reward was an increase in air time from one hour a week to ten, and the programme now broadcasts five two-hour programmes every week.[31]

# *The way forward?*

In short, radio is a relatively cheap and accessible medium, ripe for exploitation by lesbian programme makers. But before we can take full advantage we need both to overcome our commercially ill-defined status and to convince programme commissioners of the size and enthusiasm of the lesbian audience.

Past performance shows lesbians' access to radio is sporadic at best and largely subject to the editorial whims of established programmes like *Woman's Hour*. Blending in with mainstream programming may be what most lesbians want from radio, but the One in Ten survey shows that most of the lesbians who regularly listen to Radio 4 are unhappy with its coverage of lesbian and gay issues.

Radio 4 drama producer Sue Wilson is optimistic that the only thing standing in the way of greater lesbian input to BBC radio drama is the willingness of lesbian writers to submit suitable material:

> I think even less interest is taken in lesbian issues than in gay men's, and I think that's regrettable. But, to be honest I can't even say I've had bad lesbian plays submitted to me because I've never even had one. I'd very much like to see more lesbians sending in their material.[32]

So far lesbians have had most success achieving *regular* air time when working with gay men. The successes and failures of these projects have thrown up two points. First, the tastes of lesbians and gay men, while not mutually exclusive, will not always coincide. As BBC Radio and *A Sunday Outing* producer Nicola Meyrick describes it: 'Lesbians and gay men share a common repression, but do not always share common interests.' Second, keeping a balance of these disparate interests within programmes can be difficult, particularly when so few lesbian performers feel they can safely be 'out' without jeopardizing their careers. Meyrick believes lesbians who choose to be out in their professional lives: 'risk being type-cast as some sort of arbiter of lesbian experience'[33], and may lose out on mainstream opportunities.

To infiltrate the radio establishment from within women's radio groups is equally as difficult, as so few outlets exist for women-oriented programmes. In 1993 two bids for a women's radio station licence were turned down by the Radio Authority – London AM (chaired by veteran broadcaster Joan Bakewell, backed by giant publishing group EMAP) and 'VIVA!', (chaired by PR queen Lynne Franks and backed by Red Rose Communications, owners of London station Jazz FM). Eight years previously the BBC had briefly considered turning the flagging Radio London into a women's station, but at the last moment opted for a relaunch as Greater London Radio.[34]

A short-term but successful women's radio station broadcast in Bristol on a festival radio licence in March 1992. Timed to coincide with International Women's Week, Fem FM grew out of the ideas and enthusiasm of two women from Bristol commercial radio, Caroline Mitchell and Trish Caverly. Although Fem FM broadcast no explicitly lesbian-targeted programmes, lesbian perspectives tended to pop up quite naturally in coverage of the arts, entertainment and health, and several lesbian technicians and presenters were involved. The project worked well as a collaboration between straight and gay women, and between professionals and women new to broadcasting. All programmes were produced locally and roughly equal amounts of air time were given over to music, presented by local women DJs, and speech. Undoubtedly Fem FM would never have got off the ground without the inspiration and fund-raising skills of Mitchell and Caverly, who secured £20,000 sponsorship from sources as diverse as Avon County Council and Aer Lingus.

Women involved in Fem FM testify to the easy-going atmosphere at the station. Most decisions were made only after collective discussion and 'goodwill was Fem FM's most valuable resource'.[35] Several women have since got together to launch another station, this time as part of the Women in Music festival in London in March 1994. Brazen Radio aims to be London's first women's station and to 'give London a taste of what women can do'.[36] The Brazen production group already has in place a provisional programming schedule which includes a Saturday night magazine-style programme for lesbians. Brazen's Vicky Carter says: 'We want a lesbian programme which reflects lesbian interests, but we don't want to pigeon-hole people. We want lesbians to contribute across the board to different areas of the station.'[37]

Outside the radio industry, in areas of the media where lesbians have had perhaps more experience, attempts to unite lesbians into a single audience have had only limited success. Lesbians have notoriously disparate tastes, beliefs and lifestyles and form part of several different consumer groups. Although the gay press has significant lesbian content, the major newspapers and magazines are funded largely by gay men's phone lines and classifieds, and magazines for lesbians have found it a struggle to attract enough advertising of their own.

On the other hand 'ghetto media' itself can be a double-edged sword. In her article on 'pink publishing'[38] Sara Dunn expressed concern that specialized book clubs for lesbian and gay publications would lead to less cross-over between gay and straight readers. This applies equally to radio in that 'channel loyalty' discourages listeners from scanning the air waves, and so people are unlikely 'accidentally' to tune in to a station that they feel does not address them directly.

Establishing commercial confidence is not the only obstacle to lesbian exposure on radio and it would be naive not to acknowledge how mainstream radio places restrictions on pro-gramme makers. Both the BBC and commercial sector are subject to guidelines on political impartiality, taste and decency, enforced ultimately by the government. Commercial values in themselves can amount to a form of self-censorship, given that all forms of commercial media are obliged to avoid offending the advertisers who fund them. Perhaps even more significantly the personal beliefs and values of station controllers and commissioners often determine the tone of programmes – in 1983 a BBC producer came close to losing her job for daring to combine the subjects of lesbianism and religion in a feature she made for a Radio 4 religious series.

A radical way of avoiding commercial restrictions and mainstream pressures is to take control of *distribution*. Fruit FM is the provisional title of a pirate radio station planned by three young lesbians in Hackney, London, for launch in 1994. Describing their programming as, 'a mix of radical music, features, weird jingles, improper poetry and bad language' and with material '*chosen* by lesbians, but not necessarily by or about lesbians,'[39] Fruit FM challenges the view that the only way into the media is via mainstream acceptance.

Queertalk is another example of the do-it-yourself spirit. Produced with the help of the Local Radio Workshop in 1993, a series of 30-minute tapes were distributed to gay bars and cafés in London. Each tape contained a slightly uneven blend of irreverent humour, news and features. Lesbian involvement in the project was minimal and the material itself contained little of direct relevance to lesbians.

Despite some of the difficulties outlined above there are many ways lesbians can exploit radio's potential. Only rudimentary training is needed and radio offers a whole range of opportunities for creative and political expression, from drama and music to news and current affairs. Several colleges and organizations provide courses for women who wish to learn radio production skills, and some London-based ones are listed below in Radio Groups listings.

It has been said that a basic requirement of a democratic media system should be: 'that it represents all significant interests in society. It should facilitate their participation in the common domain, enable them to contribute to public debate and have an input in the framing of public policy.'[40] According to these standards lesbians are entitled to a channel of communication through which to address one another and society as a whole. Until lesbians take more responsibility for radio output we will twist the dials in vain in our effort to find a voice which speaks appropriately and independently about our culture and experience.

## Notes

1.  A. Crisell, *Understanding Radio*. Methuen, London, 1986, pp. 7–10.
2.  The results of this survey were not fully collated at the time of writing.
3.  Anne Karpf, *Radio Times*, in K. Davis *et al.* (eds), *Out of Focus*. The Women's Press, London, 1987, p. 175.
4.  Joanna Scott-Moncrief and M. Hart, *The Woman's Hour Book*. The Windmill Press, London, 1957.
5.  *Ibid.*
6.  Nancy Spain, *A Funny Thing Happened on the Way*. Hutchinson, London, 1964.
7.  *Radio Lives*, broadcast on BBC Radio 4, 17 June 1993.
8.  Biography of Nancy Spain by Rose Collis, Cassell, London, forthcoming (1995).
9.  Jill Hyem, personal notes.
10. Caroline Sheldon, 'Lesbians in film', in K. Davis *et al.* (eds), *Out of Focus*. The Women's Press, London, 1987.

11. Lorraine Trenchard and Mark Finch, Gays and Broadcasting Project, *Are We Being Served?* Hall-Carpenter Archive and London Media Project, 1985.

12. This clause of the 1988 Local Government Act prohibits the 'promotion' of homosexuality by schools and local authorities.

13. Rebecca Hardy, *Daily Mail*, 9 February 1993.

14. John Dugdale, 'Breaking up is hard to do', *Guardian*, 26 April 1993.

15. Maggie Brown, 'BBC plans to move Radio 5 down-market', *Independent*, 7 October 1993.

16. Pirate radio stations had filled the gap for local, popular broadcasting since the early 1960s and forced the hand of the BBC to move into local radio in 1967.

17. That is, 'independent' from the BBC.

18. A third independent national frequency will be allocated in 1994.

19. Tim Congdon *et al.*, *Paying for Broadcasting*. Routledge, London, 1992. p. 55.

20. Coopers & Lybrand Deloitte, *Media Climate Briefing, Investment in European Radio*, 1991.

21. Local Radio Workshop, *Nothing Local about It – London's Local Radio*. Comedia, London, 1983, p. 132.

22. Helen Baehr and Michele Ryan, *Shut Up and Listen*. Comedia, London, 1984.

23. Capital Radio plc owns 13 different stations around the country and its turnover amounts to nearly 30 per cent of the industry as a whole. See Laurie Taylor 'Mandarins with no bite', *Guardian*, 26 April 1993.

24. In interview with authors.

25. *Extending Choice: BBC's Role in the New Broadcasting Age*. BBC, London, 1992, p. 45.

26. *Ibid.*, p. 22.

27. *A Sunday Outing*, Outcast Media Productions, produced by Nicola Meyrick, 14 February 1993.

28. Trish Lesslie, 'Fleshed out radio', *Pink Paper*, 13 August 1993.

29. Peter M. Lewis and Jerry Booth, *The Invisible Medium*. Macmillan, Basingstoke, 1989, p. 105.

30. G.A.Y. broadcasts from 1 a.m. to 3 a.m. Monday to Friday on Spectrum 558am in London.

31. A lesbian presenter, Dawn Thorp, has recently been drafted in to present the Wednesday night show.

32. Sue Wilson in interview with authors.

33. Nicola Meyrich in interview with authors.

34. Lewis and Booth, *The Invisible Medium*, p. 98.

35. Vicky Carter, Fem FM, interviewed by authors.

36. Press release issued by Brazen Radio, 1993.

37.    Sara Dunn interview with author.
38.    Sara Dunn, 'Gay writes', *Time Out*, 8 September 1993.
39.    Fruit FM in interview with authors.
40.    James Curran, 'Rethinking the media as a public sphere', in *Communication and Citizenship*. Routledge, London, 1991.

## Radio groups

The Women's Radio Group, 90 de Beauvoir Road, London N1.
Ovatones Music Studios, Highgate New Town Community Centre, Bertram Street, London N19.
WAVES, Wesley House, Wild Court, London WC2.
Brazen Radio, 90 de Beauvoir Road, London N1.

# Part Four
# The Avant-Garde

Chapter seven

# Lesbian Desire on the Screen: The Hunger

**Shameem Kabir**

*Women's cinema must embody the working through of desire.*
Claire Johnston[1]

IN this essay I will offer a detailed textual reading of *The Hunger*, a Hollywood lesbian vampire film made in England and America and released in 1983. I am ambivalent about this film, for all kinds of reasons, but I welcome its lesbian content, especially as it evokes the complexity of lesbian desire. I find the film engaging and compelling even while it alienates and repels me. My pleasure comes partly from the film's attention to avant-garde practices, which is unusual for Hollywood. My displeasure is at the film's violence, the depiction of which is a duplication of a cult of destructiveness personified by the vampire in an equation of sex with death. Given this connection of vampirism with violence, and knowing it is a horror film, my disgust at certain images may seem my own inappropriate squeamishness. I think more is at stake in the consumption of violent images, and I still protest at their gratuitous use. I am put in the familiar position where I enjoy certain practices while resisting others. Though the specificities of my response will undoubtedly differ from the responses of other spectators, I think this position of ambivalence in our reception of commercial films is inevitable.

In feminist terms, this ambivalence has often been expressed in the critical recognition of a masculinist bias in filmic languages that renders the woman the fetishized object of our voyeurism. This is with the simultaneous admission of pleasure at the deployment of certain techniques we know to be operating in the classical film, techniques such as narrator involvement and spectator identifications. As an introductory detour, I will expand on this ambivalence, hoping that its presence in our response allows us some agency as spectators to enjoy or eject material according to our own social subjectivities.

The masculinist bias in filmic languages was first articulated by Laura Mulvey in her celebrated 'Visual pleasure and narrative cinema', an essay published in 1975 that set the terms of the feminist debate on film that were to follow.[2] Mulvey identified that the camera(man), the male protagonist, and the intended male spectator made the woman representable only as the object of male desire. By implication, the woman spectator could identify with the woman on the screen in a position of wanting to be desired. Or she could renounce the passivity of this position, and identify across gender with the man as the subject of desire. Or possibly the woman could do both simultaneously. What she could not usually do was identify with the woman on the screen as an active subject of desire, because the woman does not ordinarily carry the agency associated with the male gaze.[3]

What if we were to substitute these terms with a camera-woman and female director, to have women protagonists, and an intended female audience? Would this alter the bias? In theory it would, especially if the women protagonists are active agents, and if the intended spectator is posited as female. But then we come up against the problem of filmic languages themselves, which are said to be a rewriting of unconscious processes as they have been shaped by a patriarchal stranglehold over the production of meaning. Voyeurism, the pleasure in watching, and scopophilia, the pleasure in seeing, are themselves organized around the phallus.

The consequence of phallic languages is to fetishize the woman, to seek in her the phallus we lack, and to render her an object of our voyeurism, where our visual knowledge of her meets the need for mastery and control. In this system, the man cannot 'be' the phallus, in his so-called possession of it, whereas the woman in her lack cannot possess the phallus, although she is seen to 'be' it. Desire itself is introduced through the phallus, where speaking subjects take their social positions according to whether they have or 'lack' a penis. How to break out of this bind? Elsewhere, I have argued idealistically that we need to 'dismantle' phallocentrism, thereby reconstituting the ways in which our identities are negotiated.[4] This is an ambitious, possibly impossible, project.

More concretely, Mulvey has bravely wanted to disrupt narrative pleasure and spectatorial engagement as a way of breaking out of Hollywood's masculinist hold over the imaging of women. I think this is going too far, precisely because narrativity and spectatorship are so crucial to cinematic pleasure. Film theorists, including Claire Johnston, have wanted feminist film makers to oppose Hollywood with a 'counter cinema', but they also recognize the necessity for the pleasure and entertainment that Hollywood has so skilfully packaged for global consumption.

How, then, to 'counter' cinema's masculinist bias? First, we need to appropriate what gives us pleasure as women. If this involves the adoption of mainstream practices around narrativity and spectatorship, we should go ahead with this appropriation, attempting to realign such mechanisms according to our own needs. But the notion of a 'unitary' subjecthood in the spectator is to be resisted, which is where the avant-garde questioning of form and languages comes in. By resisting the appellation of the unitary subject (seen usually as white, middle-class, male and heterosexual), and by challenging filmic languages that attempt to disguise their own materiality, avant-garde strategies offer an obvious method to make certain mechanisms of pleasure fit into an alternative or 'oppositional' mode. In another essay, Mulvey outlined the common objectives between the avant-garde project and a feminist aesthetic attempting to bring about change in form and content.[5]

I sincerely believe a synthesis of the two traditions we have available to us can allow a way forward. Mainstream practices create pleasure, while avant-garde techniques are closely allied to a political project. Such a project is possible because avant-garde strategies bring in an altered perception of the filmic text. By making the spectator critical and self-conscious, I think narratorial and identificatory processes can be *consumed consciously*, without apparent contradiction, so that we can simultaneously enjoy and analyse how certain responses in us are being evoked. This is to resist cinema as a mere manipulation of response, and more to see it as a way of examining how meaning is produced. This focus on intelligibility, on how we make sense, is I think the future for cinema as it reflects on itself self-referentially. When the production of meaning is achieved by making the unknown intelligible in ways that are self-conscious, a text can be 'progressive' in allowing social subjectivity a prominent place. Our ability to make the text intelligible will depend on how our identities have been constituted, not just along the lines of gender, but of race, sexuality, class, culture, language, age, ability, and of course our political positionings. By insisting on the presence of cultural diversity, sexual dissidence, racial difference, political divergences, and other sources of power differentials, the progressive text invites a plurality of positions in our identifications. And, as I say, intelligibility, or the process of making sense, is crucial as a strategy for both producers and consumers of meaning.

As a woman who is black and lesbian, I favour oppositional or progressive practices from the vantage of being 'triply other', a status I celebrate. In terms of films, I have been a critical spectator because my identity as a black woman has meant I have often identified with screen personae at a racial remove. On the few occasions when I see images of black people in the white mainstream, they are often images of servants and criminals. Denied easy identification, I have had to reconstruct my own mechanisms of making sense. In that reconstruction is a clarification, a demystification of mythic notions of a single and stable subjectivity. I know from my position of reconstruction and resistance that truly oppositional practices remain on the periphery, but it is precisely this distance, this dissociation, that gives the oppositional its cutting edge, its ability to analyse and re-envision.

For me, pleasure is produced when I can engage in the consumption of a product while remaining aware of how it is constructed. *The Hunger* gives me pleasure even while I remain resistant to its main generic form, the horror film. I am able to enjoy the film despite the ambivalence in my response. Above all I celebrate the depiction of lesbian desire, especially given the poverty in representations of us.

I will now retell the story of *The Hunger*. The first half will be in conjunction with a discussion of the avant-garde techniques it deploys, and the second half will be in terms of its lesbian content. I am aware that this might not 'work' for some readers, given that I am negotiating two very different mediums, the verbal and the visual.

*The Hunger* begins with the MGM logo, so it is immediately identified as originating in Hollywood. There are sound effects of an audience as music begins to a black blank screen, then the first image is of a male figure in . . . a cage? We are not sure. The figure suggests something non-human. The credits of Catherine Deneuve, David Bowie and Susan Sarandon are intercut with this male figure in a cage moving to music, then on the left of the screen we get a glimpse of part of a guitar, and suddenly we realize this is a 'stage cage', a performance. The film's title appears on screen at this point of realization, in bold black capitals. We are then given shots of a disco, with Bowie and Deneuve looking alike, at first indiscernible in terms of their gender. Their visual style is similar: they are both wearing dark glasses, and the strobe lights flash intermittently as reflections, intercutting with the 'stage cage' and shots of what is later established as a monkey.

What this beginning signifies for me is that the notion of 'performance' is made explicit, so that as spectators we are immediately aware of the film as a visual product to be consumed consciously. Of course the presence of a film's credits always has this distancing effect, but in this case the punk band's performance in the stage cage at the disco frames the direction of our look as enquiring, a questing for meaning. Because we have had to supply meaning in gradual unfolding stages, the process of wanting to make sense is activated in our gaze.

The smoking of cigarettes is a recurrent activity in the film, signifying desire, appetite, hunger, as well as distress. As Deneuve and Bowie look around the disco, smoking, they see a heterosexual couple dancing. They obviously scrutinize the couple with the aim of picking them up, something the couple are also aware of. Meanwhile the punk band's vocalist is singing a song with the hook 'undead, undead, undead'. Bowie and the man signal to each other, and there is a cut to the four of them in a car, a motorway journey with more smoking intercut with the performance of the 'undead' song, in which the singer has become grotesque and batlike. The car arrives at a remote house; interior shot of a drinks cabinet. The notion of performance continues as the young woman dances in front of a screen for the visual pleasure of the others. Deneuve and Bowie exchange a conspiratorial look, signalling an agreement to proceed. The two couples split into separate rooms, Deneuve and the man, Bowie and the woman, and a sex scene begins. There is kissing, undressing, the man and woman are in extreme arousal when the film switches into slow motion and we see Deneuve and Bowie tearing off trinkets from their ankh neckchains that turn into tiny knives. The sound effects reach a sinister climax as orgasm is carried over into murder. This is intercut with shots of a mad monkey, and there are images of blood and torn flesh, but they are cut so fast that we cannot be sure of what we are seeing, although it emerges that the monkey has attacked its partner.

Cut to Susan Sarandon with a female colleague who says, 'He's gone completely crazy.' We might think this refers to the monkey, and this is revealed to be the case. There is a shot of dead monkey, flesh and blood. Sarandon says, 'Oh my God!' Cut to Deneuve and Bowie in their car, smoking cigarettes, feeling good after a murder, then back to Sarandon smoking, feeling distressed. Two different value systems are quickly established. Deneuve and Bowie drive up to their New York residence, which turns out to be a massive house.

This opening sequence of the film is highly disturbing. We are at first excluded from knowing what is going on. It is in the editing that the film's strength lies, both in its revelation and its refusal to reveal. The murder scene, for instance, shows a strategy of suggesting more than showing what happens. And what is shown is revealed gradually, a layering of our knowledge as it unfolds intermittently, so we go from unknowing to knowing to unknowing. Although the detail is not visualized concretely for us, the violence of the murders is horrendous, intercut with tearing flesh.

The next shot is of a trunk opening and clothes being burned. The artistic effects around a visual aesthetic are clear, as the flames hungrily consume the evidence of the murder. From an image of fire there is a switch to water with Deneuve and Bowie taking a shower together. 'Forever?' asks Bowie, their first words spoken together audibly on screen. The sexual content of their kissing and touching suggests a conventional complementarity in their relationship. There is a panning shot to the bedroom, to cello music, they are seen sleeping. In fact, Bowie is unable to sleep; he is hallucinating a music room where someone is playing the cello. A cut to him still unable to sleep establishes this as a hallucination. Suddenly a cigarette is lit, and without a temporal or spatial linking shot, Bowie is seen out of bed, in silhouette. There then begins an intercutting between Bowie and the monkey, and we learn more about how the latter fits in.

The monkey is the subject of a research centre's investigation; the four-party research team is composed of Sarandon, her lover Tom, the woman we saw earlier with her, and a black male doctor. They discuss the monkey murdering its partner. The way the account of the monkey's manic state and lack of sleep is intercut with Bowie suggests that there is a direct synchronization going on between the two behaviours. Sarandon wants to monitor the monkey with video equipment. There is then a romantic interlude, a hallucination or memory that Bowie has, of Deneuve appearing to him in what could be a wedding veil, she lifts it to kiss him, declaring 'For ever and ever'.

Mostly, the effect of this sequence is to establish an 'arthouse' feel to the film, not quite the same as an avant-garde practice, but still oppositional or at least different in style to Hollywood, carrying a slow and textured pace reminiscent of some European cinema. A lot of attention is paid to spectacle, from watching the research team watch the monkey to the self-reflexive decision to get in video equipment to monitor the monkey. The strategies are self-reflexive and self-referential, reflecting and referring to cinematic codes that have an established place in the relaying of images. Here, however, the effect is to make us conscious that we are consuming images, achieved partly through devices that distance us by making us aware of our spectatorship.

Cut to a close-up of part of a disfigured face being relayed on a television screen, with Deneuve watching a programme in which Sarandon is being interviewed about a book she has written, *Sleep and Longevity*, about premature ageing. Is Deneuve interested in the content of the interview? Or in Sarandon? As it transpires, she is interested in both. Bowie appears, looking the worse for wear. He opens the door of their massive New York house to admit a young woman, Alice, who takes a photograph of him and then of Deneuve with an instant camera, another self-reflexive device. Deneuve, Bowie and Alice play a musical piece in an ensemble. When Bowie is unable to play further he says 'Forgive me' and leaves the room. He has realized that he is ageing abnormally – a look in the mirror and at Alice's photograph confirms something is seriously wrong with his body.

Cut to a copy of Sarandon's book being bought by Deneuve. She looks up at a video circuit screen to see Sarandon signing copies upstairs. Deneuve goes upstairs and this is carefully established in conventional spatial and temporal terms. There is a then a sudden shift to a disjuncture in space and time: Deneuve is apparently on the other side of the room when Sarandon suddenly feels she is being addressed, then without any movement Deneuve is standing close to her. She says she would like to talk to her; Sarandon says yes, she would like that; and their first meeting ends with a look from Sarandon of enquiry, attraction, anticipation. This contact between the two women may well suggest the stirrings of lesbian desire, even though it is within phallocentric terms, in that both women are 'phallic mothers', both with the power to be and to have what they want to possess. For now, because of Deneuve's prior visual 'knowledge' of Sarandon, relayed to her on television and video screens before she actually meets Sarandon, she is the more powerful of the two women. And from the first moment of contact, power between the two women is an issue.

While Bowie is at home watching television, Deneuve goes to the sleep research centre where Sarandon works with her colleagues on monitoring monkeys. While Deneuve is negotiating her way to the centre through hospital corridors, she is heard to be already in conversation with the black male doctor at the centre; he is telling her about the links between bloodtype and ageing. The effect of this disjuncture between visual and spoken signals is to distance us from what we are watching, and we are conscious that there is a playing with temporal codes. Deneuve returns home where Bowie has been reading Sarandon's book. His hair is falling out in handfuls, and he is understandably distressed. It emerges that this has happened before, to Deneuve's previous partners, including women. Bowie asks 'Who's next?' Deneuve is upset when he asks if Alice is going to be her next lover. For us, the lesbian content is made explicit in this scene. As a shift away, there is use of the traditional horror genre as we receive images of sinister shadows and partial bodies in what will emerge as the room at the top of the house. There are images of curtains, candles, but for now we do not know how they signify, and again we have to arrive at 'knowledge' as an unfolding process.

Meanwhile Bowie goes to the sleep research centre. Sarandon is just about to go to a meeting, when she sees a sinister image of him in her pocket mirror. She turns and sees him approach. From his manner she assumes he is disturbed and she does not believe he is ageing rapidly. She manages to evade him by telling him to wait in the patients' lounge, where she leaves him for several hours.

While Bowie is waiting at the hospital, Sarandon and her colleagues are watching a video replay of the monkey's ageing, and there is a direct synchronization between the monkey as it ages 'at a rate of five years per minute', and Bowie in the waiting room, also ageing dramatically. The video screen flashes with disturbed signals as the monkey's lifesigns start to terminate, with special effects of its skeleton disintegrating. This synchronization gives us a double imaging, where one level of action visualizes for us what is happening on another level of action. It is also a prefiguring, as we will see.

Sarandon and her lover Tom discuss showing the video tapes to get more funding. Meanwhile Bowie has aged considerably. He sees Sarandon before he leaves the hospital, and she realizes he was genuine in coming to her about premature ageing. She wants to talk to him but he leaves. There are close to two murder attempts, as Bowie is hungry for human flesh.

Cut to Alice on the video security system at the house. Bowie lets her in. He has aged beyond recognition, although Alice asks if he is Bowie's father because he has the same eyes. Alice leaves a message for Deneuve, takes a picture of a statue of a naked woman, and is about to leave when Bowie asks her to play something on the violin. She agrees and starts a classical piece.

What follows is for me the film's worst 'excess', as Bowie says 'Forgive me' and then murders Alice. I find it unforgivable that this murder could have been staged at all, let alone in the slasher tradition. I think the film fails on ethical grounds at this point in allowing such a crass manipulation of response to be attempted. I am very critical of the values of violence that have come to characterize many Hollywood films, because often this violence is used to evoke a response based on brutality. I would prefer that emotional engagement be premised on human feelings, and not on the violation of human flesh. The fascination with the body as a site of pleasure is one thing, but to subject that body to physical violence is a distortion of the values we could hold to celebrate human life, that is, the autonomy of the other as well as the maintenance of our own boundaries.

Deneuve comes home. She finds that Bowie has aged grotesquely. He wants her to kiss him, which she does reluctantly, intercut with the earlier hallucinated memory of them kissing; the contrast of his youth and beauty with his age and decrepitude is evident. Deneuve effectively rejects him. He then wants her to kill him, but it is apparently not possible for the undead to die. She discovers what he has done to Alice. There is a scene in the basement with Deneuve burning the evidence. Bowie falls down the stairs, apparently deliberately. Deneuve weeps over his helpless body, now shrunken and shrivelled. She carries him into the lift and up the stairs to the room at the top of the house, which is what we have seen imaged before. She puts his still-alive body in a coffin, next to the coffins of her previous lovers. This moment belongs to the horror genre, with premature burial something directly out of Edgar Allan Poe. In terms of the narrative, this 'burial' of Bowie is effectively a removal of the male partner, and allows the film to follow another direction, the lesbian content that has been figured in the look of desire between Deneuve and Sarandon.

The sequence that follows has a lesbian content that becomes increasingly explicit. It begins with a bell ringing; we are given an image of curtains in a mirror, pan to the bed where Deneuve is resting; she goes down the stairs as the bell rings insistently; shot of Sarandon on the video security screen; again Deneuve has more power because she can see Sarandon while Sarandon cannot see her. Sarandon identifies herself as a doctor from the centre. Deneuve says, 'I know,' and opens the door. Sarandon recognizes her immediately. This is their second meeting. Sarandon says, 'Oh, hello,' and electronic sound effects signal her desire. This moment of recognition, following that first look of desire in the bookshop, conveys a thrill as Sarandon now has contact with Deneuve – she knows her name, where she lives, she has a reason of sorts to be there. In terms of narrative logic, we feel we have 'arrived'.

Sarandon tells Deneuve about Bowie's visit to the centre. Deneuve tells her he's gone to Switzerland, which could be read as a joke. Sarandon tells Deneuve that they get a lot of cranks at the hospital and that she didn't believe him. This is intercut with Sarandon's quick glance at Deneuve's ankh hanging at her neck. Deneuve is all-knowing, all-powerful. She sees a man getting out of a car and she hurries Sarandon away, saying she will tell her more about what is happening 'when we know each other better'. Sarandon gives her her home and office phone numbers; she is able to leave on a note of hope that Deneuve will call her. She walks away, the man approaches, he turns out to be a detective. A synchronicity between the two women is established as Deneuve looks at her walking away and Sarandon turns her head to look back.

While the detective questions Deneuve about Alice there is a recurrence of electronic music – as Sarandon is walking, a truck appears, obviously threatening. Deneuve takes the piece of paper with Sarandon's telephone numbers and holds it to her breast; Sarandon is narrowly saved from being run over. Cut to a scene in a shower – Sarandon imagines the telephone is ringing, then she hallucinates an image of Deneuve in the mirror. This signifies the haunting of desire, the obsessive longing for the loved object.

Mergence of the two women has begun and is visualized in a scene where Deneuve is in a mourning veil – she is playing the piano to the right of the screen, intercut with Sarandon on the left of the screen in bed. A tear falls from Sarandon's eye, as another tear forms in Deneuve's eye; it is all very artistic and aesthetic, to mournful music.

The next shot is of Sarandon in her office, smoking a cigarette. She imagines the phone is ringing again, but this time we do not hear it ring, we just see her pick it up. This is intercut with the outside of Deneuve's house. This, again, is a delightful moment of desire and wish-fulfilment. Next shot to the interior of a door opening; Sarandon is visiting Deneuve again, ostensibly to enquire about Bowie, but Deneuve's all-powerful look makes Sarandon admit 'I don't know why I'm here.' Deneuve lets her in with a quick look that recognizes her desire. The next shot is of Deneuve's back. She asks what Bowie told Sarandon about himself and her. Sarandon says he told her very little, and Deneuve says that's probably for the best. And that is the end of that. The narrative can now explore the lesbian content prefigured in the look of desire between the two women.

Double doors open from the obverse side as Sarandon declines some sherry, but Deneuve says she thinks she will like it and gets some anyway. Sarandon is in awe of all of the beautiful antiques; some are 2,000 years old. Deneuve says most of them belong to her family. She has history and wealth. Sarandon looks at a bust of a woman. She says 'I love this piece.' She tells Deneuve it looks like her, and yes, there is a resemblance. This is a double visual joke as Deneuve says the bust is Florentine, 500 years old. What is so funny is that the audience knows Deneuve is an ancient vampire and could well have been the model for the bust, but obviously Sarandon cannot know this. There is delight at both her acute observation and its apparent naivety.

There follows the seduction scene, but we cannot know who is doing what first. To begin with there is disjuncture between the spoken and the visual. At first it appears that Deneuve is talking and Sarandon is listening, but in fact neither is talking during the scene where they salute each other with their glasses while gazing into each other's eyes. The conversation that takes place during this scene is really from a future scene – one that we cut into. This disjuncture has a charming effect; it is playing with our desire, an evading of direct spectatorial address in the interest of anticipation.

While they look at each other Deneuve says offscreen, 'I'm sure we could talk for hours, you and I, but I suppose you're very busy.' Sarandon's voice is also offscreen as she answers, 'Not too busy.' We see her sipping at her sherry on the right of the screen, and we hear her ask, 'What about you?' The moment shifts into the future present with Sarandon on the left of the screen, sipping sherry for continuity, as Deneuve says, 'Me?', sitting at the piano where she is playing a piece. She tells Sarandon, 'You would think me mostly idle, I'm afraid. My time is my own.' Sarandon replies. 'That's great.'

We have here established two powerful women, one a professional, the other an aristocrat, both successful, beautiful, and desirous of each other. Together they have everything; they are phallic women in the sense of being and possessing what they desire. Later, when they have sex, they enact the completion of the fantasy of the phallic mother, that is, the child's desire for its mother whom it fantasizes as being omnipotent. To take this fantasy further, the child also desires the mother to be the subject of a desire for the child. (The more exclusive this desire, the more dangerous it is.) It is the fetishization of their *beauty* that signifies the quest for completion that their desire is about – their sexual 'possession' of each other is a finding of the phallus, not as an organ, but as an attribute of aesthetic pleasure. In their mutual beauty, their reciprocal desire conveys a closure of sorts.

Again, who is doing what? Sarandon asks, 'How do you spend your time? Do you get lonely?' Deneuve replies, 'No.' She continues to play the piano    lf-contained in the sense of containing a self that is 'full', 'whole', with its promise of plenitude. Sarandon is obviously seduced by her beauty, her wealth, her power of completion. She says, 'I, rea – , I like your pendant.' The syntactic confusion conveys her nervousness. 'It's Egyptian,' says Deneuve. Sarandon mutters a 'hm' indicating she knows this. She crosses behind Deneuve to sit perched in a chair. Deneuve says, 'You know it's the symbol of everlasting life,' again Sarandon mutters a 'hm', meaning yes.

Sarandon leans forward, obviously enjoying the music. She asks Deneuve what she is playing. Deneuve tells her it is from Delibes's *Lakme*, the story of an Indian Brahmin princess with a woman slave, Malika. Sarandon asks, 'Is it a love song?' Deneuve says, 'I told you, it was sung by two women,' Sarandon says, 'It sounds like a love song.' Deneuve says, 'Then I suppose that's what it is.' Again, the lesbian possibility is made explicit. But it still needs further spelling out. Sarandon then asks Deneuve if she is trying to make a pass at her. Deneuve says not that she's aware of, and Sarandon laughs. The music switches from Deneuve's solo playing to full orchestral score as Sarandon spills sherry on her T-shirt top. She says 'Oh no' in a deep gutteral voice. The red of the sherry stains the white top. Slow motion as she tries to wipe the stain off. Deneuve touches her shoulder and neck from behind, then sits down seductively. Sarandon uses this as a cue to take off her top, she is seen as if through a window frame as she reveals full breasts and a look of offer, of promise as well as possession, as she gazes at Deneuve, also seen through a frame as she gets up and approaches Sarandon. Deneuve puts out her right arm to touch Sarandon's neck and breast. They look at each other, kiss, look, kiss again. With the same Delibes score now in full choral flow, switch to a bedroom scene with them partially dressed, kissing. The movements are clearly orchestrated. Deneuve is the initiator, Sarandon is responsive. This scene of them kissing starts to intercut with another position of them in bed, with what we realize is Deneuve at Sarandon's right arm, though it takes a few glimpses to realize who is who, doing what. Deneuve bites into Sarandon's right arm, then we get a shot of Sarandon in a similar position biting into Deneuve's right arm. Again it is difficult to be sure who is doing what to whom, as we make the unknown intelligible.

There is a superimposed cut to a massive piece of rare meat, a visual joke that condenses sex and hunger for the flesh with hunger for food into one funny image. Indeed, this scene is very humorous. Sarandon is unable to eat. She is distracted as her lover Tom questions her about her appetite. He asks her about the chain around her neck. She explains it's an ankh and that Deneuve gave it to her that afternoon when they talked for three and a half hours. Tom is surprised that the women talked for so long, that Sarandon should have drunk sherry when she does not even like it. The scene is set in a restaurant overlooking a swimming pool, but again we have to arrive at this knowledge in a way that renders our vision a conscious look of enquiry. For instance, while Tom expresses surprise that Deneuve should have given Sarandon a present after only one meeting, Sarandon is looking at what turns out to be a diving space. She says by way of explanation that Deneuve is European, and we get an image of a diver to establish our vision – this is an 'othering' of Deneuve that the audience will laugh at, intercut as it is with lustful looks at scantily clad bodies beside the pool. The previous sex scene loads this scene with the physicality of love-making, so we know that Sarandon is in another space because she has had satisfying lesbian sex. But this lesbian sex has to be secretive, dishonest, in that Sarandon cannot tell Tom about sleeping with Deneuve, though whether she does not tell him because he is her lover is left ambiguous. Sarandon and Tom fight; he tells her to see a doctor; she tells him, 'I am a doctor.'

That night she is vomiting and the next scene starts with a shot of blood on a microscope slide. It emerges that the medical team is examining Sarandon's blood. She is ravenous but cannot eat, and has an alien strain of blood in her veins, non-human, and fighting for dominance. Sarandon is seen to have a bite on her left arm, and when twice asked how this could have happened, Sarandon lies. The sex scene with Deneuve biting into her arm is intercut, however, to show she has knowledge of how it happened, though she does not know why.

Sarandon goes to visit Deneuve. She says her colleagues think she has gone to a blood specialist, and that she wants to know what is happening – 'What have you done to me?' Deneuve says it is natural that she should be frightened because she doesn't know what is going on, but to give her time, to trust her. Sarandon says that she did trust her, but that Deneuve has done something to her. She opens her left sleeve and shows Deneuve a wound. Deneuve says it is a bruise, that it will heal. She tells Sarandon that she has given her everlasting life, but Sarandon thinks this is derisory. Deneuve tells Sarandon that it is her, Deneuve's, blood in her veins, that they each made an incision – she shows Sarandon the mark on her own right arm. Deneuve tells Sarandon 'You belong to me, we belong to each other.' Sarandon thinks all this is nonsense. She wants a straight answer, she attacks Deneuve, slow motion. Deneuve is stronger and hurls her to the ground. A table falls with papers scattering; Sarandon is stunned, reeling.

Sarandon leaves the house but goes back as Deneuve predicts. She is imaged as having heroin withdrawal because of having to feed her hunger for flesh. Hallucination again figures to convey desire. Deneuve picks up a young man and brings him home for Sarandon to feed on. There is another murder scene as Deneuve's ankh makes a severe gash in the young man's throat. This is imaged very explicitly. It transpires that Sarandon resists eating the human flesh, because when Tom arrives at the house she is still in withdrawal. We see her fighting the alien blood in her system, and this involves the resistance to becoming a vampire herself. When Tom arrives she tries to seduce him, but a glimpse of Deneuve watching makes her realize she has to resist, which she does by trying to make him escape. He struggles with her. Then, in yet another moment when a man is in danger from a woman, we see her ripping off her ankh and . . . later we see her feeding. This is the final crossover; she cannot resist human flesh, and her initiation is complete.

She appears to Deneuve downstairs with a look of satiation, a wild animal full with having fed, as imaged by the blood on her mouth and face. But we know that her position of moral strength provides a genuine space for conflict, that she cannot collude with this arrangement with Deneuve, who tells her, 'You are a part of me now. I cannot let you go.' Deneuve wants to share eternity with her. 'You will begin to love me as I do you. Forever. Forever and ever.'

Our identifications may have been shifting but the value system in operation in the film is generated by Sarandon, whose desire we share, whose seduction we enjoy, but whose ambivalence and resistance we also identify with as morally right. The conflict is genuine: Sarandon cannot become a vampire without validating destruction and the nihilism of murder. Despite desire, despite the apparent parity between the two women, power has to be asserted through resistance to a corrupt value system.

The earlier mergence we saw between the women is again operating as they kiss, then Sarandon rips off the ankh and stabs either herself or Deneuve – the ankh is caught up in flesh, which we see ripping apart although we do not know what has been done to whom, all we know is that both women are bleeding simultaneously and profusely from the neck. Deneuve says, 'Stay,' Sarandon says, 'I can't.'

To conclude, the apparently immortal Deneuve is destroyed, although we cannot be sure of this, despite seeing her face disintegrate with some of the special effects prefigured earlier. There are, for instance, images of a coffin at the end – is it being kept in storage, is Deneuve still undead? Or is the coffin for Sarandon's own use? And we wonder whether Sarandon, who survives, will be a practising vampire. There is a kiss between a young girl and Sarandon in the penultimate scene – is it a maternal kiss, a sexual kiss? Does it figure lesbian desire? We cannot be sure. Full knowledge is denied to us, leaving us in a state of closure without completion.

I conclude this account of the film summarily, because by the end it degenerates into the horror genre which holds no interest for me. I have concentrated on the use of avant-garde strategies to show how the film keeps us at a distance, makes us aware of our own activity of spectating. At the same time, there is the conventional use of filmic languages in the deployment of spectatorial identifications and narrative engagement, but this I find to be a strength, especially given that the explicit lesbian content is so fascinating. It is no coincidence that both avant-garde strategies and a lesbian sexuality are highly oppositional practices.

Our pleasure in seeing the look of lesbian desire given articulation is indeed 'oppositional', because it is so infrequent in film, and because lesbian desire is itself so revolutionizing of the heterosexual premise that dictates classical film narrative. (Would that this were the only consequence of the heterosexual institution!) In *The Hunger* we are able to see lesbian desire as a 'fiction', a representation that fits a narrative mode which moves us, but which also remains visible as a fiction in all its materiality. This dual reading is possible because the myth of the vampire is itself a fictional reading, a metaphor we deploy to convey our obsession with the buried, the hidden, the unacknowledged. Our cultural obsession with the vampire as signifying the undead connects with the psychic mechanisms of the repressed, that material that returns, re-emerges to haunt us in our adult lives.

What I think *The Hunger* enacts for us is the desire, to borrow from Lacan, to be the exclusive desire of the m/other.[6] When Deneuve and Sarandon offer themselves to each other, there is a moment of mergence, but it is illusory, elusive, it cannot last, it is the space of the imaginary, of the pre-oedipal that must break through into the symbolic order of the phallus, moment of fracture, lack, rupture, loss. Lesbian desire in *The Hunger* is as delightful as it is destructive, but what makes it an acceptable representation is its ficticity. To the question, 'What do lesbians do in bed?', the answer, in this film, is that they bite each other's arms. By this I mean that the structure of the vampire myth shapes lesbian behaviour in the film to fit into a fictitious mould. This is one advantage in avoiding attempts at authentic representations. We can accordingly take what we want for our pleasure and resist the rest for the construction it is.

Let us look again at how the lesbian is figured in the film, powerful, phallic, holding the promise of completion. First there is their desire, which is initially articulated through their looking at each other. It is the agency and affectivity assigned to the look that the women bear which gives them the power to enact lesbian desire. In phallocentric terms, when the two women acknowledge their desire for each other, and make love, they both 'are' and 'have' the phallus, the latter through the sexual 'possession' of each other's body. Then the notion of lesbianism as contamination is raised, as when Sarandon repeatedly asks Deneuve, 'What have you done to me?', an inferred accusation being that she has corrupted her sexuality by sleeping with her. The moment when Sarandon tells Deneuve, 'Don't you touch me', when she wipes a tear off the edge of her face, supports such a reading. Sarandon is frightened, in a rage because she is so vulnerable. I think this rage is the key and I think what we recognize in the women's desire is not a fear of contamination but of the rage to which that lesbian desire is prey. It is this rage that I find the most 'convincing', in terms of representations, not only because it has a narrative place, but more because it conveys the loss of control, the sense of impotence at being so much in the (usually emotional) power of the other. As the lesbians are seen in mergence, so their loss of boundaries precipitates them into that shifting space of simultaneous intimacy and invasiveness. Rage can be the only response, re-emerging from the moments of impotent dependence on the m/other. 'You are a part of me,' Deneuve tells Sarandon, drawing on the levels of both the maternal and the sexual relationship. This is the complexity of lesbian mergence.

To the question of whether there is something anti-lesbian in conveying a lesbian relationship as a configuration of mother–child mergence, I would say it depends on how sensitive is its treatment. There is, for instance, the need to maintain autonomy and independence. Despite mergence, despite parity, there must be separation, a clarification of boundaries, or else there is a danger of psychosis. More concretely, the merging could lead to feelings of engulfment at the dependency in desire. Rage again is a usual response, close to hatred because of the intensity of this dependence. Lack of self-sufficiency can lead to feelings of impotence, and one can try to compensate for the resulting rage through acts of violence. These are the worst aspects of lesbian mergence. Otherwise there is support, strength, sustenance in lesbian mergence, where the possibility of a fluidity in shifting positions in a mother-daughter dyad can be a source of empowerment. What emerges from the film is the beginning of a sympathetic treatment of the women's phallicized relationship. But because the central metaphor of the vampire dictates violence in the diegetic action, mergence is seen as destructive, where desire is 'possession' in the many senses of the word, including the meanings of invasion and occupation. In a way, to portray total mergence as destructive is a confirmation that resistance and refusal are about the need for autonomy, as well as intimacy, in relationships.

If *The Hunger* conveys so well the complexity of lesbian desire, this is achieved partly through a conventional imaging of the woman as stunningly beautiful. I think spectators 'fetishize' the woman's beauty, in so far as they see in that beauty a plenitude, a promise of completion that the search for the phallus signifies. I had hoped that by positing the intended spectator as female, and by positing female desire as the *subject* of desire, we might be able to escape the masculinist regime of representing women as objects. And yet we seem to be repeating the same languages, the same responses. There are close connections between voyeurism and fetishism, a watching and a searching or scrutinizing of the woman, just as there are implications in scopophilia of 'lookism', where the pleasure in seeing is often one about the pleasure of gazing at beauty. We cannot seem as yet to avoid this fetishization of the woman's beauty.

But maybe we can begin by being conscious of how we constitute desire.

I am aware of the danger in using the fetish as a concept to explain lesbian desire, because it merely seems to bring back the phallocentrism I would ideally like to see dismantled. Nevertheless, if we accept our 'castration', it is because we recognize our socially disadvantaged position as women under a patriarchy. Simultaneously, if we also disavow our castration, we do so with a consciousness of our power, not as women pretending to be men by adopting the phallus, but as women who have seen through the phallus as a sham. If we persist in the fascination with the phallus despite its fraudulent status, it is because we cannot operate in any social order other than the one already given to us. Our fixation with the phallus has less to do with wanting to maintain male supremacy, and more with wanting to challenge the dominant order, not for reasons of envy but of a desire for equality.

However, it would seem to be practically impossible to institute a change in phallocentrism at this time, and so quite predictably filmic languages will also reproduce the phallic term under which they are constructed. In *The Hunger* I am so pleased to see two women articulating the look of lesbian desire that I can tolerate its phallocentric framing. And there is much that pleases me about the film. It lends itself easily to simultaneous enjoyment and analysis, as we are both engaged and kept at a distance. For instance, our involvement in the narrative flow and our investment in spectatorial identifications are kept intact, while at the same time we have a space to be critical and enquiring as we construct our readings. Our knowledge unfolds intermittently in a process of making sense, so that we consciously produce meanings in the absence of given knowledge. This mirrors the process of intelligibility, whereby we attach meanings as social subjects, and our participation in such processes evokes a more conscious and critical state of spectating, a political project. In terms of agency, the spectator has the space to enjoy some practices and to resist others. I still believe in a synthesis of the pleasures of the mainstream with the political potential of the avant-garde as a way forward for filmic languages.

As I have said elsewhere, one way forward is to have closure without completion, something that the avant-garde tradition allows. The appellation of a fractured, fragmented subject is because the processes of intelligibility that are activated in the film are operating to create a possibility of preferred readings. For instance, in the attempted 'suicide/murder' scene at the end, we wonder which is which, who is the victor and who is the victim? Sarandon is seen to be dying, and yet she survives. Could the same apply to Deneuve, whose 'death' is in some doubt? The roving positions in fantasy are pertinent here, where subjects are not fixed, and where this unfixity allows for a shifting and slippage of positions and meanings. I am indebted to Kate Mackintosh for alerting me to the notion that it is the 'fixing' of positions, say in rape, that makes certain acts into the atrocities they are.[7] Therefore the 'unfixing' or oscillation of such positions allows for mobility, for freedom almost, from the otherwise constricting conditions of closure. The film's ending, with its appeal to diverse interpretations, enables a progressive reversion to the spectator as the site and source of meaning. This is indeed an avant-garde practice in calling upon the making of meaning as a self-conscious project. This is one step closer to exposing the fraudulent status of the phallus, where 'the lesbian gaze' could rewrite filmic languages if it were to reconstitute how the fetish figures in our construction of desire.

The film borrows from different traditions and genres to form an eclectic but coherent product, one which nevertheless takes away any ultimate knowledge, or 'mastery', of and over what happens. Although the narrative is full of satisfying detail that links the film together, it is also left open-ended. Consider, for instance, what could be a continuity error, when Sarandon reveals the bloodbite on her left arm, though in fact in the bedroom scene she was bitten on her right arm. Is this just an error? Or is it a deliberate insertion of uncertainty to our spectating? Either way, it serves to detract from a definitive reading. The closure without completion that the film enacts in its conclusion is also progressive. And the self-reflexive strategies, including watching television, having a video security system, taking and looking at photographs, setting up and monitoring video tapes, commenting on the resemblance of visual artefacts, are all devices which remind the spectator of the process of watching, where what is seen is constituted at a remove. Moreover, the use of both temporal synchronization and disjuncture conveys the 'uncanny', the known unknown, both familiar and frightening.

The look of lesbian desire is ultimately what has me hooked. I think the film does address the specificities of lesbian spectatorship, not just because it erotically evokes lesbian desire, but because that desire is figured as complex, it is about rage, resistance, refusal (just as much as it can be about passion and compassion). We can receive the lesbian content as both the fact of women's desire for each other, and as the fiction that this particular narrative takes. Made by a man and edited by a woman, the film feeds our hunger to see the look of lesbian desire articulated on the screen.

## Notes

1.  Claire Johnston, 'Women's cinema as counter-cinema', in Claire Johnston (ed.), *Notes on Women's Cinema*. SEFT, London, 1974, p. 31.
2.  Laura Mulvey, 'Visual pleasure and narrative cinema', in Constance Penley (ed.), *Feminism and Film Theory*. Routledge and BFI Publishing, New York and London, 1988 (originally published in 1975).
3.  E. Ann Kaplan, 'Is the gaze male?' in Ann Snitow, Christine Stansell and Sharon Thompson (eds), *Desire: The Politics of Sexuality*. Virago, London, 1984.
4.  Shameem Kabir, 'Lesbian representations in film: mermaids in the desert . . . must be seeing things', in Suzanne Raitt (ed.) *Volcanoes and Pearl Divers: Essays in Lesbian Feminist Studies*. Onlywomen Press, London, forthcoming.
5.  Laura Mulvey, 'Feminism, film and the avant garde', in Mary Jacobus (ed.), *Women Writing and Writing about Women*. Croom Helm, London, 1979.
6.  Jacques Lacan quoted by Jacqueline Rose, 'Feminine sexuality: Jacques Lacan and the *école freudienne*', in *Sexuality in the Field of Vision*. Verso, London and New York, 1986, p. 61.
7.  I am additionally grateful to Kate Mackintosh for reading a draft of this essay and for being so supportive.

## Acknowledgements

I am greatly indebted to many more women theorists than I have credited here, including Teresa de Lauretis and Judith Roof, for providing ideas without which I could not have attempted this essay.

Finally, I would like to thank Liz Gibbs for commissioning this piece, Gill Price and Lucy Whitman for their encouragement, and my sisters Priya Bano Kumar and Nasreen Munni Kabir for their love and support.

Chapter eight

# Beyond Queer Cinema: It's in Her Kiss

**Cherry Smyth**

HOW do you tell a lesbian these days, now that androgyny is a fashion statement and straight girls are impersonating dykes? Lesbians, once caricatured as the fat, hairy, ugly sisters of feminism, are experiencing the ambivalent pleasures of mainstream media flirtation. Enter the Lipstick Lesbian aka Lesbian Chic. This ethnographic gaze has invented the new lesbian. Gone are the dungarees and man-hating slogans. The new lesbian doesn't bite or scratch, she even wants to have babies and she's just like me and you . . . . Have they finally taken the outlaw out of being out? The feminist out of being lesbian?

The celebrated cover of *Vanity Fair* taken by Annie, No-One-Knows-I'm-a-Lesbian, Liebovitz, took everything straight culture ever thought about butch and femme, magnified it and made visual the notion of dyke camp. Not only do we ape heterosexual roles, we improve on them. And most lesbians got the joke. We had discovered the power of self-irony and the media had beat us at our own game and taken queer as its own.

The overblown excitement many of us felt at the discovery of the commodifiable lesbian could only have occurred in a culture where lesbianism has been so successfully erased, not only within mainstream feminism trying to clean up its act, but within broad-based visual culture. The fact that since *Desert Hearts* in 1985 there has been no major Hollywood production focusing on lesbians has driven many of us to seek out role models elsewhere, and to turn to independent film and video in the hope of seeing/creating something of ourselves.

In the bloom of the GLC-positively-imaged mid 1980s, we would never have imagined that it would have taken another ten years for a lesbian kiss on a British TV soap opera, only to find it excised from the afternoon repeat slot for being 'offensive to family viewers'. A ten-second kiss between two adult women in 1994!

Even though those chosen to represent lesbian chic have been all white, all feminine 'girls', who conform to the non-threatening stereotype of the good-looking, safe woman, we're mostly grateful. Why? After years of being seen only as the prelude to the prick in straight pornography, or as the sick predator in films – *She Gotta Have It* (Spike Lee, 1986) and *The Killing of Sister George* (Robert Aldrich, 1968) – or as Laura Ashley caressers in *Fried Green Tomatoes* (Jon Avnet, 1991) and *Coup de Foudre* (Diane Kurys, 1983), we see these images as progress. Just one look at the turkey of independent features, the lesbian-directed *Claire of the Moon* (Nicole Conn, 1993) in which it took the whole movie for the one-dimensional caricatures to fuck, and you'll run back to *Lianna* (John Sayles, 1982) with open arms. Oddly enough the success of *Claire of the Moon* rests on the fact that most viewers read it as an outrageous parody, reading irony where none was intended. It's taken several decades of coming out screaming, fighting bigotry, resisting stereotypes and invisibility to develop an irony that is only possible when a marginalized community feels confident enough to laugh at itself.

It's easy to see why glamour has become attractive to lesbians for whom in the 1980s it was a sell-out to patriarchy to be 'trendy', and how the queer project which proclaimed to move beyond the separatism of the lesbian movement and the misogyny of the gay male movement has seemed to offer something innovative to younger lesbians and older casualities of the infantalizing rigours of some lesbian feminism. In the 1970s lesbian feminism tended to strive towards erotic partnerships that emphasized sameness and dismissed butch-femme dynamics as an eroticization of power difference, a corrupt imitation of heterosexist roles, a collusion with patriarchy. In the mid-1980s it was still difficult for lesbians to wear lipstick and high heels without being labelled 'lesbians from the waist downwards'. Many of us who wanted to be out had to choose between a career and being politically active. Now younger dykes are coming out and maintaining a career, and the community in which political activism thrived is sadly much fragmented and dispersed. This has also meant that the role of culture, both popular and mainstream, to reflect and reinterpret lesbian identity has become much more important. We are just beginning to define our experience as universal: to wrest a place in popular culture in music, with out lesbian bands like Zrazy winning top music awards; in art, with the first British lesbian art show in 1992; in photography, with the publication of *Stolen Glances* (Boffin and Fraser, 1990), *Love Bites* (Della Grace, 1991) and *Postcards from the Edge* (Ainley and Budge, 1993); in theatre, with all lesbian companies like Slip of the Tongue and Red Rag; and in literature, with the mainstream success of Jeanette Winterson and the *Penguin Book of Lesbian Short Stories* (1993).

However, until I witness more professional lesbians coming out in film, theatre, TV and government and see the rewards of producers and funders recognizing the existence of an educated, culturally starved lesbian market with increasing spending power, I will continue to see lesbian chic as just another assimilating blip, a PR exercise for clients who didn't realize they needed one. As the dust settles after the galloping hype over 'new queer cinema', have we seen more lesbian features not only being produced but receiving mainstream distribution and critical acclaim? Whose cinema is it?

While there is a tendency to see queer politics as the first lesbian and gay attempts to disrupt the hegemony of the nuclear family, the oppressive sex roles and homophobic institutions that have made heterosexuality compulsory, Gay Power Activists, Radical Fairies and DAFT (Dykes and Faggots Together) were doing similar work in the 1970s. Although it's fashionable to trash the 1970s' celebration of oceanic, floral images that typified cultural feminist representations, much of this work was also pioneering and profound for women who had never seen women fucking or masturbating for their own pleasure. Barbara Hammer's explicit, iconoclastic work such as *Dyketactics* (1974), *Women I Love* (1979) and *Superdyke Meets Madame X* (1977), and Jan Oxenburg's satirical study of butch-femme and non-monogamy in *Comedy in Six Unnatural Acts* (1978) confronted deeply held taboos about women, never mind lesbians, being sexual. Not only were these artists marginalized within the male, straight experimental community, and notoriously under-funded, but they confronted massive self-censorship. Some of the work produced in the 1970s and 1980s was made under the strict proviso that it would not be screened to mixed audiences. The fear of men 'getting off' inhibited many feminist film makers and continues to be used as a reason to censor sexually explicit lesbian work. In a formal attempt to deconstruct the male gaze, work like *Je, Tu, Il, Elle* (Chantal Akerman, 1974) tried to refigure lesbian sex in a non-voyeuristic fashion, using wide shots, long takes and a disrupted narrative. Many lesbians lacked the visual language to read such work and agreed with one critic who said in retrospect that 'too much attention was paid to analysing the male gaze and not enough to what the male gaze cannot see'.

The response to what was determined as the narcissistic prescriptiveness of huggy, nurturing lesbian sex has been read by theorists like Sheila Jeffreys as a reactionary backlash, reconfiguring the lesbian as a construction of a heterosexual male fantasy, but it has been seen by others as a progressive whiplash, reinventing the bad daughter in whom the good feminist mother could inspire guilt, but not restrain. Whether you call it 'queer' or see it simply as a coming of age of a new generation of upfront lesbians, it has sparked a plethora of definitions and counter-definitions, has fuelled the politics of representation with fresh complexities and pluralities, and is teaching us to negotiate coalitions in spite of dissent.

Instead of a ghetto culture that seeks to address itself, many lesbians and gays in the 1990s are demanding to be part of popular culture on their own terms. While independent cinema of the 1970s and 1980s often defined itself apart from the popular, new film and video culture is unafraid of the contamination of the mainstream, yet insists on its historical and social specificity.

The work we could call queer seeks not only to disrupt the

ways in which lesbians and gays are seen in straight culture, but to challenge how we see ourselves. *She Must Be Seeing Things* (Sheila McLaughlin, 1987), although it tries rigorously to invent a lesbian language to articulate difference and desire, is seen as pre-queer. Had it been produced in 1991, it might have made it into the queer arena. Several independent film makers in London are not publicly out as lesbians, never mind as queers. Their work, which centres around the feminist body, has the visual elegance, formal inventiveness and pleasure quota praised in 'queer cinema', yet is distinctly 'unqueer', for it fails to disrupt a heterosexist gaze.

B. Ruby Rich marked the start of the queer film phenomenon at the Toronto Film Festival in 1990: 'There, suddenly, was a flock of films that were doing something new, renegotiating subjectivities, annexing whole genres, revising histories in their image.'[1] Others stake out a broader definition. Borrowing from Raymond Williams's phrase, 'structure of feeling', video maker Gregg Bordowitz suggests that:

> Cultural work can be considered within a queer structure of feeling if self-identified queers produce the work, if these producers identify the work as queer, if queers claim the work has significance to queers, if the work is censored or criticised for being queer. A particular work is queer if it is viewed as queer, either by queers or bigots.[2]

Commercially, this coming of age has manifested itself in the cross-over of 'new queer cinema' from art house cinemas into more commercial cinemas and burgeoning video distribution companies like Out On A Limb, Dangerous To Know and Pride, consolidating the 'queer' film market beyond the whims of a mainstream media fad. This work does not rely on mainstream approval and hence circulation, nor does it ask to be tolerated or accepted. It is less interested in converting the homophobe than in entertaining and affirming the homo. There is a growing currency for work that is iconoclastic and difficult in the face of censorship, funding cuts, paranoid interpretations of political correctness and political apathy. Some have argued that 'queer cinema' is no more than a marketing ploy, but B. Ruby Rich has drawn convincing parallels with the energy of feminist film in the 1970s and the black British workshops in the early 1980s.

There is a danger in constructing a homogenized concept of 'queer cinema', however. When you say 'queer cinema', do you mean the four gay male films celebrated as the birth of a new genre – *Poison* (Todd Haynes, 1991), *Swoon* (Tom Kalin, 1992), *My Own Private Idaho* (Gus Van Sant, 1992) and *The Living End* (Gregg Araki, 1992)? Then do you include Isaac Julien's *Young Soul Rebels* (1991), which is seen as pretty queer in the context of the black family in Britain, but considered not queer enough within the white gay male community? Women have to fight to extend the genre to include short work on video, to include very different subjectivities. As Pratibha Parmar points out, the queering of the black lesbian perspective involves constant negotiation, but is marked by a different mode of address:

> We are creating a sense of ourselves and our place within different and sometimes contradictory communities, not simply in relation to . . . not in opposition to . . . nor in reversal to . . . nor as a corrective of . . . but in and for ourselves. Precisely because of our lived experiences of racism and homophobia, we locate ourselves not within any one community but in the spaces between these different communities.[3]

Desperate to find a queer dyke film, *Rosebud* (Cheryl Farthing, 1992) has been heralded as 'queer', even though it's as conventional as *Lianna*, and borrows from a gay male aesthetic of flowers and angels, which barely translates into dyke camp. Take the Channel 4 *Out* TV series. While it may be an unprecedented intervention into mainstream television, it could never be called 'queer cinema', for in style and address it seeks to be tasteful and tolerated. Although it gave Isaac Julien and Constantine Giannaris space to make quasi-dramas, dykes have been allowed to produce only worthy documentaries which, apart from Pratibha Parmar's stunning *Double the Trouble*, took few formal risks. And what about features? We're ready, are you?

So does claiming queerness depend on a self-knowing irony

in the film maker, address, or audience interpretation? Queer in Britain is used largely by pro-sex dykes whose aesthetic owes more to SM than film noir. Liane Harris of Cinenova, a women's film distribution company, has been trend spotting:

> I don't know if there is a new aesthetic, but there is a new term that covers what's happening for men. It's based in gay male cinema and lesbian shorts seem to be tacked on to higher budget feature work by men. Lesbian work reflects a preoccupation with SM, though it's often all image and little real exploration of what power is about. It gives a hard edge, unlike all that soft focus.

Look at *Mano Destra* (Cleo Uebelmann, 1985), *Between* (Claudia Schillinger, 1989) and one of the latest British video shorts, *Kissy Suzuki Suck* (Alison Murray, 1992). Murray's student work assaults violence, voyeurism and female stereotypes, using tough language and rough physical theatre – and was loathed by her tutors. 'I've had a lot of shit since I made this work,' asserts Murray, who's twenty-one and bisexual.

> Some people call it pornographic, which I take as a compliment – it is and it's meant to be. Others find the language aggressive – that's the whole point. I don't want to be written off by a straight audience for being queer, nor do I want to preach to the converted. It's more daring to move beyond that context.

She's taken the taboos of the feminist anti-porn debate and flung them in its face. If men are saying, 'I'm a fag, get used to it', women are asserting, 'I'm a macho slut, so what?' The post-punk iconography raided by Murray references Madonna, the hooker and DV8, and whips up a trash femme cocktail that explodes the confines of feminism in an exhilarating promise of what 'queer' could mean for women.

Part of the problem of inventing a queer dyke cinema is what Kalin refers to as the 'revisionist aestheticism', which pillages and pastiches a vast store of images stretching back to Genet and

Cocteau. Gay men have a rich aesthetic heritage from Warhol and Kenneth Anger to Derek Jarman, while dykes have constantly to invent themselves in an 'alchemical' process, as B. Ruby Rich coins it:

> Whereas the gay male work is engaged in the important enterprise of archaeology, sifting through the past and salvaging what was long buried, the lesbian work must more properly be seen as alchemy, creating gold where before there was only dross. The lesbian video artist simply doesn't have the traditions to go back to: her invention faces a canvas long blank.[4]

Part of this alchemy has involved pillaging and parodying butch-femme traditions, gay male sexual iconography and SM signifiers, but also widening the net of sexual identity to include and explore issues around transgender. We're not talking simply about reading against the grain, whether it's Douglas Sirk or Maya Deren, but about analyses of images and images themselves that could only have happened now, because of AIDS, the response to a reductive feminism, an awareness of non-sexist, non-racist strategies and a refusal to condone homophobia.

In seeking past movies to parody, lost images to reclaim, icons to glorify, dykes have always had less booty to raid. Thank god for Marlene, Greta and James Dean. Feminist cinema has been appropriating like fury for 20 years, but more dykes watch *Prisoner: Cell Block H* than have seen *Un Chant d'Amour* (Jean Genet, 1950). The grimy butthole prison scene and the wide-angled ennui of the road movie have become *de rigueur* for the queer boy to the point of over-determination and aesthetic exhaustion. That's not to say when I see it coming, that long lustful look between the prison bars, those frenzied fucks stolen in the corridor, that I don't find them sexy. I do. But when will pussy-sex invent a brassiness, a power to enthral boys and, more importantly, funders, to the same degree? I was nonetheless shocked by lesbian producer Christine Vachon's admission that she colluded in 'maintaining a kind of false auteurism' to market *Poison* and *Swoon*: 'It's just so much easier to position men as the new artistic hot potato to watch.'[5]

There is no question that queer cinema has brought with it queer theory and enlivened a stale debate which had floundered under the weight of identity politics and proselytizing promises of respectability. How many times did we hear the cry, 'But this film doesn't represent me!' at screenings, and witness the film maker apologize meekly as s/he struggled to breathe under the unreasonable burden of responsibility?

Perhaps 'queer' is saying, 'No, this film doesn't represent you, unless you're a young, hip, streetwise white boy, or a dyke who's a wannabe – tough shit.' That's why queer dyke cinema will be a long time catching up with the bandwagon, 'cause dykes are not just angry with straight homophobia, and feminist hypocrisy, they're angry with being excluded by the gay boys as well.

What does a queer film look like? Has one been made yet? Queer's optimistic dream of inclusivity across race and gender has sometimes led to the mistake of queers seeing themselves as post-racist, post-sexist. Just as queer boys assume that pro-sex dykes who choose to work with them are post-feminist and that therefore they can be post-sexist, so some assume that white lesbians and gays in relationships with black partners are post-racist. Of course, a queer film is not exempt from racism. *Safe Is Desire* (Debi Sundahl, 1993), for example, a safer sex tape for dykes, reinforces rather than ruptures the stereotype of the black lesbian, who must take her lessons in safer sex from the more experienced, and morally correct white lover. The white woman loves the city, the black woman misses the wild countryside. The racially coded dynamic of civilized versus primitive renders the tape extremely problematic.

On our utopian screen there will be proof of inclusivity and plurality. B. Ruby Rich argues convincingly that:

> queers have the potential for a different *relationship* to race, and to racism, because of the very nature of same-sex desires and sexual practices . . . [there may be an argument to be made that] queerness, in its outsider guise, as a potential laboratory for the renegotiation of race relations, a place where oppressions can be not ranked in hierarchy but productively combined.[6]

Surely a queer film is one that operates a queer gaze within it, regardless of who's watching – that emerges out of necessity, out of the need to survive: films that evoke questions around gender fluidity, interracial couples, black lesbians and gays determining their own representations, queer parenting, queer celibacy being posited as normal, inevitable? If the category or site of 'normal' is constantly contested, the queer project will have won.

Queer is increasingly used in a vernacular sense as being synonymous with lesbian and gay, but surely a queer film has to posit something new about the privileging of heterosex and culture, the hegemony of the white gay man. There is a whole new generation of lesbians and gays who take it for granted that homophobia should be tolerated as little as racism or sexism, who've not only had enough of being marginalized, ignored, bashed, stereotyped and ridiculed, but who are more TV literate, more script-wise and confident that the gay and lesbian body should, and indeed must, be articulated.

The urgency that fires some queer work must be due to the awareness of the vulnerability of the body, the terrain of sex having become dangerous, indeed fatal. AIDS has forced a discussion not only of the exchange of body fluids, but of the larger relations of exchange in which sexuality occurs. What Linda Singer usefully articulates as *Epidemic Logic*[7] has heightened sexual regulations, like monogamous marriage and the back to basics mantra, and insidiously reasserts hetero male privilege, with the nuclear family presented as the exclusive site of safer sex. Those who refuse to measure up to society's ideas of legitimate sexual exchange are increasingly forced to justify their behaviour. As Paula Webster points out, 'If sex is repressed, that is condemned to prohibition, non existence, and silence, then the mere fact that one is speaking about it has the appearance of a deliberate transgression.'[8]

How often is the notion of queer dismissed as being transgressive for its own sake, rather than appraised for its ability to destabilize boundaries of sexual definition? It's hard to accept that for many lesbians and gays their sexuality does not necessarily render them oppositional or subversive. They want normalcy and acceptance, and join with heteros in dismissing the perverse 'queers' as dangerous.

Through feminism, women have long sought to re-present the body, to devise a sexual subjectivity, as well as living the risks of the sexual terrain – rape, incest, pregnancy, abortion and male violence. As Chris Straayer insists 'the contemporary stance of sex-positivity was made possible by, and builds on, feminism's reclaiming of women's bodies to empower women'.[9] Now there are the beginnings of a female sexual agency that is not only feminist but lesbian and is inviting the boys to see too.

New dyke work presents an active cunt that has nothing invested in self-reflexive separatism and heralds the self-determined dyke who compromises neither to hetero-notions of what a lesbian looks like nor to white constructions of lesbian lifestyle. Much of it is on video and most of it is short. No prizes for guessing why. It addresses how to cruise in a humorous way in Cheryl Dunye's *She Don't Fade* (1992) and how the Indian lesbian situates herself in white, racist lesbian culture in *Khush* (Pratibha Parmar, 1991). It celebrates and develops black lesbians' sexual fantasies in *24 Hours a Day* (Jocelyn Taylor, 1993) and in *Sex Fish* (ET Baby Maniac, 1993). When the character playing an actress walks off the set of a film which has positioned her yet again in the role of a submissive black woman being raped by a white man in *She Left the Script Behind* (Dawn Suggs, 1993), and then confronts a homophobe by embracing her, the interstices of race, sexuality and identity are torn apart and powerfully re-enmeshed. Much of this work is celebratory rather than angry and presents a charged rebellion not only against how straights see us, but against the ways in which we have invisibilized and caricatured each other among ourselves.

Even though I attempt to argue uneasily for a certain historical specificity of a 'queer aesthetic', Genet's *Un Chant d'Amour* (1950) could only be defined as queer, both in its formal inventiveness and its mode of address, which does not pander to the heterosexual viewer. Patricia White has argued for Ulrike Ottinger's film *Madame X: An Absolute Ruler* (1977) which takes lesbians' visual pleasure for granted as queer:

> Ottinger manipulates a visual and aural collage technique drawing on sources from the Shrangri-La's to Yma Sumac, Gustave Moreau to Man Ray, Oscar Wilde to Virginia

Woolf, to produce a feminist surrealism, or what might be called queer cinema.[10]

As film maker Pratibha Parmar insists:

> Queer cinema has been going on for decades, although not in its current manifestation – that is, a marketable, collective commodity produced by white gay men in the US . . . My sensibility comes as much from my culture and race as from my queerness . . . My personal style is determined by diverse aesthetic influences, from Indian cinema and cultural iconography to pop promos and 70s avant-garde films.[11]

Film maker Annette Kennerley does not define herself as a 'queer film maker', but admits that some of her films could be cited as 'queer'. Her latest work, *Like Mother, Like Son* (1994) for example, shows her five-year-old son dressing in girl drag while Annette discusses her life as a tomboy dyke. Jacqui Duckworth, *Prayer Before Birth* (1991), does not see herself as queer, but deals with the subject of disability with the irony, awkward humour, resistance and formal boldness associated with the 'queer aesthetic'. When her young black protagonist waltzes with a mannequin to the lilting melody of Patsy Cline's 'I Fall To Pieces', Duckworth's surreal wit defies the daily encroachment of multiple sclerosis passionately and aggressively. Another film maker working in Britain, Ruth Novaczek, is happy for her films to be shown in a queer context – especially since the word is the new buzz word of the market – but again expresses ambivalence about the influence that particular politics has on her work. *Rootless Cosmopolitans* (1990) rigorously explores notions of lesbian Jewish identity, while *Cheap Philosophy* (1993) is a superb pastiche on compulsive therapy, double identities and confessional diarist work. This is lesbian camp, a genre as contested as queer. It seems that when gay men act up it's called camp, while when dykes act up it's called over-acting. Similarly, when gay men make experimental inroads into filmic conventions they're acclaimed as unprecedented, while when lesbians do it they're seen as bad film makers.

As soon as we grasp a definition of what 'queer cinema' might be, it vanishes, transmutes into something other. Queer will be a young, affluent white boys' thing if we let it, but the energy that is being demonstrated by lesbians needs to be recognized and recorded as both important and radical. Lesbians have been bad at naming ourselves, respecting our work enough to deem it worthy of naming, to demand that it is named and thereby taken seriously. Socially encouraged to see ourselves as powerless as women, lesbians have been much more suspicious than gay men of the power that the mainstream offers, and some who have been successful on a wider scale have been hastily disqualified from a movement that equates self-effacement with political integrity. The chances for lesbians, white and more particularly black, to buy their way into social legitimacy are few and costly. Many lesbian artists have been hostage to the whims of straight white male critics, but the 1990s have marked a vital shift, in that lesbian critics and theorists are leading much of the new work around queer cultural debates and challenging the weary old confines of film and video theory.

Take Barbara Hammer for instance. Long shunned by the straight boys' avant-garde club and working as the only out lesbian in her field – is her latest work, *Nitrate Kisses* (1993), going to be ignored by the queer canon because it's not part of the butt pack? This charismatic exploration of sexual taboos is Hammer's fiftieth film and first feature-length drama-documentary. 'I named the film *Nitrate Kisses*,' explains Hammer, 'because nitrate celluloid is highly explosive material, just as lesbian and gay sexuality has been highly explosive to this repressive society.' Fifty-three-year-old Hammer claims she made the film because she wanted to make old beautiful:

> If you have wrinkles on your face you're not supposed to swing. I just want to say, 'Hey, get it straight! We're changing what old means. They think of us as asexual. Well, hey girls, I'm alive.'

The film not only challenges the erasure of lesbian and gay sexual culture in general, but also the ways in which we suppress elements of our own lives, such as SM sexuality, interracial couples and older lesbians and gays. *Nitrate Kisses* epitomizes the alchemical process of creating dyke cinema. Its seductive black and white layering opens by retracing the life of lesbian writer Willa Cather whose sexuality has been absent from the literary celebration of her work. It goes on lovingly to portray two older women having sex, one of whom describes herself as '77 in the shade'. Then Hammer captures an East Village gay male couple, one black and one white, making love, intercut with found footage from *Lot in Sodom*, a 1933 film described as the first gay film in the US. The final section explores desire between two young pierced and tattoed SM dykes in Berlin, interwoven with footage from German films of the 1930s. 'I want the audience to become archaeologists of the cinema, sift through images on the screen, the way I had to shift through life to find these images.'

Frequently creating a cinema which visualizes the erotic touch and the relationship between the natural and the social worlds, Hammer's vision is at once unique and empowering, challenging hetero audiences with her up-front sexual explicitness and attacks on bigotry, as well as shifting taboos around sex, race and age within the lesbian and gay communities themselves. Hammer is currently working on her next feature, *Tender Buttons*, about the lives and lusts of dyke hobos.

The potential of 'queer' forces us to investigate how homosexuality defines itself. The increasing number of films and videos exploring notions of transgender from *My Father is Coming* (Monika Treut, 1991), and Annie Sprinkle's *Linda, Les and Annie* (1989) to *Adventures in the Gender Trade* (Susan Marenco, 1993) suggest that as we become more secure in our identities we can embrace a wider concept of sexuality that is not based on same-sex object choice. When Annie Sprinkle has sexual intercourse with Les, an ex-radical feminist lesbian, now a man with a cunt and a manmade prick, in *Linda, Les and Annie*, is this heterosexual sex? Is it lesbian sex? The old definitions are no longer adequate to describe our broadening sexual orthodoxies.

In *Juggling Gender* (Tami Gold, 1992) a woman artist who takes radical feminism to its logical conclusions is profiled. She refuses to pluck her chin and grows a beard and moustache, thereby challenging the door policies on many lesbian clubs where she is refused entry on the grounds of being a man or a transsexual. This is one of the few tapes that successfully encapsulates the contradictions within radical feminism and points towards the radical potential of queer definitions of gender and the body. As Judith Butler asserts, 'All gender is drag, where men and women impersonate an ideal that no one inhabits.'[12]

When teenager video maker Sadie Benning put on a beard in her bedroom and crooned to 'Blueberry Hill', puffing a fat cigar in *It Wasn't Love* (1992), she wasn't confused about her lesbian desire. She wasn't afraid to femme-up and don a blonde wig and whisper along to 'Fever' and tease out the many divergent and different identities that rescued her from isolation, homophobia and the tyranny of gender.

Benning skipped the 'lesbian phase' and came straight out as a baby dyke into the eager arms of the lesbian and gay film world. 'Lesbian,' she confessed, reminded her 'of a cross between a lizard and an alien'. After a retrospective of her work at New York's Museum of Modern Art, and now working on her first feature, *Girl Power*, Benning invented herself through her work: 'When I started making videos I hadn't really come out to anyone, but it was in my head. I began to talk in front of a camera because it wouldn't talk back or judge me. I started because of the lack of imagery I could identify with.'

Shot with a Pixelvision camera, her mostly black and white work is highly textured and tightly framed. The image is set in a black mount, which has been likened to a peepshow effect. Snippets of hand-held texts are passed mechanically before the lens, giving life to words that can't be braved aloud: 'Girls can't get married.' In *A Place Called Lovely* (1991) she flaunts a school portrait with a person torn out. 'I never felt that I was learning what I wanted to learn. It was holding me back and teaching me to be racist and hate my identity, teaching me all about appearance and nothing about who I was.' Sensual, rude-positive, discreet, erotic, sharp and intimate, Benning's work represents some of the most thrilling work to emerge as queer.

Annie Sprinkle with her audacious post-porn art parodies femininity beyond camp. In *Sluts and Goddesses* (1992), directed with Maria Beatty, Sprinkle explodes the vulnerability and self-hatred of the female body. Only Sprinkle could get away with this amount of corny, often phoney and always extraordinary camaraderie between her vagina and the audience. The video stars slags of the sex world, known as 'transformation facilitators' – skinny, fat, black, white – who take the ordinary woman through the routines of the slut and goddess personas and encourage her to 'Reclaim our orgasms. To do this we have to be experimental, impolite and uncontrollable.' Sprinkle may not be breaking boundaries in celluloid, but she doesn't half disrupt the hetero/sexist gaze. The crescendo of this sexual workshopping is Sprinkle's five-minute orgasm. At no point does the video explicitly address the sexual orientation of her female viewers, which opens up a rare space in which heterosexual women, as well as lesbians, can exercise self-determined pleasure. The gay male body has been so sexually determined that some of us have been tempted to imitate it to pronounce ourselves as erotic. But Sprinkle's work promotes an erotic vocabulary that is wholly female. It also collapses the old tyranny of madonna versus whore, bad slut and good goddess, erotica versus porn, scattering those dichotomies in a frenzy of sexual self-display that confounds cultural and racial identities. The humour and lack of shame Sprinkle brings to her performance adventures have inspired a new generation of gender activists and film makers.

While *Kamikaze Hearts* (Juliet Bashore, 1988) was made before the re-naming of queer, it could be seen as a precursor to the genre in its rigorous probe at lesbian lovers working in the sex industry. This quasi-documentary follows the lusty, co-dependent relationship of Tigr and Mitch, who try to decipher real from performed passion. Its bleak, nihilistic conclusion remains non-judgemental, forcing the viewer to find her own moral position. It is a brave, uncompromising exploration of the illusions and deceptions that bind desire and was severely dissed in Britain for showing such negative images of lesbians – lesbians as drug users, prostitutes and porn stars were not the kinds of lesbian radical feminists wanted in their club.

*Flaming Ears* (Angela Hans Scheirl, Dietmar Schipek, Ursula Purrer, 1992) broke the mould for experimental dyke dramas with a cultish, wacky film which mixes animation, live action, sci-fi and horror. What the film lacks in plot coherency it makes up for in sheer visual magic. The inventive sets and props proved how the micro-approach to lesbian shorts could be extended with hilarious effect on a macro scale. The characters are positively fiendish – in fact they make Leopold and Loeb of *Swoon* looks like preppy pups. First you have roller-skating Volley, whose sexual thrill is pyromania. The phrase 'playing with fire' takes on a new dimension when she burns down the printing works of a lesbian comic artist, Spy, who seeks revenge. Enter an alligator-eating shaven nun, sporting red rubber, who is one of Volley's lovers, but then falls for Spy. The text throughout parodies the language of love and defies the finality of death. These women delight in the romance of cruelty, take pleasure in humiliation, and fight among themselves as much as with the outside world. Here are the nasty bits we would prefer not to examine. Scheirl is currently seeking funding for another full-length feature about space age fantastical mother-lover figures.

Another noticeable trend in the latest video work is a growing representation of body decoration – tattooing, piercing, scarification, cutting, in films like *Rapture* (Sara Whiteley, 1992), an extraordinary record of ecstasy rituals, and *Stigmata: The Transfigured Body* (Leslie Asako Gladsjo, 1993), which has in-depth interviews with piercers, tattooists and their clients. Whereas in the 1970s it was enough to declare 'I am a lesbian' to reclaim your body, now women are seeking an extreme auto-eroticism to demonstrate control of the self. As lesbianism as a sexuality and lifestyle becomes increasingly accepted, those who wish to be outsiders must invest in a more transgressive practise to mark their non-conformity. It signals entry into a new subcultural club in which the body is the final place where regulation and control can be exercised and celebrated. A bolt through the tongue may be transgressive visually, but is it radical, is it queer? When stick-on piercings are worn by top models, does that render the act redundant?

Lesbian features take much longer to be produced than those by gay men. The film industry is notoriously sexist, and lesbian chic does not guarantee a return in access to resources. Misogyny continues to affect how and where lesbians are seen. There are, however, more lesbian features in the production pipeline, that are still raising funding, including *Fresh Kill* (Shu Lea Cheang), with a multi-racial cast of dyke mums, computer hacks and guerrillas in a decaying urban landscape, ever-threatened by radioactive poison-ing, and *Silence of the Moon* (Midi Onodera), which tells the tale of a young pre-op female-to-male transsexual who falls obsessively in love with a lesbian.

One of the more recent features that captures the thrill of being low-budget, urban, dyke/queer/post-queer/non-queer is *Go Fish* (Rose Troche, 1994). Its charm lies in its frank, fresh tone, its self-conscious wit, its hand-held camera, shadowy black and white cinematography and jazzy soundtrack. It seems familiar, even though a feature-length drama about young contemporary lesbians has *never* been done before. In *Go Fish* not one, I repeat, not one lesbian character comes out. Nor do any seduce younger, blonde straight women, then get punished, rejected or sent away because they eat pussy. *Go Fish* is about flirting, being single, cruising, getting nookie, friendship and definitions of pussy. This is a sweet romantic comedy which deals with daily dilemmas for dykes. It never aims to represent all lesbians, nor to address the political issues of homophobia or sexism or racism or poverty. But all those issues are part of these women's lives, from the Latina lesbian who's thrown out of home, to the African-American teacher who's dealing with homophobia in her class. It's the film the 1970s would not have funded, the 1980s would not have allowed, the 1990s is more than ready for. It makes dyke dating normal and inevitable. It rings with the unapologetic irony that self-knowledge and pride bring.

While queer rides merrily into the straight media as a co-opted and diluted reference, there is no denying the unabated lesbian and gay cultural renaissance. Yet there continues to be resistance to what it appears to represent among lesbians. If lesbians were the ugly sisters of feminism, so SM dykes are the bad girls of queer. Some women think that they can't be queer unless they wear black leather caps. Conflating SM with a 'cult of violence', with fascism and anti-feminism, they dismiss the queer project as inherently reactionary and look back in angora to the fixed notion of a lesbian and gay community. Lesbians Against Pornography, for example, feel:

> fed up of so-called 'queer nation' politics presenting itself as representing the lesbian and gay community; fed up of butch-

femme, SM, porn, being misrepresented as 'new', 'radical', and 'liberated', instead of reactionary, misogynist and oppressive; fed up with terms like 'lesbian boy', 'daddy dyke' and 'chick with a dick'.

They go on to insist that 'the Gay Press preaches to us weekly that "Queer", fucking, dildos, porn and SM are the only valid forms of sexuality for us' (from a leaflet distributed in summer 1992).

This is the ground queer politics is constantly contesting, opening up a space for lesbian porn made by lesbians, consensual SM, the use of sex toys, and the right to cruise and fuck without being made to feel less of a feminist. These pro-censorship critiques which demonize masculine phallic sexuality in porn and the use of dildos as 'other' have fed the right's attacks not only on porn, but on lesbians, gays and sadomasochists. Writers like Linda Williams have argued persuasively that a new form of scapegoating has occurred where blame for a wide range of sex crimes and the spread of AIDS has broadened from pornography to include 'deviants', with legislators drawing the line between normal and perverse rather than explicit and non-explicit, thus threatening any sexual activity outside the heterosexual 'norm'.

Queer resists the cultural homogenization of lesbian and gay lives and lifestyles; it takes homo in from the margins and demands equality as well as the right to retain difference. Burgeoning queer film and video, whether or not it's made by those who self-define as queer, aims to act as an agent for social change and to rethink the sexual subject. While gay men may have brought the authority to new queer cinema, lesbians have brought diversity, daring and dissent.

## Notes

1.  B. Ruby Rich, in 'New queer cinema', *Sight and Sound* (London), September 1992.
2.  Gregg Bodowitz, in M. Gever, J. Greyson and P. Parmar (eds), *Queer Looks*. London, Routledge, 1993.
3.  Parmar, in *Queer Looks*.
4.  B. Ruby Rich, in *The Village Voice on Queer Cinema*, summer 1992.

5. Christine Vachon, in interview with B. Ruby Rich, *Out*, summer 1992.
6. B. Ruby Rich, in *Queer Looks*.
7. Linda Singer, *Erotic Welfare: Sexual Theory and Politics in the Age of Epidemic*. Routledge, London, 1993.
8. Paula Webster, in Carole Vance (ed.), *Pleasure and Danger: Exploring Female Sexuality*. Routledge, London, 1984.
9. Chris Straayer, in *Dirty Looks: Women, Pornography, Power*. BFI, London, 1993.
10. Patricia White, in *Queer Looks*.
11. Pratihba Parmar, in 'New queer cinema', *Sight and Sound*.
12. Judith Butler, in *Gender Trouble*. Routledge, London, 1990.

All other quotes are from conversations with the author.

# Part Five
# Breaking Free

Chapter nine

# *The Outside Edge:*
# *Lesbian Mysteries*

## Barbara Wilson

---

*That is what the practice of an art is, you keep looking for
the outside edge*
Ursula K. Le Guin

# *Beginnings*

I remember very well the day I began my first mystery. It was
1983 and I was sitting at my old blue-painted desk, brooding over a
novel-in-progress, a novel I was, in fact, never able to finish, the sad
story of a hopeless love triangle. I was somewhere in the middle of
my fourth draft when I ripped the paper out of my old manual
typewriter (this was in pre-computer days, when you could make
such satisfyingly dramatic sounds) and inserted a fresh sheet.
Without hesitation I typed MURDER IN THE COLLECTIVE
boldly at the top.

A friend had recently told me the story of an attempted
business merger between a lesbian grains collective and a mixed
gender fruit and vegetable collective. Several members of each
collective had not liked the idea and one day someone in the lesbian

grains group had come into work to find her desk covered with molasses. As a former member of a newspaper collective in Seattle, the anecdote appealed to my sense of the ridiculous and I thought the subject might be good for a satiric short story about leftist and feminist infighting. But as I continued to write, I realized with growing enthusiasm that I might be on to something.

I'd never read a mystery like the one I wanted to write; in fact I'd read very few mysteries at all. But I thought that if I could manage to combine politics with entertainment, I might be able to create a novel that could not only tackle some important topics, but could actually be fun and energizing to write, something that, unfortunately, my study of the interior lives of three rather depressed women was not (though some years later I took up the theme again in *Cows and Horses*).

*Murder in the Collective* appeared in 1984, at a time when the lesbian literary movement was less fixed and more fluid perhaps than it is today. Writers crossed boundaries and genres; few of us imagined mass audiences because little of what we wrote could be published in the mainstream. But the feminist presses provided homes for our work and while we were obviously marginalized we also found, in our marginalization, an unself-consciousness (sometimes embarrassing to reread now) and a thrilling freedom. We were writing words that had never been written before, describing characters and situations that had never been imagined in earlier times. There was no literary hierarchy, because as yet there was no firm notion of lesbian literature. To write in a genre was not necessarily to be a genre writer; to play with the science fiction or fantasy or mystery form was often just that – playing.

Ten years later there is a lesbian literary hierarchy, and it's not just Virginia Woolf floating above and all the rest of us down below. As lesbian literature has expanded into a larger market it has stratified, solidified and become, for good and ill, more self-conscious. There are lesbian *novels* and then there are lesbian *crime* novels. Lesbian mysteries have become a recognized genre, and one of the most popular ones. Within this genre are adventurous novels and predictable novels, but all are more easily defined as genre writing than they might have been in the early 1980s. There is less boundary-crossing these days and more encouragement (from publishers buoyed by sales and from large and often very appreciative audiences) to keep to what appears to be a winning formula. There's less talk about the mystery as a subversive form, less talk about how women have changed the genre. Perhaps this means that women have been so successful at challenging the form that all that remains to be done is to write very good mysteries. Perhaps it also hints that the days of experimentation may be over for now.

Genres, because of the layers of conventions that have shaped them, come with a heavy measure of expectation. When the reader picks up a science fiction novel she expects to be transported in time and place to another, perhaps extra-terrestrial or alien, culture where she will come across odd landscapes and unusual technology, invented words and imaginative social behaviour. When the reader picks up a crime novel she expects, if not a murder or two, then at least an unexplained disappearance, a kidnapping, a theft or a heist. She expects a wide variety of characters with hidden pasts and dubious motives; she expects even the most pleasant person in such a novel to be capable of murder or at least of cheating, stealing and dissembling. The reader also expects decent characters who are falsely accused and characters with small faults that loom large. The reader expects a central character who has curiosity and guts, and a notion of justice.

The icons of mystery writing (the dead body, the gun, the vial of poison) and the patterns (the discovery of the body, the interrogation of the witnesses, the accusation of guilt) are what make the crime novel distinctive. Precisely because of the set structure, women writers were able to move into and utilize the same icons and patterns that made the genre familiar and at the same time change some of the expectations. Lesbian writers have been able to do the same thing: to tell the familiar story of the solving of a crime from a different perspective.

Part of what defines a genre is the community it creates; before the 1980s there was no community of women crime writers, much less of lesbian crime writers. Now there is, and it has proved to be vibrant and supportive. But community is also created by readers who participate in the creation of genre and in the expectations they bring to it. I am curious about what happens when a genre which once defined itself as new and in opposition to established forms becomes its own establishment, when writers and readers who were once drawn to the form precisely because there was something new about it now turn to it because it is familiar.

There are many definitions of a literary genre, but one thing is always true – if you write in the genre form, you have some explaining to do. Over the years I've answered the question of why I chose the mystery genre in a variety of ways. Sometimes I speak of fun, sometimes of politics, sometimes of grief, sometimes of subversion or subtexts. I could also answer that I like the company. Mystery readers are remarkably eclectic and generous, and mystery writers are to an amazing degree supportive and unpretentious.

I have never felt a *true* mystery writer, however, and this has, I believe, as much to do with reasons I started to write mysteries as with my perception of the genre. I don't have to explain this to other mystery writers, who are aware of all the reasons why one could want to write in the genre, but I do have to explain it to more mainstream authors and audiences. Sometimes I hear in my voice a kind of bemusement, if not defensiveness, when I speak on panels, in workshops, in interviews and question periods after readings, about why I came to this form. Perhaps because I've written and published other sorts of fiction, my ears are tuned to another, blunter question behind the more overt one of 'Why mysteries?' The blunter question is 'Why mysteries instead of real literature?' or, 'How can you write both?' And, 'If you can write real literature, why would you want to write anything else?'

Here are some ideas, then, about what the difference may be and why 'both' may be a more interesting answer than 'this one or that one'.

## Investigations

Many novels have crimes and many more novels deal with death and loss and grief, and only some of them are called crime novels. However, thrillers and mysteries could just as well be called novels of investigation, to distinguish them from crime novels that deal with crimes but not with solutions. For the focus of the thriller is not the crime but the solving of the crime, not the mystery but the demystifying process. Crime and death do not distinguish this genre from its literary or mainstream counterparts, but the process of asking questions and looking for the truth, or at least someone to pin the blame on, does.

I grew up in the Christian Science Church, where truth is spelled with a capital T, but where any attempt to tie Truth to reality is discouraged. For Truth in Christian Science is never arrived at by looking, smelling, touching, hearing or tasting – otherwise known as the 'false sense impressions' – but by reading the Bible and the works of Mrs Eddy, and by keeping one's thoughts steadily on higher things. 'Mystery' comes from the Greek word meaning *to keep silent*, and in my family there were many mysteries and much silence. For years I postponed investigating these mysteries and breaking these silences, because I feared to learn the truth. Yet at the same time I found myself writing highly structured novels about women whose fictional role was defined by their inconvenient desire to get, once and for all, to the bottom of things.

The form of the mystery is action alternating with contemplation, enlivened by bursts of questions and answers. Sometimes the questions are sly, sometimes badly formulated; sometimes the answers are mildly misleading, sometimes outright lies. In no way are crime novels realistic, though they are meant to seem so. They are shadow plays, and what is being dramatized is not so much good and evil – for in the best thrillers good and evil shift constantly – but truth and lies.

The power of the crime novel is invested in the role of the investigator: she who asks questions and demands or puzzles out answers; she who is philosopher, detective, prosecutor and judge; she who is neither a victim nor a bystander; she who rejects the role of passive observer in favour of speech and action. The investigator takes an active role concerning death. She doesn't sit by, as we do in real life, stunned and paralysed by grief; she knows that someone is to blame and that her role is to find who that person is. It's no mistake that many investigators are orphans or widows or otherwise bereft; a very frequent motivation for sleuths is compassion for those who have lost someone. It is grief transferred, grief made manageable.

The appeal of the investigator novel to women writers and readers would seem obvious. For to be a woman is to have been silenced and socialized into passivity. To be a woman is to have been the victim or bystander of many nameless and hidden crimes: battery, rape, sexual abuse, harassment. To take the role of investigator means to open the doors upon silence, to name the crimes, to force the confessions, to call for justice and see justice done. And even, sometimes, to take justice into one's own hands.

In the 1980s, when thrillers with feminist themes first became popular, women were standing up in greater and greater numbers and telling stories of incest and abuse. In this culture of victimization, as some have called it, the investigator plays a special role. For she is of the gender that is institutionally and individually oppressed, and yet she has managed to free herself or is trying to free herself sufficiently to act on behalf of herself and other women.

Crime novels are about society and power. What changed when women began to write crime novels in the 1980s was that traditional notions of authority and justice were called into question. Could a woman who killed a man who'd been abusing her be let off the hook? Were the police and courts sometimes as much to blame for the victim's suffering as the murderer? What did the law mean when it came to women's lives? More than most protagonists in contemporary fiction, women sleuths are able to move up and down the social scale, from the back streets to the boardrooms of multinational corporations. These investigators often break the rules and put their bodies on the line. They venture into dangerous neighbourhoods and scary situations most readers would never dare explore. Unrealistic perhaps, but empowering.

For lesbian writers and readers, the appeal of novels of investigation also seems clear. Not only have most of us been silenced as women, but as lesbians another layer of silence surrounds our lives. The lesbian investigator brings this silence into her work; it protects and oppresses her. Her advantages are risks as well. If she works in a police department, she may find homophobia is a greater threat than bullets, and will continually have to juggle her loyalty to her community with fears of what will happen if she steps out of the closet. Although a few lesbian mystery writers have created private detectives who are loners, most writers provide their investigators with well-developed friendships, love relationships and families, and situate them squarely in gay and/or mixed communities. Sometimes their participation in a gay subculture is pivotal to the solution to the mystery, and sometimes it's inconsequential, but in every case it offers the writer a chance to create and the reader a chance to absorb scenes which show lesbians as actors in a realistic setting.

By definition the lesbian mystery overturns convention, and it has the power to ask questions about the nature of society and to explore what justice means in an unjust world. I know that I, child of an authoritarian religion who grew up in the rebellious 1960s, certainly was drawn to the mystery form for those very reasons.

# Pam Nilsen and issues of social justice

These are some of the conventions I took up and shook up in the three mysteries that feature printer-sleuth Pam Nilsen: murder among a small closed circle of acquaintances, a circle that happens to be a collective (*Murder in the Collective*); the search for a teenage hooker – a staple of male detective novels (*Sisters of the Road*); the murder of a prominent person with a hidden, unsavoury past that only gradually comes to light (*The Dog Collar Murders*). In these novels the question and answer method of investigator is used extensively, not only to elicit alibis and confessions, but to create a dialectic on issues like racism, prostitution and pornography. Part of what I wanted to do in the Pam Nilsen novels was to create an arena for discussion of subjects that are often part of the unexamined, but titillating backdrop to murder mysteries. Because many people are used to reading mysteries for the plot, I assumed that the audience wouldn't put the thriller down even if it came across new and unusual political perspectives.

Pam Nilsen is a youngish, liberal, middle-class, well-intentioned and fair, but sometimes naive, protagonist. She tends to be offset by friends and relatives who are savvier than she is, for instance her twin sister Penny, and their co-worker at the print shop, June Jasper, an African-American. In the first of the three novels Pam is straight, but in the process of falling in love with another woman. By the third novel (*The Dog Collar Murders*) Pam has navigated the coming-out process and is celebrating a house-warming with her lover, Hadley. Throughout the novels Pam struggles with her new identity, and with the stigma that both separates her from the straight world and allows her to identify with other marginalized people.

As an anti-authoritarian lefty, Pam has an uneasy relationship with notions of law and order. In all the books she either hides evidence from the police or assumes that they wouldn't be interested in what she knows. Her motives for investigation spring in part from curiosity and in part from her desire to help others in her subculture. She admits that she's not necessarily good at deduction or following clues; what she is good at is persistence and loyalty, and asking the kinds of question that eventually precipitate the culminating action of the books. Pam is not the all-powerful sort of investigator that readers draw inspiration from; but she is a character that many women have indentified with.

All three of these Pam Nilsen novels follow certain conventions of their own, and in this they are quite in tune with other overtly feminist crime novels of the 1980s. The crimes focus on injustice towards women and explore family secrets and institutionalized oppression. They also call into question some of the hypocrisy and rhetoric of the feminist movement. The novels show an independent but not autonomous female investigator in the process of forming and acting on feminist values. As a lesbian Pam is not immune from injustice and stigma, nor invulnerable to violence against women. Indeed, the incident at the end of *Sisters of the Road* did not shock because it is uncommon, but because it goes against what we expect in crime novels. Investigators may be threatened, drugged, beaten up, tortured and left for dead, but their sexual boundaries are never disturbed.

# Moral comedies

With my fourth crime novel, *Gaudi Afternoon*, I decided to try subversion from a different angle. The pressure I'd experienced in the 1980s to write as a social realist and to describe and discuss the issues in the lesbian community was lifting, and I wanted to be both more frivolous and more sophisticated – to joke more and ponder less. I found my new narrator in Cassandra Reilly, a forty-ish translator of Spanish and South American literature, a woman based in London and Oakland who can most frequently be found on a train to a distant country.

Although *Gaudi Afternoon* tackles as many issues as the earlier novels, the tone is very different. Transexualism, child custody, motherhood – all are treated in a much more light-hearted fashion. *Gaudi Afternoon* is a farce, a mystery without a murder, a caper in which the precious item stolen back and forth is animal, not mineral. The plot plays with the notion of disguises and false identities so dear to the hearts of crime writers. Set in Barcelona, the novel introduces an investigator who is also a working translator. As a translator myself, I see Cassandra Reilly's profession as a device that gives her a plausible reason to travel, as well as allowing her to engage in all the word games and misunderstandings that the juxtaposition of languages can create.

Just as there are degrees of outness in lesbian mysteries, so are there degrees of seriousness. Some lesbian detective writers do not regard the genre as a laughing matter. But they're probably in the minority. The stylized form of the mystery lends itself well to parody, pastiche and satire. The most obvious style of parody is to mimic the typical Chandler and Hammett hero – the hard-drinking, womanizing loner. In the person of a woman, such a voice rings provocatively and absurdly. Emma Victor's over-the-top similes have made it impossible to read Chandler in quite the same way again. Sarah Schulman in *The Sophie Horowitz Story*, Val McDermid and Elizabeth Pincus have also experimented with a tough-girl voice that mocks the genre with affection.

In the Pam Nilsen novels I had done my own share of parodying the genre and lesbian culture. I had satirized everything from collectives to current feminist debates. Although I generally meant to be thoughtful in my humour, there were always readers who took what I wrote seriously and felt personally attacked. But in *Gaudi Afternoon* I began to experience myself as a comic writer, and to see the possibilities of carrying on riotously while dealing with serious subjects. Humour could be more than satire, I discovered; it could be unrestrained physical slapstick and farce, as well as witty repartee. In the character of Cassandra, a working-class Irish Catholic who has been a lesbian all her life, I found a tolerant sense of humour that could respect many people's choices while still finding them amusing.

*Trouble in Transylvania*, the second in the Cassandra Reilly series, takes up some of the themes of the first novel – motherhood, lesbian desire and the question of home – and does so while looking at history, landscape and myth in eastern Europe. At heart it is a serious book that circles around my preoccupation with the acceptance of difference, and with loss and death, but the tone is light and the atmosphere comic. As I wrote this book I grappled constantly with the question of what was funny and what was not. Romanian orphans were not funny, but naive Americans who adopted them might be. Hungarian minority rights were not funny, but the ridiculous prejudices that Hungarians and Romanians clung to about each other were.

One of the most interesting aspects I found of writing humour (aside from the fact that a remark may sound very witty the first time you read it, and less so the twentieth), was what happened to the essential tension of the plot in a comic mystery. When farce takes over, the whodunnit energy fades. Although most people were surprised to find out who the murderer was in *Trouble in Transylvania*, not many of them actually cared. I realized that I had drifted a bit from the genre's rules when my audience said to me, 'I laughed a lot, and I learned a lot, but . . . it didn't seem so much like a *mystery*.'

Fortunately for me the mystery is an elastic and flexible form, which tolerates, and may even encourage, such deviations.

## Outside/inside

Before I began to write mysteries I defined myself as a short story writer, and during the ten years that I worked primarily in the mystery genre I also translated two works of fiction from the Norwegian and completed one novel and parts of another. I've now returned more or less to the practice of 'literature'.

It has felt, to my surprise, something of a relief, not unlike the relief I experienced when I first typed the words MURDER IN THE COLLECTIVE on the typewriter. At this moment fiction and essays appear to me to have that indefinable quality of newness and excitement, of not quite knowing where I'm going, not quite knowing what will happen.

What I carry with me from my years of thriller writing are a fascination with structure and pattern, an ability to conceal and disclose truth as necessary, and most important, a knowledge that writing can be playful, and that I can be, if I want, a humorous writer. I also learned a great deal about making things up as I went along and not working from established forms. The mystery does not encourage plumbing the depths of characters' personalities, but it does encourage creating unusual, quirky casts of people. Because the crime novel places so much emphasis on plot, it forces the writer to be inventive and action-oriented, and to keep things moving with dialogue and a minimum of analysis. As a short story writer it seemed natural to me to withhold information from the reader; mystery writing taught me something about when and how to tell the truth.

Perhaps because I was not a keen mystery reader when I began to write in this genre and had to educate myself as I went along, I did not see the limitations so much as the possibilities. But now the strictures of the genre are clearer to me: it is difficult to develop character when the plot takes such precedence, and it can be hard to negotiate one's way around the plot when dead bodies and questions about dead bodies take up so much time. In spite of one's most inventive tricks, the crime narrative can only be subverted, rarely wholly transformed. Because of its conventions, its emphasis on plot at the expense of character, its investigative drive, the crime novel can rarely express the true depth and richness of human experience – not because it doesn't invite good writing, but because it suggests that life's mysteries can be solved when, in fact, that is almost never the case.

Although there are limits to writing in the mystery genre there are limits to writing in any form, and it might be more useful to see forms and genres pollinating and enriching each other, and to see the lines of division as more fluid than rigid. In contemporary literature there are edges where specific genres blur together with mainstream fiction. Margaret Atwood, Marge Piercy, Angela Carter, Jeanette Winterson all use elements of fantasy and science fiction in their writing, and A.S. Byatt in *Possession* and Jane Smiley in *A Thousand Acres* have both used some of the traditional aspects of the mystery genre to create suspenseful plots revolving around secrets from the past.

Genre writers have, rightly, been miffed when their work is ignored, when, for instance, mainstream fiction authors are praised for their magic realism while science fiction authors are patronized. Of course one might argue that literary fiction tends to be less formulaic and better written, but the people who argue that way are generally not genre writers. One could easily assert that the writing of Elmore Leonard, Ruth Rendell, Ursula K. LeGuin and Philip K. Dick is far superior to much of what is published in the mainstream.

When I speak of fluidity and cross-pollination and experimentation, I realize that I am making a case for continued innovation in the genre of the lesbian mystery. But of course there is nothing wrong with working entirely within the realms of a genre. It would also be a mistake to believe that every lesbian author wants to be subversive or even to deal with lesbian and feminist subjects. Those few who have entered the mainstream, in fact, have often taken care to create characters who are, as one writer told me, 'lesbian, but just like anybody else'.

If I find myself working at the outside edge, it's probably because I find myself more comfortable there. However, if one pushes hard enough at the outside edge, the boundaries change, and what was once outside is now inside. If we are looking for inclusion rather than marginalization perhaps that's as it should be.

I don't see myself ever entirely abandoning the genre of the mystery, though I am choosing to work again with fiction and a memoir. I am hoping to tackle some of my stories more directly and personally and to go a little deeper than is possible with the mystery. But I think I will always be writing investigative fiction, and always looking at silence, lies and truth.

# Index

234: *Index*